EmTech Anthropology

EmTech Anthropology: Careers at the Frontier emphasizes anthropology's critical role at the frontier of emerging technologies (EmTech). The book explores the opportunities and challenges that arise as anthropologists venture into the territory of EmTech, pushing the boundaries of traditional academic approaches and methodologies.

By sharing the stories and insights of early to mid-career anthropologists working in AI, robotics, Web3, cybersecurity, and other cutting-edge fields, the book provides a possible roadmap for future practitioners seeking to make an impact in the world of EmTech. These anthropologists demonstrate how the discipline's unique perspective and skills can be applied to address the complex ethical, social, and cultural implications of emerging technologies.

The volume showcases how anthropologists can act as visionaries, innovators, and early adopters, shaping the trajectory of EmTech towards more ethical, equitable, inclusive, and sustainable futures. It highlights the importance of interdisciplinary collaboration, practical impact, and intervention in EmTech contexts while also acknowledging the need for anthropologists to challenge existing narratives and push the boundaries of the discipline itself.

EmTech Anthropology: Stories from the Frontier serves as an essential resource for anthropologists, students, and professionals from related disciplines who are interested in exploring the frontiers of anthropology and emerging technologies. By offering a glimpse into the exciting possibilities and compelling insights that emerge when anthropology meets EmTech, the book inspires and guides the next generation of anthropological innovators.

Matt Artz is an anthropologist, designer, and technologist specializing in AI product development. He is the founder of Azimuth Labs, host of the *Anthropology in Business* and *Anthro to UX* podcasts, and co-editor of *EmTech Anthropology* and the forthcoming *Anthropology and AI*. His work has been featured on TED, UNESCO, South by Southwest, and Apple's Planet of the Apps.

Dr. Lora Koycheva is an anthropologist and technologist working at the intersection of anthropology, innovation, entrepreneurship, and robotics. She is Assistant Professor at the Chair of Technoscience Studies in Brandenburg Technical University. She is also building Robots, actually! – a global initiative to rebuild the human condition with robots. From 2020 to 2023, she was a convenor of the EASA Applied Anthropology Network. She holds a PhD in Anthropology from Northwestern University.

Anthropology and Business

Crossing Boundaries, innovating praxis

Series Editor: Timothy de Waal Malefyt

Both anthropology and business work at the forefront of culture and change. As anthropology brings its concerns with cultural organization and patterns of human behavior to multiple forms of business, a new dynamic of engagement is created. In addition to expanding interest in business as an object of study, anthropologists increasingly hold positions within corporations or work as independent consultants to businesses. In these roles, anthropologists are both redefining the discipline and innovating in industries around the world. These shifts are creating exciting cross-fertilizations and advances in both realms: challenging traditional categories of scholarship and practice, pushing methodological boundaries, and generating new theoretical entanglements. This series advances anthropology's multifaceted work in enterprise, from marketing, design, and technology to user experience research, work practice studies, finance, and many other realms.

For more information about this series, please visit: https://www.routledge.com/Anthropology–Business/book-series/AAB

"Anthropology is in the throes of change as fieldwork and problem solving are expanding rapidly into organizational settings, particularly in tech. Today's trailblazers are partnering with others as active problem solvers at the 'cutting edge.' Gone is anthropology's insularity, as new theory, methods, and models are tested and put to use serving diverse communities. These anthropology innovators bring a 'solutions mindset' to their work as they reinvent what anthropology is and demonstrate its value and impact."

Elizabeth K. Briody, *Founder and Principal of Cultural Keys LLC and Chair of Anthropology Career Readiness Network*

"This book presents a compelling premise: anthropology, once a prominent public platform for voicing concerns, lost its way in higher education and society. But anthropologists in business today are intervening to create meaningful change by confronting our most vexing human problems. The authors detail how a new generation of business anthropologists are applying their knowledge to shape sociotechnical transformations in AI, robotics, genetic engineering, and other emerging technologies, while addressing what it means to be human. Readers can enjoy a series of rich, informative, and descriptive stories of careers, choices, and actions that anthropologists take to make transformational change happen, and it comes at a highly relevant time: to portend not just the future of technology but potential futures of humankind."

Timothy de Waal Malefyt, *Ph.D. Clinical Professor of Marketing at the Gabelli school of Business, Fordham University*

"Visions of the frontier run deep in anthropology. They separate the familiar from the exotic and set the stage for the anthropologist to venture beyond and bridge the gap. Today's frontiers are technological and constantly shifting. *EmTech Anthropology* offers a fascinating, personal, and deeply compelling introduction to how anthropologists can navigate our unfamiliar futures with tech like AI, robotics, or genetic engineering – and help the rest of us do the same."

Anders Kristian Munk, *Professor of Computational Anthropology, Technical University of Denmark*

"A healthy, heartfelt piece of food for thought for all anthropologists who work in interdisciplinary teams – and not least those who do not, yet! Served with humor, the authors remind us to move beyond our anthro-egos and embrace the perspectives of 'the other' to enable the impact of our discipline. The brilliance of the argument is that we must shift our own perspectives and look outwards, to enable making our own perspectives relevant for the sake of a better future of tech."

Louise Vang Jensen, *Anthropologist, co-CEO and Partner in the Strategic Innovation Agency, IS IT A BIRD*

"*EmTech Anthropology* masterfully explores the intersections between anthropology, business and engineering, and challenges anthropologists to become *anthro-solutionists* – innovators who combine anthropological knowledge and insights with the development of people-centred technological solutions that will shape our future. It acts as a catalyst for inspiration and will definitely shape the path of the next generations of students, researchers and practitioners in the dynamic landscape of emerging technologies. In short, a powerful book."

Dan Podjed, *Associate Professor, Research Centre of the Slovenian Academy of Sciences and Arts*

"This unique collection offers potential ways for anthropologists to chart new courses within the emerging technology landscape. Rather than serving as insight providers within tech business models, these authors call for anthropologists to lead the way toward developing novel forms of serving human needs through technology. Rooted in a fresh perspective of the discipline, they see a world where anthropologists drive new offerings that prioritize the dynamics of human interactions as the starting point."

Jay Hasbrouck, *Ph.D., Author of* Ethnographic Thinking: From Method to Mindset

EmTech Anthropology

Careers at the Frontier

Edited by
Matt Artz and Lora Koycheva

Routledge
Taylor & Francis Group

NEW YORK AND LONDON

Designed cover image: © Marina Hrinchuk

First published 2025
by Routledge
605 Third Avenue, New York, NY 10158

and by Routledge
4 Park Square, Milton Park, Abingdon, Oxon OX14 4RN

Routledge is an imprint of the Taylor & Francis Group, an informa business

Library of Congress Cataloging-in-Publication Data
Names: Artz, Matt, 1981- editor. | Koycheva, Lora, editor.
Title: EmTech anthropology : careers at the frontier / edited by Matt Artz
and Lora Koycheva. Other titles: Em tech anthropology
Description: New York, NY : Routledge, 2024. |
Series: Anthropology and business | Includes bibliographical
references and index. |
Identifiers: LCCN 2024016700 (print) | LCCN 2024016701 (ebook) |
ISBN 9781032603025 (hardback) | ISBN 9781032602998 (paperback) |
ISBN 9781003458555 (ebook)
Subjects: LCSH: Anthropology–Vocational guidance. |
Technology–Anthropological aspects. | Social change.
Classification: LCC GN41.8 .E67 2024 (print) | LCC GN41.8 (ebook) |
DDC 301.023–dc23/eng/20240514
LC record available at https://lccn.loc.gov/2024016700
LC ebook record available at https://lccn.loc.gov/2024016701

ISBN: 978-1-032-60302-5 (hbk)
ISBN: 978-1-032-60299-8 (pbk)
ISBN: 978-1-003-45855-5 (ebk)

DOI: 10.4324/9781003458555

Typeset in Times New Roman
by Taylor & Francis Books

Contents

Figures

Acknowledgments

This book is about AI, robots, Web3, spaceships, and genetic engineering as emerging technologies, but we do not forget that, for all intents and purposes, books themselves also fall into that category. They are a technology that is never quite finished, and they have multiple beginnings scattered throughout a wide array of encounters, conversations, formal inquiries, and serendipitous finds along the journey of any anthropologist. We want to acknowledge those who have helped us in our thinking, our writing, and our continuous meanderings into the world of emerging technologies – not only directly but also indirectly, through the sheer force of their own applied and scholarly work as anthropologists in the world of technology.

First and foremost, we want to thank the authors in this book for sharing their inspiring stories and allowing us a glimpse into their journeys. We are enormously privileged to have been able to work with them in shaping the collection, and could not be more grateful for the experience of editing their work, which has made us rediscover fascinations in oldies but goodies (the Kula ring lives!), learn something new about the world we thought we knew (beer as a medieval form of bioengineering!), and find new energy in championing EmTech anthropology.

At Routledge (Taylor & Francis), this book has found a champion in Meagan Simpson. Her expertise and assistance have been invaluable, ensuring our journey through the publishing process was as smooth and successful as possible.

A special thanks is also due to Timothy de Waal Malefyt for his unwavering dedication to the field of anthropology. His books, including his most recent, *Business Anthropology: The Basics*, have been cornerstones in our understanding of the discipline. His work not only enriches the academic community but also serves as a guiding light for practitioners in the field. Beyond his professional commitment, Timothy's generous friendship and personal mentorship have been a source of profound inspiration and support that we are grateful for.

We must also acknowledge other mentors and friends who have shared with us the generosity of their time, insights, expertise, and fundamental human kindness at various times in our individual journeys, which eventually converged in writing this book. There are far too many to list here, but we want to thank, in no particular order, Elizabeth Briody, Robert Morais, Julia Gluesing, Christine Miller, Jay Hasbrouck, Patti Sunderland, Rita Denny, Cathleen Crain, Tom Maschio, Simon Roberts, Melissa Vogel, Susan Squires, Christina Wasson, Uldarico Rex Dumdum, Anders Kristian Munk, Dan Podjed, Louise Vang Jensen, Andrew Causey, the late and inimitable Joan Erdman, Robert Launay, Helen Schwarzman, Angela VandenBroek, Rafael Hostettler, Alona Kharchenko, Inga Treitler, and Katie Hillier.

Gratitude is also due to the many Language Learning Models (LLM) for becoming newfound creative sparring partners.

Last, but certainly not least, we must sincerely thank our families and partners for their love and support in putting up with our idealist, weird, impossible obsessions, not just when writing this book but throughout our *punk*, fringe, and misfit lives.

All mistakes are, as ever, our own.

Foreword

As an anthropologist who has spent over 30 years working at the intersection of business, technology, and culture, I was thrilled when the editors approached me to write the foreword for this timely volume, *EmTech Anthropology: Careers at the Frontier*. In the realms of knowledge and technology, it is rare to encounter a work as insightful and timely as the one presented in this volume. As an enthusiastic advocate for the fusion of traditional disciplines with emerging technologies (EmTech), I find myself aligned with the book's premise that anthropologists have a unique opportunity to play a critical role in how emerging technologies shape society and to participate as innovators themselves.

I first met Matt Artz at an American Anthropological Association conference and just recently had the pleasure to hear him speak about emerging technologies and the anthropological discipline at the 2023 Global Business Anthropology Summit in Mexico City. Our recent conversations have convinced me that he is a rising intellectual leader and pioneering practitioner in the burgeoning domain of business anthropology. Matt is an anthropologist, designer, and strategist, who stands at the crossroads of user experience, service design, and product management. His work, marked by innovative design and strategic thinking, has gained recognition from prestigious platforms such as Apple's Planet of the Apps and the South by Southwest (SXSW) Pitch Competition. His podcasts, including *Anthropology in Business* and *Anthro to UX*, reflect his commitment to exploring the transformative power of anthropology in business and technology. Matt's co-editor, Lora Koycheva, has a similarly unique blend of skills and experiences in emerging technologies through her work at the intersection of anthropology, innovation and entrepreneurship, STS, and robotics. Trained as a four-field anthropologist, she has been experimenting with building a hybrid practice which spans industry and academia. She has been working proactively to introduce anthropological methods and theories to the vast field of robotics and is a known champion of applied anthropology through her recent convenorship of the Applied Anthropology Network of the European Association of Social Anthropology.

A vivid narrative of Google's journey and its anthropological undertones, sets a profound backdrop for the book's exploration of the intersection between anthropology and emerging technologies. Google has had a monumental impact on accessing and organizing global knowledge. This story is not just about technological innovation; it's an exploration of the anthropological essence in these advancements. From Google's early algorithms to its latest advancements in search experience, the authors articulate how these developments parallel anthropological endeavors in understanding human knowledge and culture.

This book raises a pivotal question: What if anthropologists had pioneered such technological ventures early on? The text contemplates the historical skepticism within anthropology towards external opportunities, suggesting a missed chance for anthropologists to lead in technological innovation. This reflection sets the stage for a broader discussion on the role of anthropologists in emerging technology, a domain rapidly reshaping our society and the very fabric of human interaction.

The book's core argument is that anthropology, traditionally engaged with frontier work, broadly defined, has often been reactive rather than proactive where the emerging technologies frontier is concerned. The authors highlight missed opportunities where anthropological insights could have been pivotal. They advocate for a proactive anthropology that not only theorizes but also enacts and innovates within the EmTech space.

The narrative then shifts to the potential roles and career paths for anthropologists in the burgeoning field of EmTech. It emphasizes the need for anthropologists to move beyond academic boundaries and engage actively with the private sector, where their expertise should be actively championed, especially in technology companies.

The editors and their contributors reimagine the role of anthropologists as innovators and early adopters in EmTech. They call for, and are exemplars of, a new breed of anthropologists who are not just observers but active participants in shaping technological futures. The innovator stories in this collection – spanning roles in startups, consultancies, social justice movements, tech firms, and academia – provide an invaluable roadmap for that future. They model how anthropological skills translate powerfully to EmTech, organically blending intellectual inquiry with pragmatic, real-world, problem-solving impact. From AI ethics to space mission planning teams, these anthropologist-innovators locate practical openings to enact positive change. They hybridize methods and theory in context-sensitive ways. And they collaborate broadly to bridge disciplines. The authors' manifesto for anthropological innovation is a clarion call for the discipline to embrace its potential in shaping technology that is ethical, inclusive, and responsive to human needs.

In essence, this book is a bold and necessary step towards bridging anthropology and EmTech. It is a guide for current and future anthropologists to navigate and contribute to the rapidly evolving technological landscape. As someone deeply invested in this convergence, I am excited about the possibilities this book opens up for the discipline of anthropology and the broader field of technology – and for the tone it sets to the next cohorts of anthropologists entering EmTech.

The book also arrives at an urgent moment. Emerging tech promises to reshape society in unprecedented ways, demanding informed, ethical guidance and alternative visions. Anthropology is uniquely positioned to provide critical interventions into the sociocultural dimensions of EmTech innovation. By getting in early as user researchers, founders, and strategists, anthropologists can steer technology towards inclusive, equitable goals, making business more responsible and human-centered. The stakes could not be higher at this historic juncture. I cannot wait for perceptive, reflective readers to deeply explore these fascinating stories and begin dynamically charting their own trajectories as engaged anthropological innovators helping responsibly direct the future of emerging technologies. Our shared tomorrow depends on anthropologists making choices today.

Julia C. Gluesing, Ph.D.
Anthropologist and Professor
Global Executive Track Ph.D.
Industrial and Systems Engineering
Wayne State University
President, Cultural Connections, Inc.
Troy, Michigan

Contributors

Matt Artz is an anthropologist, designer, and technologist specializing in AI product development. He is the founder of Azimuth Labs, host of the *Anthropology in Business* and *Anthro to UX* podcasts, and co-editor of *EmTech Anthropology* and the forthcoming *Anthropology and AI*. His work has been featured on TED, UNESCO, South by Southwest, and Apple's Planet of the Apps.

Dr. Lora Koycheva is an anthropologist and technologist working at the intersection of anthropology, innovation, entrepreneurship, and robotics. She is Assistant Professor at the Chair of Technoscience Studies in Brandenburg Technical University. She is also building robots, actually! – a global initiative to rebuild the human condition with robots. From 2020 to 2023, she was a convenor of the EASA Applied Anthropology Network.

Laura Musgrave is a lead researcher studying the relationship between people and artificial intelligence. She helps organizations to build and use AI in a socially-responsible way. Laura leads on responsible AI at SPARCK, a leading global design and innovation consultancy, part of business technology consultancy, BJSS. She is also a research scholar in digital anthropology at the Ronin Institute, specializing in socially-responsible conversational AI. Laura was named one of "100 Brilliant Women in AI Ethics[TM]" in 2022.

Lianne Potter is a cyber-anthropologist for The AnthroSecurist, and Head of SecOps for a UK retailer. Lianne combines the human and the technical aspects of security to evangelize a cultural security transformation. She is an international speaker, podcast host for *Compromising Positions*, published author, board member of a tech community enterprise, and winner of multiple security awards. She is extending her studies in 2024 by studying for a master's in AI and Data Science.

Dr. Melyn McKay is an anthropologist working at the intersection of international aid and blockchain. McKay's ethnographic research focuses on Myanmar Buddhist nationalism, social cohesion, and the impact of online hate speech on conflict affected youth. She is the founder and CEO of

Coala Pay, a blockchain company building solutions to improve money movement in the international aid sector.

Dr. Anne W. Johnson is a professor in the graduate program in social anthropology at the Universidad Iberoamericana in Mexico City. Her interests include public anthropology, the social studies of science and technology, and the intersections between science and art. On her most recent research project, which revolves around Mexican imaginaries of outer space, she collaborates with the Mexican Space Agency and a space instrumentation laboratory at the UNAM, as well as with cultural and artistic collectives.

Mujtaba Hameed is a strategist and researcher committed to solving business challenges through deep human understanding. An anthropologist by training, he has worked and lived in London, Amsterdam and New York, leading strategic research projects that involve travel all over the world. His professional practice specializes in the tech sector, with recent clients ranging from established tech giants such as Meta and Google to newer startups in cybersecurity and biotech. He has a BA in Archaeology & Anthropology from the University of Oxford, and a MSc in Social & Cultural Anthropology from University College London.

Thomas Scott Hughes is a Ph.D. Cultural Anthropologist with over a decade of experience developing innovative strategies for world-leading organizations based on a deep understanding of human behavior and what can enable teams to connect as people. Thomas is passionate about using his insights from the world of academic research to create uniquely impactful results for businesses. His work has focused on driving value for organizations though deepening their understanding of their organizational culture and the customers they serve.

Dr. Kate Sieck is director of the Harmonious Communities team within the Human-Centered AI (HCAI) division at Toyota Research Institute (TRI). Dr. Sieck is focused on integrating social theory and context to the development of novel technologies. Prior to TRI, Dr. Sieck led research teams in the nonprofit sector (RAND Corporation), in marketing and consulting (OLSON, ReD Associates), and was a faculty member at several universities (Emory, Stanford). Dr. Sieck holds a bachelor's degree in anthropology from the University of Chicago, a master's degree in medical anthropology from SOAS in London, and a Ph.D. in anthropology from Emory University.

1 Introduction

Matt Artz and Lora Koycheva

What If We Were There?

In 1998, two doctoral students founded a company with the vision to "organize the world's knowledge and make it universally accessible and useful" (Google, n.d.). A quarter-century later, that startup, Google, has had an incalculable impact, having permeated and shaped the everyday lives of billions of people. Through its search engine and related products, Google now dominates how people discover information, communicate, collaborate, exchange goods, navigate, and even conduct academic research.

At the core of Google's efforts was its search engine based on PageRank, an algorithm that counted the number and quality of inbound links to determine a webpage's relative significance (Page, 2006). While seemingly trivial, this approach to designing a search engine revolutionized information retrieval and created one of the early super unicorns – a private company with a billion-dollar or more valuation – valued at $23 billion when it went public in 2004.

Since then, driven by its vision, commitment to innovation, and its ever-expanding coffers, Google has continued its relentless march toward organizing the world's knowledge. In 2012, it announced the Google Knowledge Graph, a graph database intended to model the semantic relationships between entities and concepts. With over 500 billion facts on over 3.5 billion entities, the Google Knowledge Graph aims to imbue Google's systems with an anthropologist-like grasp of the relationships and meanings that exist in the world (Sullivan, 2020). External sources estimate this has since grown to at least 5,000 billion facts and 50 billion entities (Barnard, 2023).

Then, around 2019, Google deployed Bidirectional Encoder Representations from Transformers (BERT), integrating advanced Natural Language Understanding (NLU) capabilities into its search architecture (Nayak, 2019). This innovation enabled Google to interpret the context of search queries more holistically by analyzing words in relation to the entire sentence rather than processing them in isolation. This change significantly enhanced how the search engine comprehended and made sense of human language.

More recently, and building on the work of BERT, it introduced the Search Generative Experience (SGE) based on the Multitask Unified Model

DOI: 10.4324/9781003458555-1

(MUM), an update to BERT that better handled the nuances of human language and offered multimodal and multilingual capabilities (Pichai, 2023). As of writing this introduction, SGE is now making use of Google's latest model, Gemini, which was natively trained to offer advanced multimodal reasoning, creating a new search experience that is inherently anthropological in its multimodal, multilingual, and multivocal capabilities that are intended to holistically synthesize knowledge across cultures (Pichai & Hassabis, 2023). While it is too early to say if SGE will replace the traditional search engine, the implications of AI-based answers in search engines (Barnard & Artz, 2023) could be world-changing if it succeeds in democratizing access to knowledge by breaking down existing barriers, such as language, literacy, sight, and hearing.

In sharing this story, we acknowledge that Google's system has tremendous gaps in its knowledge, is not universally equitable for political economy reasons anthropologists are well versed in, and is plagued by daunting questions, not least those concerning accuracy, provenance, and ownership. Yet, despite those shortcomings, we still ask, why didn't an anthropologist create a solution and found a company like Google?

Anthropology's *raison d'étre* is intimately concerned with relations, language, knowledge, and its representation, and as we will argue, innovation and the insights anthropologists produce are critical to responsibly designing such systems. So then, why didn't an anthropologist create Google?

Perhaps it would have been a venture by anthropologists had anthropology at the time not been generally suspicious and dismissive of the possibilities that the world outside of academic can offer to the academically trained. Could have, would have, should have – and wasn't. Although today, Google employs many anthropologists who offer insights in various roles – from user experience to strategy to foresight – we cannot help but wonder how Google would have looked if an anthropologist had been employee number 1 to 5 – or, indeed, a co-founder.

This question is not entertained nearly enough when we consider anthropologists' roles and careers in emerging technologies and innovation more broadly. This is a blind spot, which – given the speed and scale of disruptions that emerging technologies (EmTech) spell out for billions of people – we want to start correcting in this volume.

We make the case that although anthropology regularly engages with EmTech as a field, it has missed too many opportunities to get ahead of the changes brought forth by more recent EmTech. One such example is the convergence of mobile and social media, which has contributed to a rise in misinformation, extremism, and the erosion of democratic values (Jungherr & Schroeder, 2021; Iosifidis & Nicoli, 2020).

While it may be too late to fix social media, it is not too late to get ahead of other EmTech. In fact, the chapters that follow will demonstrate that now is an even more crucial time for anthropologists to forge new paths for themselves and the discipline in EmTech, as these technologies open up new fields for inquiry and practice as they offer us ways to expand and update our methodological toolbox; and, most importantly, allow anthropology to not only theorize and critique technology but to co-opt it and own it – a fundamental shift from insights and diagnosis to enactment and innovation.

Anthropology at a Crossroads

We undertook this volume because there are increasingly internal and external headwinds complicating the status quo of academic anthropology, but there are also opportunities for anthropologists in business. Opportunities, not just in terms of *any* job but fulfilling work where we can have agency and enact meaningful change by intervening in some of the most vexing problems humans have ever faced. For the coming years are likely to be defined by rapid socio-technical transformation brought on by EmTech, such as AI, robotics, genetic engineering, nanoparticles, space travel, quantum computing, and other yet-to-be-imagined technologies that will drastically reshape what it means to be human. Further, these disruptive transformations will continue to unfold within the context of climate change and war, both of which are causing mass migrations and adding additional pressures on individuals and institutions. Collectively, the disruptive impacts of these forces present us with unprecedented challenges and opportunities that require that business – and anthropology – are not done as usual. Ways that we argue could and should involve anthropologists, though at the same time, we must also avoid the hubris of the past.

Anthropology, despite being a historically significant discipline, suffers from an innovator's dilemma to liberally take inspiration from Clayton Christensen (Christensen, 1997). We argue it has lost its leadership role in higher education and society more broadly (however polemic and contested it was). As an incumbent discipline, it has undoubtedly not remained static, as we will describe. Yet, it has struggled to establish broad and popular relevance, especially when compared to disciplines and practices such as artificial intelligence, data science, economics, psychology, and design. In broadly orienting itself inwardly toward academic insularity rather than outwardly toward applied impact, anthropology has positioned itself as an often out-of-touch discipline. Further, it has been harmed by its lack of career readiness. These issues have created identity and legitimacy crises that further disenfranchise it as a sought-after body of knowledge and practice.

Unconventionally, we believe that many anthropologists have adopted a narrative that overestimates the uniqueness and superiority of our discipline compared to others. In informal gatherings, conferences, and private conversations, an unwelcome assumption often lingers: That the value of anthropology is self-evident and unparalleled. We frequently hear people disparage other disciplines, near and far, especially those in business, tech, and engineering, leaving us to wonder, what happened to our empathy and appreciation for "the other?" Unfortunately for our discipline, the corollary that naturally follows from this reasoning is that anthropology is the greatest of all disciplines and the missing ingredient whenever there is a problem. But if that is true, why aren't more anthropologists in the room? And why, if it is so great, does everyone not immediately realize it?

To be clear, at the same time, we do firmly believe anthropology is great in that it offers humanity tremendous value, difficult to master mindset and skills, and that it can and should contribute to all of the challenges and opportunities societies face, but we also argue that we need to reach across the aisle and challenge our narrative because the paradox between what we tell ourselves when we are together and the external reality, can't be starker. This can be seen in several existential crises of legitimacy. Politicians and government officials, such as then-Governor Rick Scott of Florida and Shad White of Mississippi, have questioned why subjects like anthropology should be taught within their states (NPR, 2011; Hartocollis, 2023). Well-regarded universities like Ithaca College, Howard University, Sheffield University, and the University of Western Australia have closed anthropology departments altogether. These developments are further compounded by entrenched institutional dogmas and highly institutionalized dynamics, usually coupled with tenure-track research demands and deliverables. They, in turn, often resist a more improvisational, interdisciplinary, experimental, and practical trajectory for the discipline outside of academia.

Additionally, an academic employability crisis has emerged due to an excess of trained anthropologists relative to available academic positions, resulting in a decline in anthropologists hired for academic roles since 2007 (Speakman et al., 2018). Within this glut, highly disturbing issues are emerging, such as personal stigma, mental health struggles, and financial hardship (e.g., Fotta et al., 2020). Instead of being an exception, the adjunctification of labor – a widespread academic practice across national contexts – has become the norm, with its exploitative nature disproportionately affecting women (e.g., Bataille et al., 2017; Fotta et al, 2020).

Yet, in the face of these crises of identity and legitimacy, there are many reasons to be hopeful and inspired.

Remobilizing Anthropology's Ethos

Most notably, we are hopeful and inspired because there is no shortage of meaningful work that can benefit from anthropology, such as Google's quest to organize the world's knowledge – if we are willing and able to meet the challenge. And despite the overall sentiment about anthropology in politics and the media, private sector organizations have shown an appreciation of anthropology despite their increasing reliance on other disciplines. Nowhere is this more present than in tech, which, despite the layoffs of 2022 and 2023, continues to remain one of the sirens calling anthropologists to a fulfilling life outside of academia, contributing to the growing alt-ac (alternative-academic) movement.

Most notably, UX research, strategy, service design, and product management have been the roles attracting significant attention, with startups and large multinational companies like Meta, Netflix, Google, and Atlassian thrilled to hire anthropologists. Freelance and consulting services provided by anthropologists, such as those by Stripe Partners and IS IT A BIRD, are also growing and thriving. Finally, as highlighted in this volume, there is a growing trend of tech companies founded by anthropologists such as McKay, Koycheva, and Artz. These companies are increasingly introducing "anthropology-first" tech products to the market.

The recognition from the private sector, especially in light of the state of academic anthropology, is long overdue and directly indebted to the early trailblazers (Briody, 2023) working at the intersection of anthropology, business, innovation, and technology, such as Lucy Suchman, Jeanette Bloomberg, Genevieve Bell, Sarah Pink, Kate Crawford, danah boyd, Mary Gray, Melissa Cefkin, Tracey Lovejoy, and Ken Anderson, to name but a few. These early adopters helped to open the scholarly horizons of anthropological inquiry into the world of technology. They demonstrated how researchers can promote interdisciplinary collaboration in both industry and academia and effectively integrate the critical analysis of socio-technical systems with human-centered design to influence innovation, policy, ethics, and public discourse.

Contributing to this shift, professional initiatives like EPIC, The EASA Applied Anthropology Network, and The Anthropological Career Readiness Network are helping to overcome decades of disdain for practicing anthropology and reshaping anthropologists' perceptions of non-academic careers and employment opportunities. As a result of this shift, there has also been a steady increase in publications of inspiring books, demonstrating the value of anthropological thinking and ethnography to other disciplines and practices such as those by Paul Dourish, together with Genevieve Bell (2011), Tom Boellstorff and Bill Maurer (2015), Maja Hojer Bruun (2022), Nick Seaver (2022), and Sarah Pink (2022).

Anthropologists have also made their mark in other closely associated areas of business, such as marketing, advertising, consumer research, design, and organizational studies, with genre-defining works by Allen Batteau (2009), Timothy de Wall Malefyt and Robert Morais (2012, 2017), Timothy de Wall Malefyt (2023), Melissa Cefkin (2010), Gary Ferraro and Elizabeth Briody (2015), Elizabeth Briody, Robert Trotter, and Tracy Meerwarth (2016), Patricia Sunderland and Rita Denny (2016), Julia Gluesing (2024), and Chris Miller (2024, 2018), among others, showcasing the transferability of traditional anthropological theories to the business sector.

Within this context, efforts to translate anthropology to a broader range of publics and professionals by demonstrating how to "see" and "think" like an anthropologist have gained much appreciated and needed popularity. Books like *The Ethnographic Mindset* by Jay Hasbrouck (2018), *Why the World Needs Anthropologists* edited by Podjed et al. (2020), *Anthropologists Wanted,* edited by Bakker et al. (2021), and *Anthro-Vision: A New Way to See in Business and Life* by Gillian Tett (2021) offer a range of perspectives on the usefulness and applicability of anthropological thinking, including its ability to collaborate with other fields. Tett, editor of the *Financial Times* and a trained social anthropologist, argued that in the age of artificial intelligence, the world needs *anthropological intelligence*, a unique perspective that anthropologists bring to any domain (Tett, 2021).

Additionally, career-oriented books exist on applying anthropology in professional settings, specifically the works of Riall Nolan (2003, 2017) and Sherylyn H. Briller and Amy Goldmacher (2020). These texts offer direction to those seeking a career in anthropology by exploring themes like defining professional aspirations, obtaining necessary expertise, securing positions across diverse industries, and implementing anthropological principles in various workplaces. Furthermore, they underline the significance of cooperation, collective effort, continual development, and substantial contribution to the profession and the field.

Finally, digital media, such as podcasts like *Anthropology in Business, Anthro to UX, This Anthro Life*, and *Response-ability.tech*, as well as blogs and newsletters, are extending the reach of anthropological insights to a broader audience than ever before. For example, Artz (this volume), in designing the architecture of his website, made use of knowledge graph and semantic search concepts to increase the discoverability of his blogs and the *Anthropology in Business* and *Anthro to UX* podcasts in search engines.

Concomitantly, new institutional formats are emerging, carving out much-needed space within academia to integrate anthropological knowledge and mindsets in technical realms, particularly engineering. Programs like the Cybernetics School at the Australian National University, The Emerging Technologies Lab in Melbourne, and the Techno-Anthropology Lab in Denmark are pushing the boundaries of anthropology, especially into disruptive emerging technologies.

This volume builds upon all of these previous efforts to inspire, educate, and make anthropology public, and aims to guide those trying to forge an alt-ac career and maintain an innovative anthropological practice that has impact, and gives meaning to the practitioner. To that end, we contend that business broadly, but EmTech specifically, allows anthropologists to remobilize their relationship with several key concepts and principles in anthropology. Further, it forces anthropologists to refocus instead on their own sense – and capacity – of agency, as professionals and as individuals, and their trademark anthropological ethos in enacting change in the world. In doing so, EmTech offers anthropology novel opportunities to examine how to innovate and expand on its trademark approaches – relativism, critique of capital and (post)colonial systems, and systems of power – and do something about them by mobilizing what the discipline has already established through studying them in a critical, theoretical vein.

To accomplish this, the volume highlights alternative career paths for anthropologists at the intersection of technology, culture, and society, as demonstrated through practitioners' stories from the EmTech frontier. In doing so, we hope to encourage other anthropologists to adopt and perform the role of early adopters (Rogers, 1962), albeit applied to a research space. Our goal is for them to position themselves as invaluable early contributors responsible for shaping EmTech, as an anthropologist should have been at Google. We want more employees, 1 to 5. Better yet, we want founder-anthropologists!

To that end, this volume is as much about anthropology's role in EmTech as it is about the stories of emerging anthropologists forging a career at technology's ever-expanding frontier. More to the point, it is about the intersection of the two, where improvisation happens, tensions arise, and new opportunities are born. The volume charts what these opportunities can be: For anthropology as a discipline, for emerging tech utilizing anthropology, and for the career of anthropologists working at this intersection. It is in this frontier space – the cutting edge of technological development – that anthropologists discover, abandon, and realize possibilities for the future – not just the future of technology but the future of anthropology.

The EmTech Opportunity

As a technology classification, EmTech represents a rapidly evolving area without a universally agreed-upon definition. Popular business and innovation publications often define such technologies based on their disruptive potential, a common business trope that owes its origins to Christensen (1997). For instance, the MIT Technology Review described EmTech as "radically transforming business, disrupting the technological status quo, and reinventing the way people work" (Ivory-Ganja, 2020).

Scholars of other disciplines have often emphasized various characteristics such as potential economic impact, uncertainty, novelty, and growth (e.g. Rotolo, Hicks, & Martin, 2015; Boon & Moors, 2008; Porter & Detampel, 1995; Small, Boyack, & Klavans, 2014). The concept of emergence is also a notable trait, given that these technologies are frequently depicted as being on the verge of realization.

This is exemplified by publications such as *MIT Tech Review, Popular Science, WIRED*, and others that release annual compilations of the most notable or imminent technologies set to revolutionize our lives that year. In recent times, these lists have primarily featured a diverse array of AI, biotech, Web3, robotics, automation, and other technologies examined in this volume. While many of these technologies have materialized to some extent, past EmTech seldom disrupted life as predicted and often failed to emerge as anticipated. Despite this, the discourse continues yearly, resulting in an emergent frontier that continually pushes out into the future.

The evolving landscape of technology, marked by these ever-changing predictions and innovations, presents a perfect opportunity for anthropology to engage with the frontier once more. Anthropology has long been familiar with the concept of emergence and frontiers in both physical and existential terms. As the discipline's history shows, it has a long albeit conflicted and well-critiqued tradition of going where no contact had yet been made in an ostensible effort to understand "others" and often fueling, intentionally or not, early modern ideas of European civilizational superiority that still endures today (e.g., Launay, 2018). Perhaps more radically still, what we might call early forms of anthropological thinking have been shown to shape the practices and endeavors of colonial officials as well as New World missionaries and adventurers (e.g., Laven, 2012; Montero, 2012), going as far back as Herodotus as the first example of an anthropologist making sense of a foreign world, at the edge of the map (e.g., Roberts, 2011). From the anthropological encounter as a knowledge practice coopted by colonialism (Asad, 1973) to the anthropological encounter as a means to decolonize anthropology (Faier & Rofel, 2014), anthropology's relationship to the frontier is in many ways indelible, not only in spatial but also in practical terms. Anna Tsing has succinctly suggested that frontiers are "not just discovered at the edge; they are projects in *making* geographic and temporal experience" (Tsing, 2005, 53; our emphasis).

In this sense, the frontier has always been both an antecedent and a product of anthropology. It is something that we both discover and that we make through our work as anthropologists. As a discipline, anthropology often relies on thinking with and working through outlying cases. What we call "everyday life" can be easily seen as what happens under the bell curve, and anthropologists regularly claim "everyday life" as their domain of inquiry and excel at it. Yet, it could be argued that the virtuosity of the discipline is to extract insights about everyday life precisely from outliers, outcasts, bellwether figures, models, and even events (e.g., Whitington, 2013).

Moreover, such a peripheral positioning also represents the continued marginal positions of such practitioners, whether seen from the center of tech or anthropology. In tech, anthropologists are rarely in as early as employees 1 to 5. Even those who join later rarely rise to highly influential positions capable of enacting significant change related to the organization's strategic intent. In anthropology, those who work at the EmTech frontier are just as often either regarded as traitors of sorts, working with otherwise demonized corporate entities, or else accused of falling prey to techno-solutionism and naive optimism.

And yet it is precisely this vantage point – on the edge of things – which we find full of potential for the future of anthropology as a discipline and for the relevance of the anthropological career as a professional role. Veena Das and Deborah Poole have paradigmatically argued that anthropology's position in the margins of the state has allowed the discipline to gain critical distance from its operations in pursuit of theorizing it (Das & Poole, 2004). The discipline's equally marginal position to emerging tech would afford it critical proximity in pursuit of practical impact and intervention. The workings of how such critical proximity might look are what the authors demonstrate in this volume.

The frontier represents, therefore, not only the temporal orientation of the work of these anthropologists in an anticipatory (English-Lueck & Avery, 2020; Stephan & Flaherty, 2019), future-oriented (Pink, 2022), and even untimely (Rabinow, 2011) vein. It also represents the personal risks such practitioners take in opting out of the familiar, if deceptive, comforts of the academic track and designing a career outside of existing templates, much in the sense of edgework as taking risks (Lyng, 2014).

Navigating this uncharted territory, anthropologists are increasingly venturing into studying EmTech and its societal implications. Yet despite long-standing theoretical conversations around emergence (e.g., Fischer, 2020), the exploration of EmTech from an interventional anthropological perspective has received relatively limited attention. Only recently has the topic garnered an increasing interest, most notably from Sarah Pink (e.g., Pink, 2022) and in design anthropology more broadly (e.g., Otto & Smith, 2020).

These trailblazers work at the crossroads of anthropology, business, innovation, and technology and have taken the lead in broadening the scope of anthropological inquiry in this domain. They have investigated crucial aspects such as the cultural dimensions of technology, AI ethics, social implications of machine learning, technology's intersection with society and youth culture, and the influence of EmTech on labor and identity. Their work has enriched our comprehension of the intricate relationship between technology, society, and culture and underscored the significance of interdisciplinary research and collaboration in understanding and shaping the future of these emerging technologies.

Sarah Pink especially stands out in her extensive and prolific dedication to the topic of both emerging technologies, such as artificial intelligence and automated decision-making systems (Pink et al., 2022), and a future-oriented, interventionist anthropology (Pink & Salazar, 2017; Pink, Akama, & Sumartojo, 2018; Lanzeni & Pink, 2021; Lanzeni et al., 2022). Situating her agenda at the intersection of both EmTech and an interventional exploration of possible futures, her work is a notable example of how anthropology can actively contribute to EmTech's development and ethical considerations.

It is also notable for her call to anthropologists to rethink, rework, and reposition their work vis-à-vis questions of how the discipline moves forward. She notes, "We must *become players in the same futures-focused spaces* as other stakeholders in the future of emergent technologies, create new collaborations and bring different, diverse and everyday stories to the center" (Pink, 2022: 11; our emphasis). And while she pursues this agenda through the design anthropological perspective, which she helped to pioneer and champion, in this volume, we have compiled a more diffuse collection of perspectives that borrow on a range of approaches: From design anthropology to speculation to software engineering, all the while pushing forward novel forms of being an anthropologist in and for the world.

We are, of course, aware of the old trope (or, more harshly, critical caricature) of "the anthropologist as hero" working in the gloried exotics (Sontag, 1994 [1963]). But in the lack of a practical alternative suggestion on how to intervene and be active in the world beyond representational efforts, we take a cue from Sarah Pink. We advocate for a proactive and engaged anthropology that immerses itself in the dynamic world of EmTech, forging new collaborations and amplifying diverse and everyday narratives to shape the future of technological development. By positioning anthropologists as active innovators, visionaries, and creators, we can ensure that the discipline remains at the forefront of ethical, inclusive, and responsible innovation, ultimately guiding the trajectory of technology, society, and our discipline.

To accomplish this goal, we delve deeper into how anthropologists turn to the art and science of innovation, examining the methods, practices, and collaborations that have enabled them to make significant contributions to EmTech fields. By giving voice to their successes, challenges, and perspectives for navigating interdisciplinary landscapes at the frontier, we hope to inspire and guide the next generation of anthropologists to build on these foundations.

Finally, it is essential to remember that we often introduce concepts, modes of work, and practical collaborations, which are often viewed as antagonistic to the corporate world. This is especially true of those working in academia. Yet, in this volume, we contend that anthropology has always been an innovative discipline, and anthropologists are often innovators who help to push the boundaries of academia and industry. They just don't realize it. But the time has come for that to change and for us to embody and perform the role of the innovator at the edge of all future frontiers.

Anthropology and the Innovator's Turn

The evolution of anthropology is often mapped out in relation to schools of thought responding to one another and departing, redressing, or even vehemently disagreeing with one another. These "turns," in theory, have often been colored by national schools of thought, especially the US versus Great Britain. The early disciplinary focus on comparing and contrasting civilizational models of culture through cataloging gave way to preoccupations with social structures and organization. That was followed by a focus on meaning, culture, and theories of how society and culture reproduce, as well as a period of coming to grips theoretically and empirically with the profound effects of neoliberal capitalism on global societies.

It is only more recently, however, that anthropology has seen a novel turn in method and practice. For example, as a speculative and intermediary object to think with, interact with, and learn from, the prototype has made a jump from engineering into ethnography (e.g., Marcus, 2014; Corsín Jiménez, 2014; Estalella, 2015; Corsín Jiménez & Estalella, 2017). Speculative anthropology – which investigates the possibilities and potentialities of the kinds of worlds "we could or should inhabit" (Anderson et al., 2018), actively engages imaginaries and science fiction as a genre (Wolf-Meyer, 2018; Lempert, 2018; Attari et al., 2021). As noted, design anthropology emerged as a distinct "style of knowing" and an intentionally interventional approach that aims to use co-creation and participatory practices to address complex socio-cultural challenges (Otto & Smith, 2013; Miller, 2020; Miller, 2018). Yet, despite these changes, much of anthropology remains steadfast in its commitment to field-work, self-reflexivity, critique, and ethical responsibility in speaking truth to power. While these enduring values are relevant, they also pave the way for exploring new frontiers, such as innovation.

Arguably, a replotting of this intellectual landscape of ideas and arguments reveals that in being adaptive, curious, and creative, anthropologists have always been innovators already well before these novel approaches gathered speed in recent years, even when focused on classic scholarly prerogatives rather than interventional ones. Though no single introduction could sum-marize the many anthropologists whose work qualifies for that label, a few notable examples will illustrate this alternative remapping. The outbreak of World War I forced Bronislaw Malinowski's extended stays in Papua New Guinea and created an opportunity out of the crisis, which largely shaped the way extended fieldwork still looks and is conducted today: An innovation by necessity.

Another example could be Dell Hymes' *Reinventing Anthropology* (1999 [1972]). It brought together several anthropologists who actively explored ways to move beyond the confines of its ongoing disciplinary dogmas at the time. Notably, Laura Nader's essay "Up the Anthropologist" (1972) from that collection catalyzed the shift that led to anthropologists moving away from studying hunter-gatherers and indigenous tribes and considering instead boardrooms and modern organizations as field sites and bona fide anthro-pological topics: An innovative move which created not only the anthro-pology *of* organizations but equally paved the grounds for organizational anthropologists in a more applied vein.

Paul Rabinow's *Reflections on Fieldwork in Morocco* (2007 [1974]) offers another trailblazing example in which he wrote about the ethnographic pro-duction of knowledge in the highly personal terms we take for granted – and standard – today but which were found to be near-scandalous and dangerous to his academic career at the time.

One general tendency in these non-exhaustive examples of doing something new with and within anthropology has been to move the discipline in schools of thought that incrementally increase anthropological theory through a par-ticular stripe of thinking. Another has been to do so in turns, which marks a radical break from the dominance of such schools of thought. The former is often vested in ideological garbs, often opposed to one another.

As the work featured in this volume will illustrate, working with emerging tech and innovating anthropology from within the EmTech context requires different kinds of methodological and theoretical moves. It requires that EmTech anthropologists are school-of-thought agnostic. Although ideology-aware, they remain ideology-indifferent. Their work does not necessarily pledge to defend a theoretical canon or respond to a different intellectual camp. Instead, they have the humility to approach problems and challenges flexibly and adaptively, carefully selecting the most suitable theoretical perspectives and methodological approaches for the task.

Anthropologists in this space read what they must, where they must, and how they must, and not from within the familiar comfort of their preferred theoretical and ideological sympathies. This includes literature from business and entrepreneurship, information systems and engineering, and other social and human sciences, to name a few. In remaining non-committal but attuned to the needs of the problem space, they aim to design contextually appropriate solutions.

To be clear, this is not an argument for techno-solutionism, which refers to the belief that technology alone can solve complex social, political, and environmental issues. However, it is an unabashed argument for urgently needed *solutions* to address complex, ill-defined, and difficult-to-solve problems. These types of problems have been called "wicked problems" and have multiplied in recent decades. Reasons for this are numerous, from the scale and scope of technological advancement to the backdrop of the volatile, uncertain, complex, and ambiguous (VUCA) (Barber, 1992) social context that has arisen since the end of the Cold War (Bennis & Nanus, 1985). Increasingly and frighteningly, many of these problems could aptly be defined as existential crises, as noted earlier.

Likewise, we contend that solutions are needed. By this, we mean the proactive pursuit of interdisciplinary, culturally sensitive, and anthropologically attuned approaches to address these multifaceted challenges, leveraging not only technological advancements but also insights from the social sciences, humanities, and other fields to create comprehensive and effective resolutions.

Although we recognize the potential for controversy in using the term solutions given the connotation of solutionism, it is important to acknowledge that a problem without a solution is just that. It's a problem for one or more groups, often those who are disempowered. Though we are well aware that there are equity issues in determining who gets to define what is a problem and what is a solution, we contend that a discipline averse to contributing to the betterment of society is not a discipline at all. And so, we call on anthropologists to act like innovators and work toward shaping these emerging technologies.

To do that, we argue that we need more anthropologists willing to work at the frontiers within industry leadership positions outside the confines of higher education alone. We need these individuals to act now – as early adopters within EmTech – to get in early on developing new technologies as one of the first employees or, ideally, as the founder so that we can play a role in shaping future possibilities. More importantly, we need to do this in successive waves to establish a sustained normalized critical mass of anthropologists within the field, at each new frontier, as innovators capable of strategically influencing long-term visions and directions of EmTech.

To achieve this, we suggest interested anthropologists learn from the journeys and practices exemplified by the authors in this book. Their stories, detailed in the subsequent chapters, serve as a testament to the profound potential impact of anthropological insight in EmTech and provide a blueprint for future practitioners.

In Chapter 2, Laura Musgrave demonstrates how her work ensures a more responsible AI development. She takes the reader through the many aspects that can and often do make AI intransparent and biased and how, through her direct engagement in shaping conversational AI technology and policy, she can better guide the development of the technology and its attendant processes.

Similarly, Matt Artz picks up the AI conversation in Chapter 3 and shares his journey toward designing a gamified participatory recommender system as a co-founder of an art tech startup. Through his research, Artz discovered that existing recommender systems tend to amplify inequality by favoring creators with more economic, social, and cultural capital. To address this, he designed an alternative model that gives all creators, regardless of their existing access to capital, an opportunity to gain visibility in the recommender system through their participation. Presenting a multidisciplinary and mixed-methods approach, Artz shares how he combined ethnographic research with computational methods to reimagine a transparent and equitable machine learning recommender system model.

In Chapter 4, Lianne Potter lifts the veil on the world of an anthropologist in the cybersecurity sector. She discusses how she has become a cybersecurity professional from a background in photography and anthropology and how, in her work, she advocates for an anthro-centric approach. Drawing on concepts like reciprocity and storytelling, she outlines practical applications of an anthropological lens for understanding security culture, behaviors, and risk.

Melyn McKay, in Chapter 5, draws on theories of value, exchange, and extra-state relations to outline how anthropology can guide the trajectory of blockchain-based products, such as in the payments sector. Noting how anthropological theory has helped her overcome her own biases about cryptocurrencies, her chapter serves as a powerful example of how anthropologists as innovators and early adopters shaping emerging tech like Web3, can direct it toward equitable alternatives that serve excluded communities.

Also working from a founder perspective, in Chapter 6, Lora Koycheva shares why an anthropologist might want to commit to building robots in the hybrid spaces between academia and venturing. She argues for turning the ethnographic imagination into anthropological speculation as a basis for creating emerging hardware. She provokes how anthropological theory can make the jump and inform new, much-needed beyond-human paradigms for climate change mitigation with robots.

Speculation plays a role also in Chapter 7, where Anne Johnson demonstrates how an anthropologist can navigate the boundaries of academia and the space industry. She outlines an engaged anthropology shaping the trajectory of NewSpace in the postcolonial context through her interdisciplinary work "alongside" space engineers and enthusiasts, and she puts the trademark anthropological reflexivity, experimentation, and grassroots inclusion.

Mujtaba Hameed, in Chapter 8, tackles the meaning of "doing good work" as an anthropologist within the consulting sector in a highly polemic field such as genetically engineered food. In discussing his journey, he offers a glimpse into how anthropologists balance their own ethical aspirations for the world while simultaneously delivering value to clients in the consulting sector by deploying classic anthropological methods such as semiotics analysis.

Similarly attuned to ethics is Chapter 9, in which Thomas Scott Hughes takes the reader to the fast-paced innovation cycles of biotech. His work addresses an important nexus between ethics, organizational culture, and DEI policies, and he showcases how his work has contributed to directing a biotech company toward equitable, ethical outcomes.

Finally, to wrap it all up in the concluding chapter, Kate Sieck offers a compelling meditation on the many ways anthropology and EmTech come together and can continue together in the future, challenging us to rethinking our relationships with emerging technologies.

Across these chapters, readers will find many similar themes, such as agency, enactment and problem-solving, persuasion, intervention, reflexivity, engagement, experimentation, iteration, speculation, hybridizing, collaboration, co-creation, and organizational culture, all in the spirit of innovating. These are all required, though not sufficient. To responsibly innovate, we also must acknowledge the practical implications and real-world challenges that arise from our innovation work, and part of that entails acknowledging the equity issues of solutioning emerging sociotechnical systems. To that end, we have endeavored to demonstrate the importance of ethics to our future by weaving such discussions into each chapter. Rather than leave ethics for the last chapter, as many books do, we felt it was imperative to situate the ethical challenges in the context of the discussion on emerging technologies.

When taken together, this volume emphasizes the value of studying and incorporating anthropology into EmTech and EmTech into anthropology, demonstrating the significant contributions each field can impart to each other. Furthermore, the volume explores how anthropologists can leverage their unique perspectives to promote more responsible, inclusive, and people-centered technological innovations, enriching the field and its relevance in today's rapidly evolving landscape. By embracing these opportunities, anthropologists can contribute to shaping a future where technology serves the needs and values of diverse societies, ensuring that innovations are developed ethically, sustainably, and with a deep appreciation for the complexities of the human experience.

Anthropologists must embrace emerging tech in ways that are more than just a field site but also a domain for anthropology. Furthermore, they need to contribute to the development of anthropological practice by embracing careers at the fuzzy front end of innovation and incorporating some of these technologies into our methodological practice. By doing so, they can become innovator anthropologists, or even *Anthro-Solutionists*, who combine the strengths of anthropology with business and technology acumen, emphasizing the importance of anthropological perspectives in technology development, ethical considerations, and lasting impact. Through their innovative approach, Anthro-Solutionists contribute to shaping a more ethical, inclusive, and responsible future.

And so, we look forward to your feedback on this volume and hope that you will reach out and engage with all of the authors, but before turning to the chapters, we want to leave you with a radical call to action.

An Anthropological Innovators Manifesto

We believe anthropologists must turn to innovation to address the most pressing challenges and opportunities, especially those presented by EmTech. Likewise, and generously taking inspiration from the Agile Manifesto (Beck et al., 2001), we have put together an anthropological manifesto to help guide this necessary shift.

We value:

Agency over dogma.
Enactment over critique.
Collaboration over confrontation.
Experimentation over orthodoxy.

We commit to:

Hybrid roles spanning industry and academia that create social impact.

Interdisciplinary cross-pollination.

Appreciate businesses and acquire organizational acumen.

Leadership and teamwork.

We pledge to act as innovators shaping emerging technologies toward more ethical, equitable, inclusive, and sustainable futures that serve the needs of diverse global societies.

We vow to intervene at technology's expanding frontiers as innovators creating solutions that combine anthropology's strengths with strategic thinking and action.

We are anthropological innovators.

Bibliography

Anderson, Ryan B., Emma Louise Backe, Taylor Nelms, Elizabeth Reddy, and Jeremy Trombley. 2018. "'Speculative Anthropologies.' Theorizing the Contemporary." *Fieldsights*, December 18. https://culanth.org/fieldsights/series/speculative-anthropologies.

Asad, Talal, ed. 1973. *Anthropology & the Colonial Encounter*. Vol. 6. London: Ithaca Press.

Attari, Sanya, Charley Scull, and Mahboobeh Harandi. 2021. "Leveraging Speculative Design to Re-Imagine Product Roadmaps." In *Ethnographic Praxis in Industry Conference Proceedings*, Vol. 2021, no. 1, pp. 190–207. https://doi.org/10.1111/epic.12068.

Bakker, Laurens, Masja Cohen, and Walter Faaij. 2021. *Anthropologists Wanted: Why Organizations Need Anthropology*. Amsterdam University Press.

Barber, H. F. 1992. "Developing Strategic Leadership: The US Army War College Experience." *Journal of Management Development* 11 (6): 4–12.

Barnard, Jason. 2023. 2023 E-E-A-T Google Knowledge Graph Update. October 25. https://www.youtube.com/watch?v=RhJlCP-gymY.

Barnard, Jason, and Matt Artz. 2023. "Search Marketing in the Age of AI: Understanding the Marketing Implications of Search, Assistive and Answer Engines." *Journal of Digital & Social Media Marketing* 11 (3): 244–260.

Bataille, Pierre, Nicky Le Feuvre, and Sabine Kradolfer Morales. 2017. "Should I Stay or Should I Go? The Effects of Precariousness on the Gendered Career Aspirations of Postdocs in Switzerland." *European Educational Research Journal* 16 (2–3): 313–331.

Batteau, Allen W. 2009. *Technology and Culture*. Long Grove, IL: Waveland Press.

Beck, Kent, et al. 2001. *The Agile Manifesto*. Agile Alliance. http://agilemanifesto.org/.

Bennis, Warren, and Burt Nanus. 1985. *Leaders: The Strategies for Taking Charge*. New York, NY: Harper & Row.

Boellstorff, Tom, and Bill Maurer. 2015. *Data: Now Bigger and Better!* Chicago: University of Chicago Press.

Boon, Wouter, and Ellen Moors. 2008. "Exploring Emerging Technologies using Metaphors – A Study of Orphan Drugs and Pharmacogenomics." *Social Science & Medicine* 66 (9): 1915–1927.

Briller, Sherylyn H., and Amy Goldmacher. 2020. *Designing an Anthropology Career: Professional Development Exercises*. Lanham, MD: Rowman & Littlefield Publishers.

Briody, Elizabeth. 2023. *Trailblazing Anthropology*. Termini Distinguished Anthropology. March 23. https://www.youtube.com/watch?v=OYMpo4UWByc.

Briody, Elizabeth, Robert Trotter, and Tracy Meerwarth. 2016. *Transforming Culture: Creating and Sustaining a Better Manufacturing Organization*. New York: Palgrave Macmillan.

Bruun, Maja Hojer. 2022. *The Palgrave Handbook of the Anthropology of Technology*. London Borough of Camden: Palgrave Macmillan, 2022.

Cefkin, Melissa, ed. *Ethnography and the Corporate Encounter: Reflections on Research in and of Corporations*. New York: Berghahn Books.

Christensen, Clayton. 1997. *The Innovator's Dilemma*. Cambridge, MA: Harvard Business School Press.

Corsín Jiménez, Alberto. 2014. "Introduction: The Prototype: More than Many and Less than One." *Journal of Cultural Economy* 7 (4): 381–398. https://doi.org/10.1080/17530350.2013.858059.

Corsín Jiménez, Alberto, and Adolfo Estalella. 2017. "Ethnography: A Prototype." *Ethnos* 82 (5): 846–866. https://doi.org/10.1080/00141844.2015.1133688.

Das, Veena, and Deborah Poole. 2004. "Anthropology in the Margins." In: *Santa Fe: School of American Research Seminar*.

Dourish, Paul, and Genevieve Bell. 2011. *Divining a Digital Future: Mess and Mythology in Ubiquitous Computing*. Cambridge, MA: MIT Press.

English-Lueck, J. A., and Miriam Avery. 2020. "Futures Research in Anticipatory Anthropology." In *Oxford Research Encyclopedia of Anthropology*.

Estalella, Adolfo. 2015. "Prototyping Social Sciences: Emplacing Digital Methods." In: *Digital Methods for Social Science: An Interdisciplinary Guide to Research Innovation*, pp. 127–142. London: Palgrave Macmillan UK.

Faier, Lieba, and Lisa Rofel. 2014. "Ethnographies of Encounter." *Annual Review of Anthropology* 43 (2014): 363–377. https://doi.org/10.1146/annurev-anthro-102313-030210.

Ferraro, Gary, and Elizabeth K. Briody. 2015. *The Cultural Dimension of Global Business*. New York: Routledge.

Fischer, Michael M. J. 1999. "Emergent Forms of Life: Anthropologies of Late or Postmodernities." *Annual Review of Anthropology* 28 (1): 455–478. https://doi.org/10.1146/annurev.anthro.28.1.455.

Fischer, Michael M. J. 2020. *Emergent Forms of Life and the Anthropological Voice*. Durham, NC: Duke University Press.

Fotta, Martin, Mariya Ivancheva, and Raluca Pernes. 2020. *The Anthropological Career in Europe: A Complete Report on the EASA Membership Survey*. European Association of Social Anthropologists. https://doi.org/10.22582/easaprecanthro.

Gluesing, Julia C., Christine Z.Miller, and Helga Wild. 2024. *Innovation in the Anthropological Perspective: Insights and Consequences for the Theory, Practice, and Design of Innovating*. New York: Routledge.

Google. n.d. About Google. https://about.google/.

Hartocollis, Anemona. 2023. *Can Humanities Survive the Budget Cuts?*November 3. https://www.nytimes.com/2023/11/03/us/liberal-arts-college-degree-humanities.html.

Hasbrouck, Jay. 2018. *Ethnographic Thinking: From Method to Mindset*. New York: Routledge.

Hymes, Dell. 1999 [1972]. *Reinventing Anthropology*. Ann Arbor: University of Michigan Press.

Iosifidis, Petros, and Nicholas Nicoli. 2020. *Digital Democracy, Social Media and Disinformation*. London Routledge. https://doi.org/10.4324/9780429318481

Ivory-Ganja, Abby. 2020. *The Business of Emerging Technologies*. April 28. https://www.technologyreview.com/2020/04/28/1000760/the-business-of-emerging-technologies/.

Jungherr, Andreas, and Ralph Schroeder. 2021. "Disinformation and the Structural Transformations of the Public Arena: Addressing the Actual Challenges to Democracy." *Social Media + Society* 7 (1). https://doi.org/10.1177/2056305121988928

Lanzeni, Debora, and Sarah Pink. 2021. "Digital Material Value: Designing Emerging Technologies." *New Media & Society* 23 (4): 766–779. https://doi.org/10.1177/1461444820954193.

Lanzeni, Débora, Karen Waltorp, Sarah Pink, and Rachel C. Smith, eds. 2022. *An Anthropology of Futures and Technologies*. Abingdon, Oxon: Routledge.

Launay, Robert. 2018. *Savages, Romans, and Despots: Thinking about Others from Montaigne to Herder*. Chicago: University of Chicago Press.

Laven, Mary. 2012. "Jesuits and Eunuchs: Representing Masculinity in Late Ming China." *History and Anthropology* 23 (2): 199–214. https://doi.org/10.1080/02757206.2012.675794.

Lempert, William. 2018. "Planeterra Nullius: Science Fiction Writing and the Ethnographic Imagination." Theorizing the Contemporary, *Fieldsights*, December 18. https://culanth.org/fieldsights/planeterra-nullius-science-fiction-writing-and-the-ethnographic-imagination.

Lyng, Stephen. 2014. "Action and Edgework: Risk Taking and Reflexivity in Late Modernity." *European Journal of Social Theory* 17 (4): 443–460. https://doi.org/10.1177/1368431013520392.

Marcus, George. 2014. "Prototyping and Contemporary Anthropological Experiments with Ethnographic Method." *Journal of Cultural Economy* 7 (4): 399–410https://doi.org/10.1080/17530350.2013.858061.

Miller, C., 2020. *Design Anthropology.* https://oxfordre.com/anthropology/view/10.1093/acrefore/9780190854584.001.0001/acrefore-9780190854584-e-7.

Miller, Christine. 2018. *Design + Anthropology: Converging Pathways in Anthropology and Design.* New York: Routledge.

Montero, Paula. 2012. "The Contribution of Post-colonial Critique to an Anthropology of Missions." *Religion and Society* 3 (1): 115–129. https://doi.org/10.3167/arrs.2012.030107.

Nader, L. 1999 [1972]. "Up the Anthropologist: Perspectives Gained from Studying Up." In: Hymes, Dell. *Reinventing Anthropology.* Ann Arbor: University of Michigan Press.

Nayak, Paul. 2019. *Understanding Searches Better than Ever Before.* October 25. https://blog.google/products/search/search-language-understanding-bert/.

Nolan, Riall W. 2003. *Anthropology in Practice: Building a Career Outside the Academy.* Boulder, CO: Lynne Rienner Publishers.

Nolan, Riall W. 2017. *Using Anthropology in the World: A Guide to Becoming an Anthropologist Practitioner.* New York: Routledge.

NPR. 2011. Fla. Gov. Rick Scott Slams Anthropology Degrees. October 13. https://www.npr.org/2011/10/13/141305593/fla-gov-rick-scott-slams-anthropology-degrees.

Otto, T., and Rachel Charlotte Smith. 2013. "Design Anthropology: A Distinct Style of Knowing." In: *Design Anthropology: Theory and Practice.* pp. 1–28. London: Bloomsbury Academic, doi:10.4324/9781003085195-1.

Otto, Ton, and Rachel Charlotte Smith. 2020. "Design Anthropology: A Distinct Style of Knowing." In: *Design Anthropology*, pp. 1–29. New York: Routledge.

Page, Lawrence. 2006. *Method for Node Ranking in a Linked Database.* United States Patent US7058628B1. June 6.

Pichai, Sundar. 2023. *Google I/O 2023: Making AI More Helpful for Everyone.* May 10. https://blog.google/technology/ai/google-io-2023-keynote-sundar-pichai/#ai-products.

Pichai, Sundar, and Demis Hassabis. 2023. Introducing Gemini: Our Largest and Most Capable AI Model. December 6. https://blog.google/technology/ai/google-gemini-ai/.

Pink, Sarah. 2022. *Emerging Technologies/Life at the Edge of the Future.* Abingdon: Routledge.

Pink, Sarah, and Juan Francisco Salazar. 2017. "Anthropologies and Futures: Setting the Agenda." In: Salazar, Juan Francisco, Sarah Pink, Andrew Irving, and Johannes Sjöberg, eds. *Anthropologies and Futures: Researching Emerging and Uncertain Worlds.* London: Bloomsbury Publishing.

Pink, Sarah, Yoko Akama, and Shanti Sumartojo. 2018. *Uncertainty and Possibility: New Approaches to Future Making in Design Anthropology*. London: Bloomsbury Publishing.

Pink, Sarah, Martin Berg, Deborah Lupton, and Minna Ruckenstein. 2022. *Everyday Automation: Experiencing and Anticipating Emerging Technologies*. Abingdon: Routledge.

Podjed, Dan, Meta Gorup, Pavel Borecký, and Carla Guerrón Montero, eds. 2020. *Why the World Needs Anthropologists*. New York: Routledge.

Porter, Alan L., and Michael J. Detampel. 1995. "Technology Opportunities Analysis." *Technological Forecasting and Social Change* 49 (3): 237–255.

Rabinow, Paul. 2007. *Reflections on Fieldwork in Morocco: With a New Preface by the Author*. Berkeley: University of California Press.

Rabinow, Paul. 2011. *The Accompaniment: Assembling the Contemporary*. Chicago: University of Chicago Press.

Roberts, Jennifer T. 2011. *Herodotus: A Very Short Introduction*. Vol. 272. Oxford University Press, USA.

Rogers, Everett M. 1962. *Diffusion of Innovations*. New York, Free Press of Glencoe.

Rotolo, Daniele, Diana Hicks, and Ben R. Martin. 2015. "What is an Emerging Technology?" *Research Policy* 44 (10): 1827–1843.

Seaver, Nick. 2022. *Computing Taste: Algorithms and the Makers of Music Recommendation*. Chicago: University of Chicago Press.

Small, Henry, Kevin W. Boyack, and Richard Klavans. 2014. "Identifying Emerging Topics in Science and Technology." *Research Policy* 43 (8): 1450–1467.

Sontag, Susan. 1994 [1963]. "The Anthropologist as Hero." In: *Against Interpretation*, pp. 69–81. New York: Picador.

Speakman, Robert J., Carla S. Hadden, Matthew H. Colvin, Justin Cramb, K. C. Jones, Travis W. Jones, Isabelle Lulewiczet al. 2018. "Market Share and Recent Hiring Trends in Anthropology Faculty Positions." *PloS ONE* 13 (9): e0202528.

Stephan, Christopher, and Devin Flaherty. 2019. "Introduction: Experiencing Anticipation. Anthropological Perspectives." *The Cambridge Journal of Anthropology* 37 (1): 1–16. https://doi.org/10.3167/cja.2019.370102.

Sullivan, Danny. 2020. *A Reintroduction to Our Knowledge Graph and Knowledge Panels*. May 20. https://blog.google/products/search/about-knowledge-graph-and-knowledge-panels/.

Sunderland, Patricia L., and Rita M. Denny. 2016. *Doing Anthropology in Consumer Research*. New York: Routledge.

Tett, Gillian. 2021. *Anthro-Vision: A New Way to See in Business and Life*. New York: Simon and Schuster.

Tsing, Anna Lowenhaupt. 2005. *Friction: An Ethnography of Global Connection*. Princeton, NJ: Princeton University Press.

de Waal Malefyt, Timothy. 2023. *Business Anthropology: The Basics*. New York: Routledge.

de Waal Malefyt, Timothy, and Robert J. Morais. 2012. *Advertising and Anthropology: Ethnographic Practice and Cultural Perspectives*. New York: Routledge.

de Waal Malefyt, Timothy, and Robert J. Morais, eds. 2017. *Ethics in the Anthropology of Business: Explorations in Theory, Practice, and Pedagogy*. New York: Routledge.

Whitington, Jerome. 2013. "Fingerprint, Bellwether, Model Event: Climate Change as Speculative Anthropology." *Anthropological Theory* 13 (4): 308–328.

Wolf-Meyer, Matthew. 2018. "The Necessary Tension between Science Fiction and Anthropology." Theorizing the Contemporary, *Fieldsights*, December 18. https://culanth.org/fieldsights/the-necessary-tension-between-science-fiction-and-anthropology.

2 Everyday Life, Ever-Present AI
Data and Privacy in Voice Assistants and Chatbots

Laura Musgrave

Introduction

"Where is that sound coming from?" My colleague asked. Apparently, the sudden interruption to our meeting was my mobile phone's voice assistant, which was inside my bag, across the room. This was a new and unsettling experience for me. However, my participants had previously shared similar stories with me. Some had described unexpected actions like this as "creepy." It also made them wonder how much their ever-present voice assistants knew about them.

I was working in industry, and the use of voice assistants and chatbots was growing rapidly. Despite this popularity, I learned that questions persisted about data use and privacy. This is why I went on to study anthropology.

Since then, 36% of UK households now own a smart speaker (Kunst, 2023), compared to just 10% in 2018 (Feldman, 2018). Conversational AI's presence in everyday life has continued to grow, with the public release of generative AI chatbots in 2022. One popular example, ChatGPT, garnered over 100 million users in the first two months after its launch by Open AI (Hu, 2023).

While I have conducted research internationally during my career, my AI studies have focused on participants in the UK. These have mainly been in industry, with some in academia. Over the years, questions about manufacturers' collection, use, storage, and sharing of consumers' data have increased. My participants have traced growing public awareness of privacy concerns back to the Cambridge Analytica data scandal (Criddle, 2020) and the introduction of the General Data Protection Regulation (GDPR) in Europe.

The intention behind GDPR was to ensure that people ultimately had control over their own data. It was a catalyst for new data protection and privacy laws around the world, including the California Consumer Privacy Act (CCPA), the Brazilian General Data Protection Law (LGPD), and Canada's Personal Information Protection and Electronic Documents Act (PIPEDA). Several countries, including Australia, South Korea, and Singapore, updated their existing data protection laws to include similar provisions (Marsh, 2020; Bryant, 2021). Beyond GDPR, regulation on the use of AI is also underway in Europe and the USA.

DOI: 10.4324/9781003458555-2

Conversational AI is now omnipresent in automated systems we interact with within our homes and workplaces. What can we do to address enduring data protection and privacy issues? Furthermore, what does this mean for the future of conversational AI?

Questions like these have formed a core part of my work. I am Lead Researcher in Responsible AI at SPARCK, a leading global design and innovation agency, part of the technology and engineering consultancy BJSS. I am also a Research Scholar in Digital Anthropology at the Ronin Institute, specializing in socially responsible AI. In 2022, I was honored to be named on the list of "100 Brilliant Women in AI Ethics"[TM] (Walters, 2022a). In addition to research, I put my creative and technical skills to use as a professional songwriter, musician, and producer.

As more anthropology graduates consider careers in AI, I share my journey in this chapter in hopes of sharing the lessons I've learned and insights on why anthropologists are needed in conversational AI.

From Music and Communities to Anthropology and AI

> There is a lot to be said for transferable skills. Many different skills have value and can be applied in this work. There is an opportunity for people with anthropological training to have a real impact in the field [of conversational AI].
>
> (Artz, 2021)

My story is a little unusual because I went into industry before studying anthropology. As a result, I saw first-hand the value anthropology can bring to this work. I also learned how the skills and knowledge I developed along the way, even if they seemed unrelated initially, would eventually support my work in AI research.

From an early age, I was fascinated by social science and music, studying both at school. To me, these were complementary interests, both focused on understanding and interpreting human experience. Music ultimately won when I applied to university to study for a Bachelor of Science in Music Composition and Technology. I did not know it at the time, but learning how to quickly adapt to using new technology would eventually become a useful skill in my research career. Through music, I also gained an understanding of copyright laws, which would later be relevant to generative AI ethics discussions. I would go on to experiment with AI in my music production workflow, such as using machine learning to remove noise from recordings. This hands-on experience would help me understand the benefits, such as speed and convenience, that AI could offer.

In the final year of my degree, our cohort completed a year-long community project with a local primary school. This experience led me back to anthropology, as I enjoyed learning about and working with the local community. This prompted a new phase of my career in community engagement. I worked on the ground with people from all walks of life. Like an anthropologist, I had to learn how to respectfully understand people's lived experiences and to work responsibly. My community engagement roles took many different forms over the years. Along the way, I learned that gaining people's trust is key to meaningful communication. This proved useful in my anthropological fieldwork, where trust is vital.

My first research role was a hybrid of research and community engagement and focused on museum redesign. It quickly became clear that there was a gap between some museum staff's view of the galleries and objects and visitors and the local community's interactions with them. There were also community stories from local history that had not been heard before. We needed to take a participatory design approach to ensure that the final galleries met the needs of visitors and better represented local communities. The project timeline was ambitious, so our small team working on the gallery content worked in short sprints of weeks rather than months. This is a common project management approach in the technology industry and would later help me adapt quickly to that world.

I followed researchers on social media who had more experience than me so I could learn about their approaches. I was particularly impressed by the anthropologists and ethnographers working in industry. They were able to not only explain their work but also comment on news and current events in a way that demonstrated a deep understanding of human behavior. I wanted to know how to do what they did.

While my work left little time for study, I realized that I needed to expand my toolkit. The social science skills I'd learned previously were rusty and designed for passing exams rather than applying in practice. This prompted me to study Social Science Research Methods and Statistics at the University of Amsterdam. I also took online short courses in Global and Digital Anthropology with the University of Melbourne and University College London (UCL), respectively.

With more confidence as a result of my studies, I began to conduct ethnographic research and "deep hanging out" on the museum floor and in local communities. By the time my museum work came to an end, I knew research was where I wanted to be, and anthropology was my "home" among the social sciences.

I carried my experience to my next role in co-producing public services for children and young people with Special Educational Needs and Disabilities (known as "SEND" in England). My previous work with people of many different backgrounds, lifestyles, and ages helped me adapt to a new sector, a new organization, and a new geographical area fairly smoothly. This was the first time I had worked on research specifically for technology projects. This included designing an accessible and engaging website for young people and their families. My interests in technology and social science began to officially intersect.

My next role was with an online team for a global retailer and FTSE 100 company. By this point, I was not worried about moving into another sector or another organization. I realized that my skills would simply travel with me, and I could use them to learn quickly about the world I had landed in. For the first time, my research studies began to focus on conversational AI, such as voice assistants and chatbots. I found this area particularly interesting, especially the ethical aspects, such as privacy.

I got promoted to Senior Researcher within a year. However, I started to realize I had gaps in my knowledge. I took Ethnographic Praxis in Industry (EPIC) courses, which helped me to develop my research skills and establish that I needed more social theory training. This prompted me to begin my studies in Digital Anthropology alongside my job. I quickly made AI my key research interest and smart speakers, privacy, and convenience the focus of my ethnographic research. At the time, I could not have guessed it would lead me to chair and convene the "Priorities for AI Ethics, Law and Governance" panel at the Royal Anthropological Institute conference (Musgrave, 2022). My next role, as Lead Researcher in Responsible AI at SPARCK, would bring together all of the skills and knowledge from my journey so far.

"Alexa, How Did Voice Assistants and Chatbots get to This Point?"

"Artificial Intelligence" was established as a named discipline by the end of the 1950s (Wooldridge, 2021, 35). During its history, AI development has fluctuated, with several "winters" or periods where little technological progress was made. During these times, it seemed unlikely that AI would ever progress beyond being a niche technology.

Despite its "winters," AI has also experienced several periods of rapid progress. These AI "summers" have fuelled technological hype, which Gemma Milne cautioned "is useful to capture attention… but snake oil is an inevitable by-product" (Milne, 2021, 120). Without careful analysis of new technology, marketing, or public relations, hype can obscure some of the dangers of AI. In the United States of America, the Federal Trade Commission introduced a new Office of Technology in 2023 to review marketing claims made about AI (Coldewey, 2023).

Conversational AI simulates conversation through Natural Language Programming (NLP) and provides an "agent" for the human using it to "talk" to. Voice assistants and chatbots have gained in popularity in recent years, although conversational AI has existed since the 1950s.

Bell Laboratories developed the voice assistant Automatic Digit Recognizer, better known as "Audrey," in 1952, which could recognize digits from 0–9 (Spicer, 2021). However, there were significant drawbacks to the technology at the time. Audrey was physically rather large at 180cm tall and required sizable production and maintenance costs (Moskvitch, 2017). While this technological development would prove useful for future conversational AI assistants, initially, the convenience and practicality of pressing buttons to dial, rather than using Audrey, won. IBM produced its own "Shoebox" recognizer ten years later, at the same time that laboratories around the world were creating similar voice assistants (Spicer, 2021).

Between 1964 and 1966, the "chatterbot" ELIZA was created at the Massachusetts Institute of Technology (MIT) by computer scientist Joseph Weizenbaum (Weizenbaum, 1966). The goal of Weizenbaum's experiment with ELIZA was to gain a better understanding of communication between people and machines. Named for the character of Eliza Doolittle in the play "Pygmalion," and musical "My Fair Lady," ELIZA the chatbot was designed to take on the role of a person-centered psychotherapist for the human participant. This choice of role was deliberate, as Weizenbaum wrote, "The psychiatric interview is one of the few examples in which... one of the participating pair is free to assume the pose of knowing almost nothing of the real world" (Weizenbaum, 1966).

ELIZA was built using NLP and worked on a pattern matching and substitution process. This process worked by detecting a selection of 200 keywords from the participants' responses and linking them to pre-prepared scripts to respond to them (Wooldridge, 2021; Adamopoulou & Moussiades, 2020). Weizenbaum had anticipated that the experiment would show that communication between people and computers was superficial. However, he was surprised to learn how quickly participants formed an emotional connection to the chatbot and anthropomorphized it (Weizenbaum, 1976). This response to machines with a text interface, such as chatbots, would later be given a specific name in computer science. "The ELIZA effect" has been described as the perception of human-like "intrinsic qualities and abilities which the software controlling the agent cannot possibly achieve" (King, 1995). Some researchers considered that the human name of the chatbot had contributed to this response (Dillon, 2020).

The ELIZA participants "genuinely thought that they were sharing private information in a therapy session with the computer. They were subsequently mortified that Weizenbaum and his team were reading the entire exchange" (Faber, 2020, 6). Weizenbaum was so alarmed by the participants' response to ELIZA that it prompted him to think deeply about the impact of AI. He was also concerned by the positive response to the idea of automated therapy from some practicing psychiatrists, responding that an "engaged human" therapist was very different from "an information processor following rules" (Weizenbaum, 1976). The study not only had a significant impact on AI as a field but also on Weizenbaum himself. As a result, he spent years afterward writing about his concerns for the relationship between people and computers (MIT News 2008).

Another early example of conversational AI, Dragon NaturallySpeaking, was released to the public in 1997 by Dragon Systems, a company founded by Dr. James Baker and Dr. Janet Baker (Spicer, 2021). The Windows PC speech recognition program allowed voice commands for text input, editing, and control of PC or mobile. This was particularly useful for people with accessibility needs, allowing text entry without needing the person to physically type.

Conversational AI became part of the mainstream in 2010 when question-answer systems were introduced more broadly to the public. A memorable example of this is IBM's Watson system joining the USA television quiz show, "Jeopardy!." The bot was able to beat some of the best "Jeopardy!" champions in total points with the help of a human assistant, known as a "human-in-the-loop." The human assistant provides feedback to the system, which "can help improve its predictions, can verify the accuracy of the predictions, and can improve the performance… overall" (Duke, 2023, 96).

In 2011, Apple's Siri digital assistant app launched, initially on iOS (Faber, 2020, 161). Siri had originally been developed as a spin-off to the US Defense Advanced Research Projects Agency (DARPA)-funded "Cognitive Assistant that Learns and Organizes" (CALO) project (Allan, 2021). Siri would go on to become one of the world's most famous voice assistants, embedded throughout Apple Operating Systems (OS), although its functions would not develop at the same pace as later competitors (Tilley & McLaughlin, 2018; Vincent, 2021). A few years later, in 2013, Google launched its own digital assistant, Google Now, followed just a year later by Amazon's Alexa and Microsoft's Cortana. Conversational AI has now moved from science fiction and secret defense projects to the palm of your hand, embedded in smartphones and other devices.

Starting in 2014, smart speakers with integrated voice assistants were launched to the public. This began with the Amazon Echo, which featured Alexa and was followed by Google Home, with Google Assistant, and Apple Homepod, with Siri.

These smart speakers could assist people with multitasking in everyday life, such as "finding out the weather, helping with recipe measurements, learning new jokes, helping a blind couple to set timers, playing the news, and compiling shopping lists" (Turow, 2021, 3).

The smart speakers could also be connected to other smart home devices, which offered a new level of convenience for owners. It allowed connected devices to be voice-activated using the smart speaker or the associated mobile (cell) phone app. In this way, a resident of the smart home could ask Alexa to boil the kettle or ask Google to send the home's robot vacuum to clean the floor while they were out or busy with other tasks. Common smart speaker tasks broadly fell into "content provision… household management functions… control [of] smart devices in their homes, and… [communication]" (Community Research 2022).

Smart speakers were not only popular in home settings, but later also spread to some workplaces (Finnegan, 2018) and hotels (Amazon, 2023). The use of smart speakers further increased during the quarantine periods of the COVID-19 global pandemic, when many people were spending more time at home (Perez, 2020; Deloitte, 2020).

Despite the opportunities offered by convenience, concerns arose about data use and privacy, particularly as they were permanently located in the most private space of all, our homes (Hill & Mattu, 2018). Questions included whether all those present, such as guests visiting the home, could consent to their data being collected (De Conca, 2020), how connected smart devices might play a role in datafying children (Barassi, 2020, 93–112), and how smart homes can provide new ways for power abuse and domestic abuse to take place (Bowles, 2018).

The year 2016 heralded the era of website and social media-based chatbots, many of which followed decision trees with a rigid structure. This meant that they were not very responsive to their human conversational partners. These types of chatbots could perform simple tasks that follow a script, such as booking services, confirming order status or tracking, providing account balances, or facilitating searches in FAQs (Adamopoulou & Moussiades, 2020). However, the rigidity of the systems led to "unsatisfactory encounters" for customers (Adam et al., 2020) when their expectations were not met.

In 2022, advanced generative AI chatbots started to be made available to the public, beginning with Open AI's Chat Generative Pre-Trained Transformer (ChatGPT), and followed by Google's Bard and Baidu's ERNIE in 2023 (Nature Machine Intelligence, 2023; David, 2023). Also announced and leaked, but not officially released, in 2023 was Meta's Large Language Model Meta AI (LLaMA) (Nature Machine Intelligence, 2023; Vincent, 2023).

These large language model (LLM) chatbots were much more sophisticated and flexible than the more limited chatbots publicly available before. As prompt text-to-text generators, they worked by predicting the next word in the series. They could be used for a much wider range of tasks than earlier chatbots. For example, generating ideas or text on a variety of topics, assisting developers with coding, creating questions, and re-writing text in different tones of voice. Very quickly, additional uses were identified, including conversational role-play for learning, adopted by the language tool Duolingo (Marr, 2023).

The LLM technology itself was not new, having been developed several years earlier. Some tools using this technology were previously available to the public, such as digital marketing tool Jasper (formerly named Jarvis, Conversion AI). However, these tools did not have the same level of widespread adoption as ChatGPT would later have (Wiggers, 2022; Chow, 2023).

The public releases of these "blockbuster" LLM chatbots were the subject of much publicity and hype (Sundar & Mok, 2023), but the introductions to the world were not without concerns. As the first of its kind to be made publicly available, the launch of ChatGPT was marked by a widely reported ban on its use in Italy. The reasons for the ban centered around privacy concerns about who had access to data entered and how that data was being used. ChatGPT was also subject to a probe by a federal privacy watchdog in Canada (Nature Machine Intelligence, 2023). Some companies also had significant concerns about proprietary information being entered into ChatGPT and that same proprietary data resurfacing for other users outside the company. One high-profile case of this was reported when an Amazon lawyer saw examples of confidential internal data being accidentally leaked in this way and warned employees not to enter sensitive company data into ChatGPT (Kim, 2023). Versions GPT-2 and GPT-3 were also found to leak private data "without malicious prompting," including phone numbers, email addresses, and technical information (Weidinger et al., 2022).

Variations on these LLMs, known as multi-modal language models, have also been developed, allowing for a combination of image, voice, and text prompts to be entered. Some examples have included Google's Multitask Unified Model (MUM) for its search engine (Perez, 2021) and Google's Pathways Language Model Embodied (PaLM-E), which incorporated robotic sensor data (Nature Machine Intelligence, 2023). In 2023, Google added image input to its publicly accessible chatbot Bard, powered by PaLM2. This was followed by the ability for Bard to pull information from Google apps to give personalized responses (Nuñez, 2023). In the same year, Open AI announced public access to the image and voice features of its multi-modal GPT-3.5 and GPT-4 models through its ChatGPT Plus and Enterprise packages (Edwards, 2023b). The public release of the image features had been delayed for months due to privacy concerns (Edwards, 2023a).

Making Meaning Visible in Conversational AI

Conversational AI offers a rich field for anthropologists to find practical and intellectual purposes for their skills and knowledge.

Building, deploying, and using AI responsibly requires a range of expertise and perspectives. Anthropologists apply their own training in this emerging space and also develop through collaboration in multidisciplinary teams. Nick Seaver puts this well: "Expertise is neatly split: engineers know about functions, social scientists know about consequences. But, if we're willing to muddy the waters a little, a space opens up for engineers and social scientists to critically engage with algorithmic systems together" (Seaver, 2019, 420). Beyond project teams, anthropologists are able to offer meaningful contributions more broadly to their organizations and the wider AI industry.

Anthropology's ethnographic lens is incredibly valuable in understanding the everyday lives of people interacting with conversational AI. This might include consumers and residents of smart homes or smart workplaces, customer service employees working with a chatbot, crowd workers labeling data or training AI systems, or knowledge workers trying to improve their productivity with LLMs. Anthropologists might also undertake exploratory research before a conversational AI system is developed or launched in order to understand the social and cultural context. Direct observation of human behavior, the context in which it occurs, and interpretation of this through an anthropological lens produces a compelling, in-depth understanding of people's lived experiences. This is not a perspective that everyone in the technology industry has regular access to, and it is really powerful, especially as an evidence base for decisions about how, where, and when AI is used.

Anthropologists are well-placed to examine the cultural meaning of conversational AI, with their training in "making the strange familiar and the familiar strange." As Sam Ladner once described it, "Most of this meaning is invisible to most people" (Ladner, 2014, 189). This is where anthropological theory and conceptual frameworks can really shine, helping anthropologists to quickly make connections and interpret them. For example, personhood and value's roles in datafication (Walters, 2022b) and concepts of networked tools and humans in workplace use of generative AI (Stripe Partners, 2023). Anthropologists make that meaning visible in conversational AI and highlight ethical issues, such as privacy and bias, through their social and cultural knowledge.

What is "artificial intelligence"? What is "privacy"? These are not just theoretical questions but are important in practice to be able to interpret meaning, inform actions, and align teams. It is easy to assume that all stakeholders are on the same page. This exercise helps to create crucial shared understanding across multidisciplinary teams, and assist individual members to "[examine] the role of our own assumptions and points of view and [interrogate] what we think we know, and why we think we know it" (Sunderland & Denny, 2007, 47–48). Through ethnographic approaches and analysis, anthropologists learn how participants present themselves and the meaning of privacy first-hand. These observations highlight critical gaps in understanding, such as assumptions made about people by organizations building or using AI or errors in algorithmic inferences about them.

Responsible approaches to conversational AI really benefit from holistic perspectives, and this is an area in which anthropologists excel. The ability to expand vision beyond the individual "end user," which has long been a focus in the technology industry, is crucial. This broader context aids understanding of each aspect of a system and the relationships between them. It also helps explore ways to make the most of the opportunities AI offers and reduce the risks.

In practice, taking this holistic view means looking at not only voice assistants or chatbots themselves but also the interface or device they're housed in. It means considering the wider context of a system, including potential environmental, social, and ethical impacts. When looking at privacy in conversational AI in particular, it's important to explore how data flows through the system, what happens behind the scenes, and the unseen human "ghost work" (Gray & Suri, 2019, 7–9) that forms part of that system. Sometimes, a difference between data flows and participants' perceptions of how the system works highlights a need for greater transparency about how data is used.

Anthropology's powerful holistic perspective not only applies to research projects but also to the organizations or contexts in which they are situated. There are two key parts to this.

First, conversational AI systems are products of the environment in which they are developed. It is vital to understand the way that culture and values play out in their design, use, and deployment. This can play a significant role in the intended or unintended consequences of the release of that system. Some AI researchers have also noted that, to date, responsible AI development and governance, more broadly, "has been dominated by anglophone actors. This is starting to change as more countries develop their own AI strategies. But they are entering a space shaped by anglophone Western assumptions" (Cave & Dihal, 2023, 5). This risks AI development being shaped by a specific linguistic and cultural context yet applied worldwide. It also undermines initiatives to regulate AI without a critical understanding of cultural contexts. Anthropologists' training in social and cultural analysis is extremely valuable in addressing this gap.

Second, it is important to learn the culture of the organization in which the work takes place. This helps to identify where the research fits in and to ensure the work has the greatest impact possible. Anthropology assists in understanding the role of formal or informal silos in organizations and seeing the potential for productive connections between people or teams. Sometimes, the official structure or hierarchy of an organization is not how the power or decision-making flows in practice. Studying the organizational culture, including the organization's rituals, language, and power dynamics, assists in clarifying this. Examples of rituals might include daily team update meetings held each morning or a weekly company update, where, as Sam Ladner describes it, everyone "[gathers] around the numbers" (Ladner, 2014, 51).

Organizational culture might be influenced by the dominant project management approach. Organizations may, for example, use either the traditional "waterfall" approach, the "agile" approach, or some hybrid of the two. The agile approach, or operating in shorter-term cycles, is a popular style of working for many technology companies.

If an organization or team runs on an agile project management framework (Association for Project Management, n.d.), there are certain cadences, milestones, and rituals common to cycles of working. In the Scrum agile framework, these include "ceremonies" or meetings for the team to plan, review, and track work, as well as communicate and reflect on work completed (Schwaber & Sutherland, 2020). As a researcher, it has been crucial to understand the importance of these, particularly to stakeholders that use them to measure work completed. The Scrum approach was created for software development cycles, so it fits certain roles well, such as developers, product owners, and business analysts. Research, especially exploratory qualitative research, does not always map neatly to blocks of two-week "sprints" in a Scrum project. However, it is important to work out strategies to build trust with stakeholders and set project timeframes accordingly, even if research indicates that they will need to be changed later to account for additional time or further studies.

In addition to the dominant project management style, it is important to identify what matters to individual stakeholders. For example, their goals and interests, level of influence, and what they consider valuable. This helps to understand how to communicate research, plan projects, and manage time most effectively.

All of this has been relevant to both in-house and consultancy roles. However, in a consultancy setting, it is also essential to prepare to learn the organizational culture of clients and understand how to work productively within that. As Brigitte Jordan wrote, "the outside consultant can often see patterns and connections that for the insider are 'invisible in plain sight'" (Jordan with

Lambert, 2009, 107). However, to be able to influence change, as an outsider, demonstrating awareness of an organization's culture, politics, and language is critical to build trust.

Organizations often value stability, and many business leaders want certainty. However, the AI space, especially with the rate of growth in development (Chui, 2023), can mean that many technical experts struggle to predict very far into the future. This uncertainty can also be further complicated when new AI regulation is on the horizon but is not yet law. How do we prepare for potential futures when those futures are unknown?

Anthropology, ethnography, and related areas, such as semiotics, futures thinking, strategic foresight, and speculative design, thrive in these areas of ambiguity and uncertainty about what is to come. Strategic foresight and futures thinking help organizations to understand how AI is evolving. They provide evidence for strategic planning, particularly through understanding how AI may impact everyday life and, therefore, people, consumers, and clients, in addition to how it may impact their own work. Commercial semiotics can also provide valuable analysis of consumer culture and context for conversational AI business strategy (Hunt & Barton, 2014, 447–462). These disciplines offer rich opportunities for responsible AI and innovation, bringing new perspectives and possibilities.

By exploring potential futures for conversational AI and privacy, we can shape the future we want to see. As Woodrow Hartzog put it, "Tomorrow's privacy depends on what we build today" (Hartzog, 2018, 279). So, what are some of the risks and rewards of this type of work for anthropologists?

It is important to understand where an anthropologist's philosophy may differ from that of the organization they are in. Many businesses and organizations run on a positivist philosophy, where "truth" is either observable or not. It can be hard work to be "an interpretivist stranger in a foreign positivist land" (Ladner, 2014, 43). It is key to learn strategies and techniques to build trust and communicate that you empathize with the positivist position. It is also important not to abandon one's own philosophy because that is a perspective that is less common in organizations, and much-needed. It can take time and patience to build trust between you, your stakeholders, and colleagues from different disciplines.

There can, sometimes, too, be tensions between an organization's ethical stance and that of an anthropologist. Kathi R. Kitner advocated for anthropologists to "draw our own limits," acknowledging that "while my work... does not resemble in the least... the Human Terrain System (Forte, 2011) work... It is important to explore and understand what potential harm one's research may cause in both the long and short term" (Kitner, 2014, 316). Kitner encouraged anthropologists to "work as effectively as possible to influence the processes and products within the organization" and "offer guidance when necessary or requested" (Kitner, 2014, 318).

Being a professional insider-outsider can be difficult at times, especially if one is aiming to bring about culture change within an organization, or the wider technology industry. It is important for anthropologists to have compassion for themselves and focus on defining success through action rather than results, especially initially. Change is not an overnight endeavor. It is crucial to learn ways to avoid burnout and preserve a passion for the work.

In light of the risks, you might wonder why anthropologists would want to take on this type of work. For the curious anthropologist, the opportunity to grow their own knowledge in an emerging field can be exciting. There is always more to learn, whether as an individual or in collaboration with multidisciplinary teams. Putting their skills and knowledge into practice in these different ways can prove an enjoyable challenge. Each project brings a new opportunity to explore how to apply their anthropological lens and skill set. It is particularly rewarding when you find "you can effect incremental change in tiny nuggets and slivers of hope" (Ladner, 2014, 82). In terms of conversational AI, it is also satisfying to be able to use the skills and knowledge you have trained in to maximize the benefits of the technology and identify and mitigate risks, such as privacy.

Privacy and Other Risks

Anthropology, with its established ethical framework, is perhaps exactly the science needed to help AI become socially responsible. Without understanding the risks, we cannot work to mitigate them, and we cannot build or use AI responsibly. AI risks span a variety of categories, including ethical, social, political, reputational, legal, and environmental. The dangers are not hypothetical, ranging from an eating disorder chatbot giving harmful advice (Hoover, 2023) to facial recognition misgendering women and darker-skinned individuals (Buolamwini & Gebru, 2018), and a self-driving car killing a woman (Blackman, 2022, 4).

Many categories of AI risks are not new to technology more broadly. However, AI can provide novel ways for these problems to occur. In addition, AI is often applied on a large scale and has the potential to cause great harm in a short space of time (Blackman, 2022, 5).

As with other forms of technology, AI is "not neutral in terms of politics or power" (Coeckelbergh, 2022, 17) and "depends entirely on a much wider set of political and social structures... Once we connect AI within these broader structures and social systems, we can escape the notion that artificial intelligence is a purely technical domain" (Crawford, 2021, 17).

Some key considerations in conversational AI, in particular, are privacy, false information, copyright, transparency, bias, and security. The history of voice assistants and chatbots explored earlier in this chapter, sheds light on ways privacy might raise concerns. For example, "the ELIZA effect" demonstrates the risk of humans quickly anthropomorphizing conversational agents and sharing more information than intended. Smart speakers and devices living permanently in homes, workplaces, and even hotels highlight concerns around data collection and use. Particularly people's legal rights to have control over their own data and additional risks to those who might be considered vulnerable (Barassi, 2020, 103–112; Boddington, 2023, 54–55).

In my studies on smart speakers, it seemed there was a significant transparency issue in which data were being collected and how they were used and stored. As Carissa Véliz put it, "Consent to data collection is very rarely informed" (Véliz, 2023, 187). Participants had taken steps to try to protect their own privacy, such as muting, unplugging, or moving their devices or moving their conversations to other rooms in the home.

The scale of data collection also provides opportunities for device manufacturers to make inferences about people living or working alongside smart devices (Wachter, 2018). This can be problematic, regardless of whether the inferences are true, and you did not want to share that information, or whether they are false, and might lead to incorrect perceptions of you.

LLM chatbots present new types of risks, such as privacy leaks. These are crucial to address for both personal data and sensitive corporate data. Producing false information, also known as "hallucinations," is another risk with LLMs and is an intrinsic result of the way they are built (Metz, 2023). They have also produced false references to support the inaccurate information provided (Neumeister, 2023). The vast datasets LLMs are built on means that it is difficult for even those building them to understand transparently how an output was produced. Copyright is a known issue, too, both in terms of copyrighted source material from datasets being reproduced in the outputs (van der Meulen, 2023) and who can copyright the outputs of LLMs (Ozcan, Sekhon, & Ozcan, 2023).

Another big risk in conversational AI is bias or discrimination towards certain individuals or groups. This is often unintentional but can have a significant impact. It is important to note that bias can occur anywhere in the AI system, not just in the training dataset. Bias can occur even before the system is created within the team, environment, and culture in which it is constructed (Srinivasan & Chander, 2021; Blackman, 2022, 13–14). Concerns have been expressed about the dangers of hegemonic teams building, using, and deploying AI and dominating Western AI ethical perspectives, narratives, and approaches (Cave & Dihal, 2023, 5). Examples of cultural bias have included gendering of voice assistants and chatbots (Strengers & Kennedy, 2021; Faber, 2020; Palmiter Bajorek, 2019), poor detection of diverse regional accents (Wiggers, 2021), and black voice recognition (Metz, 2020).

Security is an area of concern for organizations, and this is where anthropologists contribute to addressing this issue (Potter, 2024). The *Wall Street Journal* reported an early case of generative AI being used for fraud, where an independent UK energy company was targeted (Stupp, 2019). A group used AI to copy the CEO's voice and fraudulently obtained a wire transfer to the equivalent of $243,000. While this was a novelty at the time, crimes like this against companies and individuals are becoming more commonplace.

Safety measures, known as "guardrails," can be added into AI systems to try to address some of these issues, though they cannot remove them completely. This process itself raises ethical questions, as human moderators are an essential part of reviewing the data and labeling them correctly so that the "guardrails" can work. The data they review can include extreme content, such as descriptions of violence or abuse. This behind-the-scenes work to make conversational AI safer and less discriminatory can be grueling, psychologically disturbing, and emotionally challenging. It also raises questions about appropriate payment for the work and availability of psychological support for the trauma experienced by workers (Perrigo, 2023; Hao, 2023). Mary L. Gray and Siddarth Suri described this invisible human labor as "ghost work" (Gray & Suri, 2019, 7–9).

Anthropology's formal ethical training and strong ethical commitment to research participants is especially vital in cases like this (Kitner, 2014, 317–318; Whiteford & Trotter, 2008, 3). Anthropologists' expertise in social factors and holistic approaches means they quickly make connections between AI, power, and social and political systems and work to address them. Their theory knowledge and analytical training can make a significant contribution to reducing bias, preserving privacy, and understanding cultural variations in the meaning of privacy. Anthropological understanding of social and cultural context is critical to identifying and mitigating risks as conversational AI becomes further embedded into our professional and personal lives.

Four Things I Wish I had Known when I Started

Reflecting on our practice is a hugely important part of being a researcher and an anthropologist. Looking back at my career so far, there are several things I wish I had known earlier.

In the "Fuzzy" Emerging Technology Space, Trust your Instincts

When I first began studying conversational AI, I was keen to understand how I could put my new knowledge into action. However, for organizations seeking certainty, investing time, energy, and finances into emerging technologies felt risky. It was hard not to feel discouraged, but it was clear from my research that AI was *already* relevant. It was having a huge impact on people's daily lives, and the dangers were not being fully addressed (O'Neil, 2016; Bowles, 2018). It was only a matter of time before its full impact would be felt.

Find a Balance in your Standpoint… and Have Courage

On the one hand, no one likes "doom and gloom." On the other hand, unchecked AI hype can be very dangerous. It can be quite hard sometimes in the technology industry to strike the right balance between the two, but a lot of it comes down to building relationships and reading culture, particularly in organizations. Something that anthropologists are trained to do. From this informed position, you can find ways to carefully challenge established ways of thinking and working in a "non-threatening way" (Ladner, 2014, 82).

Build a Support Network of People who "Get It"

Connect to others who understand and support the area you are working or studying in. When you are working to get to where you want to be, they will be the folks who give you the strength and support to keep going. This may be through social media or in-person events. You will also need to get out of your comfort zone from time to time to better help you understand the realities of emerging technologies. For example, if you work on the technical side of conversational AI, attend talks specifically on ethics or social impact. If you work on the ethics of conversational AI, follow people who work on regulation. If you work in the private sector, connect with people in the public sector or non-profits.

Keep Learning

The technology industry, and AI in particular, keeps moving at a rapid pace. You will find some things largely stay the same, such as the common risks of conversational AI. Some things move slowly, such as regulation, and other things move quite quickly, such as technological developments. You will need to find ways to keep up-to-date with the daily or weekly news in the technology industry.

Socially-responsible approaches to conversational AI are not just a "nice to have." They are a must-have. Anthropologists add great value to this work and can find rewarding opportunities to apply their knowledge and skills.

Bibliography

Adam, Martin, Michael Wessel, and Alexander Benlian. 2020. "AI-based Chatbots in Customer Service and their Effects on User Compliance." *Electronic Markets* 31, 427–445. https://doi.org/10.1007/s12525-020-00414-7.

Adamopoulou, Eleni, and Lefteris Moussiades. 2020. "Chatbots: History, Technology and Applications." *Machine Learning with Applications*Volume 2, 100006. https://doi.org/10.1016/j.mlwa.2020.100006.

Allan, Jennifer. 2021. "10 Years of Siri: The History of Apple's Voice Assistant." *Tech Radar*, October 4, 2021. https://www.techradar.com/news/siri-10-year-anniversary.

Amazon, 2023. "Alexa Smart Properties for Hospitality." *Amazon*, July 30, 2023. https://developer.amazon.com/en-US/alexa/alexa-for-hospitality.

Artz, Matt. "Laura Musgrave on Anthro to UX with Matt Artz." *Anthro to UX*. April 12, 2021. Podcast, Anthro to UX, 1:06:08. https://anthropologytoux.com/podcast/laura-musgrave-on-anthro-to-ux/.

Association for Project Management. n.d. "What is Agile Project Management?" *Association for Project Management*. Accessed October 1, 2023. https://www.apm.org.uk/resources/find-a-resource/agile-project-management/.

Barassi, Vanessa. 2020. *Child Data Citizen: How Tech Companies Are Profiling Us from Before Birth*. Cambridge: The MIT Press.

Blackman, Reid. 2022. *Ethical Machines*. Boston: Harvard Business Review Press.

Boddington, Paula. 2023. *AI Ethics: A Textbook*. Singapore: Springer.

Bowles, Nellie. 2018. "Thermostats, Locks and Lights: Digital Tools of Domestic Abuse." *The New York Times*, June 23, 2018. https://www.nytimes.com/2018/06/23/technology/smart-home-devices-domestic-abuse.html.

Bryant, Jennifer. 2021. "3 Years In, GDPR Highlights Privacy in Global Landscape." *International Association of Privacy Professionals (IAPP)*. May 25, 2021. https://iapp.org/news/a/three-years-in-gdpr-highlights-privacy-in-global-landscape/

Buolamwini, Joy, and Timnit Gebru. 2018. "Gender Shades: Intersectional Accuracy Disparities in Commercial Gender Classification." *Proceedings of Machine Learning Research* 81:1–15. https://proceedings.mlr.press/v81/buolamwini18a/buolamwini18a.pdf.

Cave, Stephen, and Kanta Dihal. 2023. "How the World Sees Intelligent Machines: Introduction". In: *Imagining AI*, edited by Stephen Cave and Kanta Dihal, pp. 5–6. Oxford: Oxford University Press.

Chow, Andrew R. 2023. "How ChatGPT Managed to Grow Faster Than TikTok or Instagram". *Time*, February 8, 2023. https://time.com/6253615/chatgpt-fastest-growing/.

Christian, Brian. 2020. *The Alignment Problem: Machine Learning and Human Values*. New York: W. W. Norton and Company.

Chui, Michael. 2023. "The State of AI in 2023: Generative AI's Breakout Year." *McKinsey*, August 1, 2023. https://www.mckinsey.com/capabilities/quantumblack/our-insights/the-state-of-ai-in-2023-generative-AIs-breakout-year

Coeckelbergh, Mark. 2022. *The Political Philosophy of AI*. Cambridge: Polity Press.

Coldewey, Devin. 2023. "FTC Warns Tech: 'Keep your AI claims in check'." *Tech Crunch*, February 28, 2023. https://techcrunch.com/2023/02/27/ftc-warns-tech-keep-your-ai-claims-in-check.

Community Research. 2022. "Smart Speakers Research with the Public: Research Report." *Ofcom*, December 13, 2022. https://www.ofcom.org.uk/research-and-data/multi-sector-research/general-communications/smart-speaker-research.

Crawford, Kate. 2021. *Atlas of AI*. New Haven: Yale University Press.

Criddle, Cristina. 2020. "Facebook Sued Over Cambridge Analytica Data Scandal." *BBC News*, October 28, 2020. https://www.bbc.co.uk/news/technology-54722362.

David, Emilia. 2023. "Baidu Launches Ernie Chatbot After Chinese Government Approval." *The Verge*, August 31, 2023. https://www.theverge.com/2023/8/31/23853878/baidu-launch-ernie-ai-chatbot-china.

De Conca, Silvia. 2020. "Between a Rock and a Hard Place: Owners of Smart Speakers and Joint Control." *Scripted* 17 (2). DOI: https://10.2966/scrip.170220.238.

Deloitte. 2020. "UK Adults Purchased up to 21 Million New Digital Devices During Lockdown in Desire to Stay Connected." *Deloitte Press Release*, July 25, 2023. https://www2.deloitte.com/uk/en/pages/press-releases/articles/uk-adults-purchased-up-to-21-million-new-digital-devices-during-lockdown-in-desire-to-stay-connected.html

Dillon, Sarah. 2020. "The Eliza Effect and Its Dangers: From Demystification To Gender Critique." *Journal for Cultural Research* 24 :(1): 1–15. DOI: https://doi.org/10.1080/14797585.2020.1754642.

Duke, Toju. 2023. *Building Responsible AI Algorithms: A Framework for Transparency, Fairness, Safety, Privacy, and Robustness*. California: Apress.

Edwards, Benji. 2023a. "Report: OpenAI Holding Back GPT-4 Image Features on Fears of Privacy Issues." *Ars Technica*, July 18, 2023. https://arstechnica.com/information-technology/2023/07/report-openai-holding-back-gpt-4-image-features-on-fears-of-privacy-issues/.

Edwards, Benji. 2023b. "ChatGPT Update Enables its AI to 'see, hear, and speak,' According to OpenAI." *Ars Technica*, September 25, 2023. https://arstechnica.com/

information-technology/2023/09/chatgpt-goes-multimodal-with-image-recognition-a
nd-speech-synthesis/.

Faber, Liz W. 2020. *The Computer's Voice: From Star Trek to Siri.* Minneapolis:
University of Minnesota Press.

Feldman, Russell. 2018. "Smart Speaker Ownership Doubles in Six Months." *YouGov,*
April 19, 2023. https://yougov.co.uk/topics/politics/articles-reports/2018/04/19/sma
rt-speaker-ownership-doubles-six-months

Finnegan, Matthew. 2018. "Alexa for Business: What It Does, How to Use It". *Com-
puterworld*, June 13, 2018. https://www.computerworld.com/article/3279733/alexa
-for-business-what-it-does-how-to-use-it.html

Forte, Maximilian C. 2011. "The Human Terrain System and Anthropology: A
Review of Ongoing Public Debates." *American Anthropologist* 113 (1): 149–153.
https://doi.org/10.1111/j.1548-1433.2010.01315.x, quoted in Kitner, Kathi, R. 2014.
"The Good Anthropologist: Questioning Ethics in the Workplace." In: *Handbook of
Anthropology in Business.* Edited by Rita Denny and Patricia Sutherland, pp. 309–
320. Walnut Creek: Left Coast Press.

Gray, Mary L., and Siddharth Suri. 2019. *Ghost Work: How to Stop Silicon Valley
from Building a New Global Underclass.* Boston: Harper Business.

Hao, Karen. "The Hidden Workforce That Helped Filter Violence and Abuse Out of
ChatGPT." *The Journal,* 11 July 2023. *The Wall Street Journal* 25 (16). https://
www.wsj.com/podcasts/the-journal/the-hidden-workforce-that-helped-filter-vio
lence-and-abuse-out-of-chatgpt/ffc2427f-bdd8-47b7-9a4b-27e7267cf413

Hartzog, Warner. 2018. *Privacy's Blueprint: The Battle to Control the Design of New
Technologies.* Cambridge: Harvard University Press.

Hill, Kashmir, and Surya Mattu. 2018. "The House That Spied on Me." *Gizmodo,*
February 7, 2018. https://gizmodo.com/the-house-that-spied-on-me-1822429852.

Hoover, Amanda. 2023. "An Eating Disorder Chatbot is Suspended for Giving
Harmful Advice." *Wired.* June 1, 2023. https://www.wired.com/story/tessa-chatbot-
suspended/.

Hu, Krystal. 2023. "ChatGPT Sets Record for Fastest-growing User Base - Analyst
Note." *Reuters,* February 2, 2023. https://www.reuters.com/technology/chatgpt-sets-
record-fastest-growing-user-base-analyst-note-2023-2002-01/

Hunt, Cato, and Sam Barton. 2014. "Decoding Culture: Cultural Insight and Semiotics in Britain." In: *Handbook of Anthropology in Business.* Edited by Rita Denny
and Patricia Sutherland, pp. 447–462. Walnut Creek: Left Coast Press.

Jordan, Brigitte, with Monique Lambert. 2009. "Working in Corporate Jungles:
Reflections on Ethnographic Praxis in Industry." In: *Ethnography and the Corporate
Encounter.* Edited by Melissa Cefkin, pp. 95–133. New York: Berghahn Books.

Kim, Eugene. 2023. "Amazon Warns Staff Not to Share Confidential Information
with ChatGPT." *Business Insider,* January 24, 2023. https://www.businessinsider.
com/amazon-chatgpt-openai-warns-employees-not-share-confidential-information-m
icrosoft-2023-2021.

King, William Joseph. 1995. *Anthropomorphic Agents: Friend, Foe, or Folly.* Technical
Memorandum M-95-91. University of Washington. http://citeseerx.ist.psu.edu/view
doc/download?doi=10.1.1.57.3474&rep=rep1&type=pdf

Kitner, Kathi R. 2014. "The Good Anthropologist: Questioning Ethics in the Workplace." In: *Handbook of Anthropology in Business.* Edited by Rita Denny and
Patricia Sutherland, pp. 309–320. Walnut Creek: Left Coast Press.

Kunst, Alexander. 2023. "Smart Home Device Ownership in the UK as of June 2023." *Statista*, August 25, 2023. https://www.statista.com/forecasts/997845/smart-home-device-ownership-in-the-uk.

Ladner, Sam. 2014. *Practical Ethnography: A Guide to Doing Ethnography in the Private Sector.* New York: Routledge.

Marr, Bernard. 2023. "The Amazing Ways Duolingo is Using AI and GPT-4." *Forbes*, April 28, 2023. https://www.forbes.com/sites/bernardmarr/2023/04/28/the-amazing-ways-duolingo-is-using-ai-and-gpt-4/

Marsh. 2020. "Two Years On, The GDPR Continues to Shape Global Data Privacy Regulation." *Marsh*, August 2020. https://www.marsh.com/us/services/cyber-risk/insights/GDPR-two-years-on-continues-to-shape-global-privacy-regulation.html

Metz, Cade. 2020. "There Is a Racial Divide in Speech-Recognition Systems, Researchers Say." *The New York Times*, March 23, 2020. https://www.nytimes.com/2020/03/23/technology/speech-recognition-bias-apple-amazon-google.html.

Metz, Cade, 2023. "What Makes A.I. Chatbots Go Wrong?" *The New York Times*, April 4, 2023. https://www.nytimes.com/2023/03/29/technology/ai-chatbots-hallucinations.html.

Milne, Gemma. 2021. "Uses (and Abuses) of Hype". In: *Fake AI*. Edited by Frederike Kaltheuner, pp. 115–122. Manchester: Meatspace Press.

MIT News. 2008. "Joseph Weizenbaum, Professor Emeritus of Computer Science, 85." *MIT News*. March 10, 2008. https://news.mit.edu/2008/obit-weizenbaum-0310.

Moskvitch, Katia. 2017. "The Machines That Learned to Listen." *BBC Future*, February 15, 2017. https://www.bbc.com/future/article/20170214-the-machines-that-learned-to-listen.

Musgrave, Laura. 2022. "Priorities for AI Ethics, Law, and Governance." *Anthropology, AI and the Future of Human Society*. Conference Panel, Royal Anthropological Institute of Great Britain and Ireland. https://nomadit.co.uk/conference/rai2022/p/11196.

Nature Machine Intelligence. 2023. "What's the Next Word in Large Language Models?" *Nature Machine Intelligence* 5, 331–332. April 24, 2023. https://doi.org/10.1038/s42256-023-00655-z.

Neumeister, Larry. 2023. "Lawyers Submitted Bogus Case Law Created by ChatGPT. A Judge Fined Them $5,000." *AP News*, June 22, 2023. https://apnews.com/article/artificial-intelligence-chatgpt-fake-case-lawyers-d6ae9fa79d0542db9e1455397aef381c

Nuñez, Michael. 2023. "Google Bard Can Now Tap Directly into Gmail, Docs, Maps and More." *Venture Beat*, September 19, 2023. https://venturebeat.com/ai/google-bard-can-now-tap-directly-into-gmail-docs-maps-and-more/

O'Neil, Cathy. 2016. *Weapons of Math Destruction.* New York: Crown Books.

Ozcan, Sercan, Sekhon, Joe, and Oleksandra Ozcan. 2023. "ChatGPT: What the Law Says About Who Owns the Copyright of AI-generated Content." *The Conversation*, April 17. 2023. https://theconversation.com/chatgpt-what-the-law-says-about-who-owns-the-copyright-of-ai-generated-content-200597.

Palmiter Bajorek, Joan. 2019. "Voice Recognition Still Has Significant Race and Gender Biases." *Harvard Business Review*, May 10, 2019. https://hbr.org/2019/05/voice-recognition-still-has-significant-race-and-gender-biases.

Perez, Sarah. 2020. "COVID-19 Quarantine Boosts Smart Speaker Usage Among U.S. Adults, Particularly Younger Users." *Tech Crunch*, April 30, 2020. https://techcrunch.com/2020/04/30/covid-19-quarantine-boosts-smart-speaker-usage-among-u-s-adults-particularly-younger-users

Perez, Sarah. 2021. "Google is Redesigning Search Using AI Technologies and New Features." *Tech Crunch*, September 29, 2021. https://techcrunch.com/2021/09/29/google-is-redesigning-search-using-a-i-technologies-and-new-features/.

Perrigo, Billy. 2023. "OpenAI Used Kenyan Workers on Less Than \$2 Per Hour to Make ChatGPT Less Toxic." *Time*, January 18, 2023. https://time.com/6247678/openai-chatgpt-kenya-workers/.

Potter, Lianne. 2024. "Towards an Anthro-Centric Cybersecurity." In: *EmTech Anthropology: Stories from the Frontier*, edited by Matt Artz and Lora Koyocheva. New York: Routledge.

Schwaber, Ken, and Jeff Sutherland. 2020. "The 2020 Scrum Guide." *Scrum Guides*. https://scrumguides.org/scrum-guide.html#scrum-definition.

Seaver, Nick. 2019. "Knowing Algorithms." In: *DigitalSTS: A Field Guide for Science and Technology Studies*, edited by Janet Vertesi and David Ribes, pp. 412–422. Princeton: Princeton University Press.

Spicer, Dag. 2021. "Audrey, Alexa, Hal, and More." *Computer History Museum*, June 9, 2021. https://computerhistory.org/blog/audrey-alexa-hal-and-more/.

Srinivasan, Ramya, and Ajay Chander. 2021. "Biases in AI Systems: A Survey for Practitioners." *ACM Queue* 19 (2): 45–64. https://doi.org/10.1145/3466132.3466134.

Strengers, Yolande, and Jenny Kennedy. 2021. *The Smart Wife*. Cambridge: The MIT Press.

Stripe Partners. 2023. "This Month's Frame: Using Actor Network Theory to Rethink Work in the Age of Generative AI." *Stripe Partners: Frames*, February 7, 2023. https://stripepartners.substack.com/p/this-months-frame-using-actor-network.

Stupp, Catherine. 2019. "Fraudsters Used AI to Mimic CEO's Voice in Unusual Cybercrime Case." *Wall Street Journal*, August 30, 2019. https://www.wsj.com/articles/fraudsters-use-ai-to-mimic-ceos-voice-in-unusual-cybercrime-case-11567157402

Sundar, Sindhu, and Aaron Mok. 2023. "If You Still Aren't Sure What ChatGPT is, This is Your Guide to the Viral Chatbot That Everyone is Talking About." *Business Insider*, August 21, 2023. https://www.businessinsider.com/everything-you-need-to-know-about-chat-gpt-2023-2021.

Sunderland, Patricia. L., and Rita M. Denny. 2007. *Doing Anthropology in Consumer Research*. New York: Routledge.

Tilley, Aaron, and Kevin McLaughlin. 2018. "The Seven-Year Itch: How Apple's Marriage to Siri Turned Sour." *The Information*, March 14, 2018. https://www.theinformation.com/articles/the-seven-year-itch-how-apples-marriage-to-siri-turned-sour

Turow, Joseph. 2021. *The Voice Catchers*. New Haven: Yale University Press.

van der Meulen, Rob. 2023. "Gartner Identifies Six ChatGPT Risks Legal and Compliance Leaders Must Evaluate." *Gartner*, May 18, 2023. https://www.gartner.com/en/newsroom/press-releases/2023-05-18-gartner-identifies-six-chatgpt-risks-legal-and-compliance-must-evaluate

Véliz, Carissa. 2023. "Governing Privacy." In: *Privacy*, edited by Steven M. Cahn and Carissa Véliz, pp. 177–190. Hoboken: Wiley Blackwell.

Vincent, James. 2021. "Hey Siri, What Happened?" *The Verge*, October 4, 2021. https://www.theverge.com/22704233/siri-apple-digital-assistant-10-years-development-problems-why.

Vincent, James. 2023. "Meta's Powerful AI Language Model has Leaked Online — What Happens Now?" *The Verge*, March 8, 2023. https://www.theverge.com/2023/3/8/23629362/meta-ai-language-model-llama-leak-online-misuse

Wachter, Sandra. 2018. "Normative Challenges of Identification in the Internet of Things: Privacy, Profiling, Discrimination, and the GDPR." *Computer Law and Security Review.* 34. 436–449. https://doi.org/10.1016/j.clsr.2018.02.002.

Walters, Dawn. 2022a. "Episode 40: Understanding Data and Privacy as a UX Researcher. With Laura Musgrave." *Response-ability.tech* 27 (44): February 9, 2022. https://response-ability.tech/understanding-data-and-privacy-as-a-ux-researcher/.

Walters, Dawn. 2022b. "Episode 41: Anthropology and Artificial Intelligence. With Veronica Barassi." *Response-ability.tech* 29 (52): April 20, 2022. https://response-ability.tech/anthropology-and-artificial-intelligence/.

Weidinger, Laura, Jonathan Uesato, Maribeth Rauh, Conor Griffin, Po-Sen Huang, John Mellor, Amelia Glaese, Myra Cheng, Borja Balle, Atoosa Kasirzadeh, Courtney Bileset al. 2022. *"Taxonomy of Risks Posed by Language Models."* Paper presented at FAccT '22, Seoul, Republic of Korea, June 21–24, 2022. https://doi.org/10.1145/3531146.3533088.

Weizenbaum, Joseph. 1966. "ELIZA – A Computer Program For the Study of Natural Language Communication Between Man and Machine". *Computational Linguistics* 9 (1). *Communications of the ACM.* Edited by Oettinger, A. G.https://cse.buffalo.edu/~rapaport/572/S02/weizenbaum.eliza.1966.pdf.

Weizenbaum, Joseph. 1976. *Computer Power and Human Reason.* San Francisco: W. H. Freeman and Company.

Whiteford, Linda. M., and Trotter II, Robert. T. 2008. *Ethics for Anthropological Research and Practice.* Long Grove:Waveland Press, Inc.

Wiggers, Kyle. 2021. "AI Weekly: These Researchers are Improving AI's Ability to Understand Different Accents." *VentureBeat*, March 5, 2021. https://venturebeat.com/business/ai-weekly-these-researchers-are-improving-ais-ability-to-understand-different-accents/

Wiggers, Kyle. 2022. "AI Content Platform Jasper Raises $125M at a $1.5B Valuation." *Tech Crunch*, October 18, 2022. https://techcrunch.com/2022/10/18/ai-content-platform-jasper-raises-125m-at-a-1-7b-valuation/.

Wooldridge, Michael. 2021. *Artificial Intelligence: What It Is, Where We Are, and Where We Are Going.* New York: Flatiron Books.

3 Reimagining Recommender Systems

Towards a More Equitable Model for Creators

Matt Artz

Introduction

Over the last three decades, recommender systems have become an undeniable and ubiquitous catalyst of cultural transformation, governing how we share ideas, exchange products and services, form social networks, find our life partners, and establish our place in society. From the personalized suggestions of other users to content suggestions in the form of social media posts, search results, movies, music, scholarly articles, and books, these systems are arguably one of the most successful behind-the-scenes information technology (IT) products (Dong et al., 2022). In fact, you likely discovered this book while shopping on Amazon or doom scrolling on LinkedIn because of a recommender system.

Notably, these systems also govern consequential life decisions, sometimes resulting in unintended and undesirable outcomes. For example, in recent years, there have been numerous reports in mainstream media highlighting a rise in discriminatory practices affecting crucial civic functions such as loan determinations (Hale, 2021), college admissions (Paykamian, 2021), policing tactics (Heaven, 2020), and conditions of bail (Callahan, 2023). While these issues present worthy challenges for anthropologists to intervene in, my focus has been on a less discussed aspect of recommender systems. Much of the existing literature and innovation is dedicated to enhancing recommendation accuracy for consumers, accompanied by growing critiques regarding the accuracy and fairness of these systems. However, my research and entrepreneurial endeavors have been directed not towards the consumer aspect of recommender systems but rather towards the perspective and impact on producers (Artz, 2022).

The catalyst for my work in this space was initiated by an entrepreneurial opportunity but also grounded in a personal interest that caused me to want to get involved and try to design for change. As a podcaster and musician, I understand what it is like to be a "creator" on the producer side of the recommender system equation, contributing content only to see it not recommended on platforms due to the tyranny of the "cold start problem."

Unfortunately, my experience is not unique and has wide-reaching consequences for the creator economy. This sector is only a decade old but is

DOI: 10.4324/9781003458555-3

already the fastest-growing small business segment, comprised of at least 50 million creators (SignalFire, 2021). A segment that is likely to experience rapid growth based on the results of a 2019 Harris Poll/LEGO® survey of children in the US, UK, and China that found children are "three times more likely to aspire to be a YouTuber (29%) than an Astronaut (11%)" (Parker, 2019).

Therefore, the consequences of getting recommender systems wrong go beyond the very valid critiques of the accuracy and fairness that impact the recommendations being made to consumers. They also include issues of equity as it relates to producers. Consequently, I argue that we need to take a holistic look at the impacts of recommender systems on production and consumption and suggest this is a worthy challenge for anthropologists to intervene in and make a difference in the world.

Likewise, I ask – if algorithms stand to shape our culture and the aspirations and livelihoods of millions of creators today and into the future, what responsibility do we bear as anthropologists to move beyond critique and intervene in this socio-technical issue? Further, how might we engage with and reimagine the continual emergence of recommender systems so that, with each new technological iteration, they become more transparent and equitable? Finally, and quite significantly, how might anthropology intervene if we were willing to roll up our sleeves and contribute to ethical innovation?

In the following sections, I endeavor to address these questions as I share my efforts to research and design a more transparent and equitable recommender system model that attempts to address some of these concerns in the art community. But first, I wish to share my anthropological origin story and what led me to this work. Following that, I will provide an overview of recommender systems and the problems of algorithmic bias, which, as I argue, are often exacerbated by the forms of capital – economic, social, and cultural (Bourdieu, 1986). I then discuss my work practice as a co-founder of an art tech startup that I will refer to throughout this chapter as ArtTech. Finally, I close with a discussion on ethics and my vision for the future. A vision that seeks to ensure our continued involvement and influence at the much-needed frontier of EmTech.

My Anthro Origin Story

My journey to anthropology was both unintended and circuitous. A journey, I should add, that is nothing to be ashamed of – because, as I've learned, it is the norm. I know this because, as the host of the *Anthropology in Business* and *Anthro to UX* podcasts, I have heard the same origin story from roughly 100 guests. I often hear stories of people discovering anthropology in college, typically by happenstance.

My story is similar, and though it may look like I made decisions with intention in the rear-view mirror, I admit getting into anthropology wasn't initially by design. In fact, I selected a different undergraduate program because I wanted to work in a management role within the tech sector. So, I opted for a Business of Bachelors Administration in Computer Information. Somewhere around my fourth year, I decided to add a Bachelor of Science in Biotechnology under the assumption that biotech, a relatively new emerging field at the time – considering the Human Genome Project had just wrapped up – was sure to be an opportunistic area for innovation and entrepreneurship (Artz, 2024).

While enrolled in my biotech program, I wanted to study primatology abroad. So, in July of 2005, I landed in Managua, Nicaragua. While there, I had many memorable experiences – an earthquake and subsequent volcanic activity, a tropical storm, and the opportunity to study primates, which I have been interested in for many years. It is there that my discovery of anthropology began.

One might suspect that I would have known what anthropology was before leaving, but sadly, that was not the case. Thankfully, though, the field site instructor asked me if I was an anthropologist, and after replying, "No, what is that?" she proceeded to explain what anthropology is and what anthropologists do, I was like: 😵

I remember it like it was yesterday, down to where I was standing. The idea of being an anthropologist rang out like a bell in a monastery, calling me to a vocation I didn't know I was seeking.

When I returned to the States, this newly implanted seed germinated, though I would not immediately act on it. While intrigued by the allure of studying all things human, I was still very much invested in tech and business and went on to get a dual-concentrated MBA in Management Information Systems and Finance and Investment – hardly an expected path to anthropology!

Thankfully, in time, anthropology would synergize with another of my emerging interests: Design. Like anthropology, I didn't study design, but I was fortunate that many of my friends were art school students majoring in the various design professions. For whatever reason, this group attracted me. Maybe it was my counter-culture leanings or the idea of creating, which I did with many of my friends in the form of bedroom-band music, indie films, and photography exhibits. I am not sure. Thankfully, it did because my first formal job during grad school was in a digital marketing agency, where I had the opportunity to merge my academic background and personal interest in the creative arts and technology.

During this period, I also developed a keen interest in the *Harvard Business Review* (HBR), an apparent vestige of my business school upbringing, and one that I will be forever grateful for because it is in HBR that my divergent interests in business, tech, design, and anthropology would converge, and come to support my early career path. This convergence, in part, was influenced by the growing popularity of IDEO and Design Thinking, and though there are valid criticisms of Design Thinking for being overly prescriptive, I am thankful for its popularity as it served a significant role in my anthropology journey by bridging these diverse schools of thought and practice.

By 2009, with this newfound transdisciplinary vision in mind, I was confident I would eventually get an anthropology degree; however, it was still not the right time. The world was in the midst of the Great Recession, and I had just started my own digital marketing agency, which I was working to scale-up as quickly as possible. Undeterred, my journey of self-education continued, acquiring a copy of *Business Anthropology* (Jordan, 2003).

This introductory text helped to define my future happy path and, by 2012, I enrolled at the University of North Texas (UNT), where Jordan had taught, to pursue a Master of Science in Applied Anthropology. I was drawn to the program because it was one of the three programs in the U.S. that mentioned business, technology, and design anthropology. While at UNT, I had the good fortune to study under Susan Squires and Christina Wasson, learning from their work in design and tech (Squires & Byrne, 2002; Wasson, 2000).

My UNT education would prove to pay off, for only a year earlier, I sold my digital marketing agency to a software engineering firm and began a new career trajectory within software development. As part of the sale of my business, I took on a leadership role in the software firm and introduced design into its historically engineering-led approach. Building on those successes, and with some UNT coursework behind me, I began to incorporate the methods of anthropology.

By 2015, these efforts had grown into a formal UX research practice, and though that practice was successful, I would argue it was yet to be complete because I had yet to mature beyond method to theory. This evolution would take another few years and an applied thesis project to achieve, but soon enough, I moved beyond just extracting user needs to synthesizing insights through theoretical frameworks like diffusionism, biosociality, reciprocity, or the forms of capital (Artz, 2018).

Both in my academic research and my industry work, this allowed me to reveal richer explanations of the sociocultural forces shaping user behaviors, values, and relationships. Anthropological theory became my tool for transforming observations into actionable opportunities guided by a nuanced understanding of the cultural contexts.

This theory-informed approach to researching, designing, and developing EmTech is demonstrated through my work with ArtTech, a mobile app for the art community connecting artists, galleries, museums, and collectors. As a co-founder, I had the opportunity to exert my anthropological agency and influence in an entrepreneurial context, a privilege that can be hard-won in other contexts. But similar to Koycheva and McKay (Koycheva, 2024; McKay, 2024), in this volume, I was in a position to use anthropology to influence all aspects of the business, including but not limited to the business model design, brand and strategy formulation, organizational culture, marketing, and new product development efforts.

The application of anthropology to this problem space proved to be beneficial because ArtTech would ultimately enter a market that was not only fraught with complex market behaviors that would be considered "irrational" from a classic economic perspective but would also be in a position to reimagine what equity might look like within the context of the historically unjust art market that favored the privileged, a phenomenon that, as I would learn, has been amplified online given the biases of recommender systems.

In the following section, I will delve into the history and design of recommender systems and examine their impact on consumers and producers, drawing on my experience with ArtTech and as a creator.

The Promise and Pitfalls of Recommendations

Before I formally explain the goals and mechanics of recommender systems, I first wish to briefly address the fact that recommender systems are not new. As noted in the opening of this chapter, these systems are at least three decades old. Yet, as discussed in the introduction of this volume (Artz & Koycheva, 2024), recommender systems have been in a perpetual state of emergence, a reflection of the norms governing the development of many information technologies. That is to say that recommender systems have continued to transform and reemerge with each new technological advance – collaborative and content-based filtering, analytics, mobile, cloud, AI models, and graph neural networks.

Yet, with each iteration, the task remains the same – to sift through large information spaces and suggest personalized recommendations for potentially relevant items or users. As such, these systems have been designed to handle a wide array of items such as websites, text, media, products, and services (Ricci et al., 2011; Zhang et al., 2019). Additionally, they extend to suggesting users – other individuals within digital platforms. For instance, they are instrumental in guiding choices ranging from search results and social media posts to movies, music, books, and scholarly articles. They also connect users with potential friends or professional contacts on platforms like LinkedIn (Dong et al., 2022). Emphasizing their impact, studies indicate that these systems drive a significant portion of user engagement on major platforms; for example, 80% of movies watched on Netflix and 60% of videos viewed on YouTube result from such recommendations (Zhang et al., 2019).

Recommender systems can generate these personalized suggestions by analyzing explicit or implicit user interactions such as stated preferences, behavioral traces, and contextual data such as geodata. They also incorporate item and user attributes such as metadata to predict potential matches. The list of potential matches is then ranked and narrowed to suggest items or users tailored to individual needs and interests (Artz, 2022).

The origins of recommender systems are sometimes traced back to the 1960s engineering and information sciences work on "Selective Dissemination of Information" (Hensley, 1963). However, more often, information filtering and retrieval (Salton & McGill, 1986) are cited as the origins. These efforts are frequently mentioned in the context of Usenet. This early worldwide distributed discussion system used information science techniques to assist users in filtering the increasingly overwhelming amount of unstructured text in the newsgroups on Usenet.

Based on these early efforts, Grundy, the first true, albeit simplistic, recommender system, emerged in 1979 as a digital librarian. Grundy was an early attempt at personalization. It operated by asking users a series of questions to determine their preferences, and then, based on their responses, it assigned users to stereotype groups and recommended books tailored to these categorized preferences. This method, though problematic for its focus on stereotyping, was nothing short of groundbreaking at the time (Beel et al., 2015).

However, by the 1990s, the demand for recommender systems had surged with the explosion of new IT systems and ever-larger datasets. This need became even more critical with the advent of the World Wide Web in 1991. Since then, the two most common methods for generating recommendations have been grounded in collaborative and content-based filtering. Collaborative filtering leverages the similarities between users and content to make recommendations. Content-based filtering uses item features such as the style of a piece of art or the genre of music to recommend other content similar to what a user likes based on their previous actions or input (Google, 2021).

One of the early seminal papers on these methods was authored by researchers at Xerox PARC. They put forward the collaborative filtering method as part of the development efforts of Tapestry, an experimental mail system that attempted to address the deluge of unwelcome mail users were starting to receive (Goldberg et al., 1992). The researchers sought to accomplish this based on the premise that people should be involved in the filtering process, and through the power of crowds, a more useful filtering system could be created.

Other foundational collaborative filtering research papers and use cases quickly followed, including GroupLens for filtering news on the Internet (Resnick et al., 1994), Ringo and Firefly for music (Shardanand & Maes, 1995), Video Recommender and MovieLens for media (Hill, Stead, & Rosenstein, 1995; Harper & Konstan, 2015), and Net Perceptions for e-Commerce solutions that powered marketing efforts for Amazon, 3M, Best Buy, Kmart and JC Penney (University of Minnesota, n.d.). At the same time, content-based filtering approaches were being advanced for needs such as website filtering (Pazzani, Muramatsu, & Bill, 1996).

Over time, both of these approaches have demonstrated strengths and weaknesses, which sometimes vary between lab tests and industry applications (Beel et al., 2015). Broadly, though, collaborative filtering appears to benefit from the wisdom of crowds, and likewise, it can make recommendations to an existing user that differ from their past actions. A benefit, to be sure, and one many of us have benefited from in the form of discovering new music and movies on streaming platforms. However, the ability to accomplish this task implies that the system can accurately associate a user with a similar community of users, a challenge that is difficult when any new user comes into a system – a problem known as the cold start problem. There are also concerns related to scalability and, importantly, data privacy, as the data needs to be shared and compared across all system users.

Content-based filtering, on the other hand, relies on data such as the metadata that describes the content and the ratings of items and users, and as such, scales better and avoids the privacy concerns of collaborative filtering. It also may avoid some of the aforementioned cold start problems, however, that require that metadata or ratings are present and accurate. It may also result in users being recommended content overly similar to previous selections, thus limiting opportunities for novel discovery. Further, both approaches have also been shown to suffer from numerous forms of algorithmic bias – popularity, over-specialization, and homogenization – resulting in unfair treatment and lack of exposure for certain items or users (Roy & Dutta, 2022; Stinson, 2022; Abdollahpouri et al., 2017; Steck, 2011; Liu et al., 2019; Ge, 2021), a dilemma that is arguably problematic in all use cases, but especially to the livelihood of creators.

Popularity bias results in already popular content being disproportionally recommended over niche and less common items and leads to a "rich-get-richer" effect that limits exposure and exacerbates existing inequalities. Over-specialization provides overly obvious and narrow recommendations within a user's known tastes rather than expanding their discovery potential. Homo-genization bias reduces the systemwide diversity as the same subset of popular items is suggested to users (Brynjolfsson, Hu, & Smith, 2006; Abdollahpouri & Mansoury, 2019). It is also worth repeating that the cold start problems can hinder recommendation performance and, thus, may be viewed as a form of bias impacting some items and users. Finally, there are other issues impacting these approaches, including but not limited to the Shilling attack, synonym, latency, sparsity, and gray sheep problems (Roy & Dutta, 2022).

Given all of these potential limitations and problems, as well as the respective strengths and weaknesses of collaborative and content-based filtering methods alone, efforts in recent years have frequently made use of hybrid approaches combining multiple techniques and technologies into ever-larger ensembles of complex and sometimes contradictory approaches. Commonly, that involves making use of artificial intelligence models to augment traditional filtering approaches with association techniques, clustering approaches, Bayesian net-works, neural networks, and most recently, graph neural networks (Roy & Dutta, 2022; Dong et al., 2022; Wu et al., 2020).

Techno-solutionists increasingly favor these complex hybrid approaches. They argue that advanced engineering solutions are necessary to overcome the inherent limitations and unintended consequences of singular approaches (Zhao et al., 2013; Steck, 2011; Stinson, 2022; Abdollahpouri et al., 2017; Adomavicius & Kwon, 2012). However, these engineering-centric strategies, while well-intentioned, often focus narrowly on technical and organizational needs. They prioritize the ability to generate accurate recommendations quickly and at scale. However, frequently left out of these innovation efforts are concerns for consumers' and producers' perceived satisfaction and the more systemic considerations of well-being, agency, transparency, and equity that impact individuals, organizations, and society at large.

To be clear, I am not suggesting there is no research and development occurring that attempts to address such concerns. There are, in fact, many well-intentioned researchers, technologists, and organizations working to create fair and equitable recommender systems, but the idea of what is fair and equitable is itself culturally mediated and thus means many things to many different groups. Likewise, there are typically unintended and undesirable consequences of recommender systems, a reality that has led to vigorous and well-founded critiques, causing proponents to respond with even more engineering-based justifications and remedies.

For example, it has been suggested that we should aim to correct problems such as bias further upstream by addressing training data bias, algorithmic focus bias, algorithmic processing bias, transfer context bias, and interpretation bias (Danks & London, 2017). Similarly, other technical solutions have been proposed for debiasing through modified ranking formulas, reweighting certain user groups, or directly optimizing fairness metrics (Singh & Joachims, 2018; Geyik et al., 2019).

However, approaching issues of bias from a narrowly computational perspective overlooks the broader social and political contexts at play. Harms online cannot be divorced from unjust human practices, norms, values, and structures offline. These are not distinct domains, and to assume that recommender systems are neutral and divorced from the inequities of society through complex engineering is to negate the inherent phygitalness of these systems.

For example, let us take an overly simplistic use case to illustrate how unequal social structures offline contribute to producing unintended consequences for creators online. Imagine a music streaming platform of your choice. If, on this platform, the music recommendations that listeners received were only for artists that they previously liked, the results might be auditorily pleasing and potentially "useful" in that they are being suggested music they are likely to like based on past performances. However, such recommendations will result in the listener not discovering new artists, and more systemically, the recommender system will harm new artists since they would have no previous likes on the platform and thus can't be recommended.

Admittedly, that is a very narrow example that intentionally excluded as many variables as possible, as well as the state-of-the-art in recommender systems, but despite its simplicity, it speaks to how complex the challenges are. In such a model, the consumer may more or less be happy with the recommendations, unaware of what musical potential lurks beyond the familiar hits. However, all new artists would starve, unable to earn a living since their music would not be recommended. Therefore, in this hypothetical example, some artists (producers) would be compensated at the expense of others, all because it was designed to cater to the known needs of existing listeners (consumers).

Now, let's advance the complexity engineers and designers of recommender systems face, this time, using a real-life example of bias based on my experiences as a creator. As I alluded to earlier, during my undergraduate studies, I could most frequently be found creating things. Of all the projects I engaged in, music was the most resonant. I found audio to be an enigmatic medium in its ability to convey emotions and stories, and since then, I have spent countless hours sculpting audio for my music and podcasts. Sadly, I am here to report that Malcolm Gladwell must be wrong about his 10,000-hour rule because I am not an expert, as my music stream earnings apparently attest to.

What I am, however, is an enthused creator, yet despite my enthusiasm, I struggle to gain visibility with my music. That is because enthusiasm alone is not enough to succeed. The problem is that I have no brand recognition as a musician and don't want to spend money to advertise my music. The most I am comfortable doing is sharing my songs with a very limited group within my personal network and the occasional posts on LinkedIn. Unsurprisingly, then, when I release music to streaming platforms, it is simply not recommended. Unless I am willing to pay to advertise it, submit it to playlists, or blast it out to my "followers," it will not receive listens and, in turn, prime the proverbial recommender system pump.

But, if I were to do any or all of those, the recommender systems would then start to suggest my music to other users, albeit in relatively small numbers, given my stature. Now, if my songs were contemporary pop hits, which they are most certainly not, they would plausibly continue to be recommended as people relisten, like, share, and save to playlists. But alas, that is not the outcome for my genre-jumping outsider music, and within very short order, from hours to a few days, it recedes back into the algorithmic ether, rarely to be recommended.

The result of this conundrum is that creators like myself, including many of the artists and gallerists who upload art into online art marketplaces, cannot earn a living doing what we love. This is at least partially because recommender systems, for all of the complex engineering, reflect societal norms offline. Though there is undoubtedly an aspect of quality that factors into the relative performance of content within these systems, the fact of the matter is that one's ability to succeed online is often governed by some of the same forces – economic, social, and cultural capital – that govern their ability to succeed offline, as I will shortly share.

Accordingly, in the following section, I will share how my work with Art-Tech gave me the opportunity to identify this problem through anthropologically informed research and, notably, how, as an Anthro-Solutionist (Artz & Koycheva, 2024), it gave me a space to try and intervene to the benefit of creators, as well as consumers. In doing so, I will describe the high-level discovery research process I use at the outset of innovation efforts in new fields or with new companies. Importantly, I will also show how this work coalesced into the design of ArtTech's pending patent for a gamified participatory recommender system (Artz & Speicher, 2023) and why this model is relevant to the dilemma that impacts the estimated 50 million creators.

Intervening as an Anthro-Solutionist

When we started ArtTech, I didn't have a sense that I would be studying recommender systems. That naturally arose out of the research. Nevertheless, once the opportunity presented itself, I knew I wanted to try and do something about it. I say try because often inventions will fail to become transformational innovations, be they disruptive or incremental in nature. But failure is no reason to sit on the sidelines and let engineers and businesspeople build EmTech without us.

This is a point that I think is particularly important because, as Nick Seaver portrayed in his thorough book, *Computing Taste*, the way engineers and businesspeople think about and approach recommender systems (Seaver, 2022) is quite different from how anthropologists do. Now, I should be clear: I greatly appreciate how they approach problems, but that doesn't mean we should let them build EmTech alone. Just like our provocation in the introduction to this volume – what if there were anthropologists who were involved early on in Google – we could muse what recommender systems might look like if anthropologists were involved early enough to think about all parties involved in the data exchange that takes place in recommender systems, especially markets where content is exchanged between producers and consumers.

In my case, I certainly was not involved in the field of recommender systems early, but in my worldview, it is also never too late to try, and so I did with ArtTech, a spin-out pandemic-era product started during the first year of COVID-19. At the time, we – the founding team – had no solution in mind, nor did we have the faintest idea of a business model. Instead, we simply set out to explore and make sense of this new space, a task that any anthropologist would be perfectly at home doing because, whether we realize it or not, anthropology is inherently entrepreneurial (Koycheva, 2020) in its iterative and divergent exploration of a problem space that converges into a solution, be it "writing culture" or a product.

To start, I created a research question: "What are the key pain points and structural inefficiencies of the traditional art market, and how might a tech solution contribute to addressing those problems?" I began putting together a plan for my initial discovery phase. Keeping in mind that this was during the pandemic, the research included traditional secondary research, virtual in-depth interviews and observations, and netnography, but being a technologist, I also planned to make use of computational approaches.

Broadly, I planned to map the art market ecosystem through market research to gain a foundational understanding and then immerse myself in the lived experiences of the community through digital ethnographic research. I first sought out leading industry market reports, such as those from UBS and Deloitte. I typically use these types of reports to establish an understanding of the market size, key actors and institutions, and trends, as well as to get a sense of the language and norms when I am new to a problem space.

A quick glance at the Art Basel & UBS Art Market reports from previous years made it abundantly clear that the art market was a significant global economic force and was increasingly going digital. In 2018, the market grew 6% year-over-year (YOY) to reach an estimated $67.4 billion valuation, and though 2019 saw a 5% dip, the market was still valued at an estimated $64.1 billion (Art Basel & UBS, 2019; Art Basel & UBS, 2020). Similarly, in 2018, online sales grew 11% YOY to $6 billion globally, and though 2019 saw a 2% YOY decline, online transactions still accounted for $5.9 billion in sales, with 57% of those sales being to new buyers. Notably, 77% of the sales were between buyers and sellers who were more than 1,000 kilometers apart, with only 11% being between parties less than 50 kilometers apart. Collectively, these stats pointed to a robust market that is increasingly younger, digitally mediated, and physically distributed. Encouraging data for a potential new art tech entrant, especially given that an estimated $380 million was invested in art tech startups by late 2020 (Fuelarts, 2020).

However, we also identified problems related to equity, inclusion, and access. The distribution of sales was highly concentrated at the top end of the market, with high-net-worth (HNW) collectors spending the vast majority of the money on purchases from a relatively small group of artists and gallerists with established reputations. This left emerging artists and galleries in a precarious position, struggling for visibility and sales in an increasingly competitive and saturated market. Furthermore, though the 2019 report noted an 8% YOY growth, female artists represented only 44% of artists and 40% of global sales. Complicating matters the art market is historically relationship-based, creating a scenario that favors empowered and entrenched incumbents over new entrants.

While these are significant problems under normal circumstances, they were made worse during COVID when art fairs and physical galleries, once the loci of economic, social, and cultural exchange had closed, many for good. In their place, we saw the emergence of online viewing rooms and virtual galleries, many of which were gated, requiring special access, often set aside for the elite actors of the market. While these digital counterparts could have offered an alternative venue for more artists and gallerists to showcase and sell their works, what we were noticing at the time was that, in practice, they served to reinforce some of the existing structural barriers that created inequalities. Notably, we noticed that successful online offerings, NFT-mania aside, were often created by actors and institutions that were already well-known and capitalized. In other words, despite the potential for technology to expand and democratize access, it was being used to restrict access even further in a market that was no longer able to have a physical footprint due to COVID-19.

To better explore the dynamics of how these digital initiatives were disrupting the art market before and during the pandemic, I next set out to gain a sense of the breadth of digital offerings, including the aforementioned emerging online viewing rooms and other common platforms. These included traditional online art marketplaces, crowdfunding, factional investing, auctions, and Web3 platforms. I also looked at art investment funds, data and analytics providers, and arts education initiatives. Finally, I explored emerging trends of applying technologies like AI and blockchain to use cases such as fraud detection and establishing provenance.

With a sense of the type of art tech offerings, I then began to identify the key companies within each space. My goal with the competitive analysis was not to benchmark us against other organizations, for we still didn't have a business idea in mind. More so, it was to create a visual market map that we could use to discuss the competitive landscape as a team. I typically find visual aids always enable a more robust conversation than bullets on a slide deck or, worse, long reports.

Aside from the market map, the competitive analysis also sought to explore critical organizational drivers for each of the identified companies, such as the business models, vision, mission, articulated strategy, founding team, company size, and the amount of venture capital raised. I also looked at the marketing efforts and positioning, team composition, customer feedback, and proficiency in search engine and app optimization. Last, but certainly not least, I reviewed the intellectual property positions and the user experience of the products to understand the current state of art tech and, importantly, to look for gaps. While I had yet to conduct in-depth interviews and observations, I was already starting to think about uncontested market spaces. My goal was to, in time, define a differentiated strategy that would sidestep some of the companies that were already deeply entrenched.

Once the secondary research was complete enough, and with my newfound, albeit still limited, understanding of the art market, I kicked off my ethnographic work. I conducted 30 in-depth virtual, semi-structured interviews with various actors across the art world. This included ten galleries, ten artists, five curators, two critics, two art educators, and one art consultant, most of whom could be described as mid-market actors aside from a few emerging artists and two HNW collectors. My goal at this stage was to develop an inside perspective on the key challenges and opportunities facing the different actors involved in the art market. I also observed some of the participants as they used existing and established art tech platforms like Artsy and Saatchi Art, as well as others who were repurposing platforms like Instagram and TikTok – favorites among artists – for direct networking and sales.

Throughout these interviews, I was struck by anecdotes that spoke to how challenging it was to survive in the art market. I heard stories of galleries only lasting months and artists having to work jobs they deplored because they were unable to earn a living doing what they loved. Strikingly, both gallerists and artists spoke to how difficult it was to make money on the existing platforms. Most gallerists were on Artsy not because they sold art but because they felt they needed to be seen there. It was viewed somewhat like a loss leader. More than a platform for earning money, it was one to signal your status – given the monthly cost, if you could maintain your profile, it demonstrated you were a more established gallery. Artists had similar things to say about platforms such as Saatchi Art, and collectors generally found both overwhelming.

In both cases, the takeaway was that it was hard to buy and sell art on these established marketplaces. Specifically, what I learned from my inter-views is that sales on these platforms had a strong correlation to established credibility and price, creating a U-shaped curve (see Figure 3.1).

Online Sales Potential vs Price

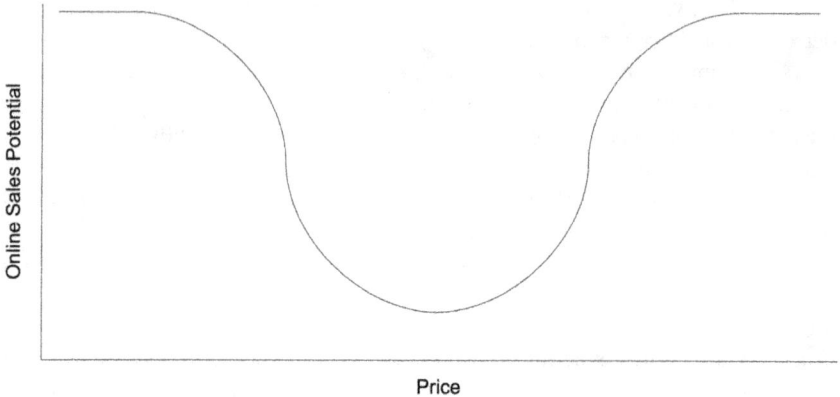

Figure 3.1 Online Sales Potential vs. Price in Art Marketplaces

Sure, artists and gallerists would make an occasional sale, but it wasn't a common occurrence for most that I spoke with, especially those in the mid-market. If the art was cheap enough, somewhere sub $3,000 USD, the credibility didn't matter as much, and so consumers were more likely to purchase works from lesser-known artists or galleries based purely on aesthetics. However, as the prices increased into the mid-market range and above, artists and galleries needed ever-greater credibility to drive sales. This trend only increased as the price went up, and buyers were more likely to be art collectors, looking at the piece as an investment versus a truly aesthetic purchase.

Likewise, without established credibility, such as name brand recognition, or previously public sales data, such as the data that comes from auctions, the mid-market sellers I interviewed struggled to sell their artwork. Ultimately, it seemed that these platforms catered best to either high-end established artists and galleries who could command premium pricing or very affordable emer-ging artists, but made it difficult for mid-market artists and galleries to gain traction.

Credibility also factored into another blatant admission from a gallerist. They described a business relationship with an artist who was described as not being exceptionally skilled but of good pedigree. To overcome the apparent lack of skill and, more importantly, their lack of credibility, the artist's wealthy family provided economic capital to buy press that praised the artist's work. In turn, this artist gradually gained greater exposure and, with the eventual anointing from tastemakers, gained access and became an accepted and successful artist.

These stories struck me not just for the difficulty of the art experience for all, not least those who might be historically disempowered, but more so because of how that experience can be modulated by access to economic, social, and cultural capital. Those with more, such as Grimes, who sold an estimated $6 million in NFTs (Kastrenakes, 2021), have a greater ability to break in and be accepted, somewhat irrespective of the intrinsic quality of their work. Those without, however, often struggle, sometimes regardless of an abundance of talent.

Alongside this anthropologically satisfying theoretical observation about capital, the initial findings that were bubbling up in my iterative analysis of transcripts from gallerists and artists primarily dealt with social connectivity, cultural alliances, equity, and inclusion. Notably, artists and gallerists had a very challenging time identifying ideal partners who shared similar needs and interests and, in turn, rarely found sustainable business partners who would contribute to each other's success, a trend that was often made worse by geographic access for those in underdeveloped geographic art markets.

From the perspective of many artists, gallerists were too transactional, only interested in the sale and not in helping to develop the artists' brands and assisting with services traditionally thought of as marketing. From the gallerist's perspective, they felt artists didn't do enough to help themselves and found it challenging, even annoying, to have to respond to all of the requests they received. Unsurprisingly, these relationships often went through fits and starts, reluctantly collaborating, often to the detriment of both parties, who frequently felt misunderstood or undervalued by the other.

Collectors, on the other hand, had different needs and goals that coalesced into themes around confidence and acceptance. Many expressed concerns about fitting in – often feeling intimidated or out of place given their lack of art education and ability to speak the language. They frequently described the art community as cold and unwelcoming and expressed a reluctant need to develop a more sophisticated understanding of art if they were to be accepted. I myself can attest to experiencing these thoughts and feelings many times in galleries in places like Chelsea, NY. Notably, though, the personal anecdote that most succinctly makes the point involves a visit to one of the leading art fairs during my later definitional research for ArtTech.

In December of 2020, I attended Art Basel Miami. While there, not a single gallerist asked me if I needed help when I entered their booth, and the overwhelming majority wouldn't even look at me. To make things worse, one gallery, the famously elite Gagosian Gallery, didn't even list the names of the art, almost implying that if you didn't already know what the piece was, then you didn't deserve a chance to know. Frustrating as this experience was, it also spoke to the norms, beliefs, and behaviors of the high-end luxury art market, reinforcing the sentiment I heard in my interviews.

To supplement the qualitative data I collected as part of the virtual interviews and observations, I also employed netnography and digital methods to observe and collect data from various online art communities, forums, and social media platforms. This approach allowed me to make sense of the broader conversation and sentiment as expressed in digital spaces. I focused on platforms like Reddit, Quora, Twitter, and Instagram, where artists, collectors, and art enthusiasts frequently interacted and shared their experiences and opinions. I also looked at the mobile app marketplaces to get a sense of how art tech apps were performing. To analyze all of my data, I combined coding and affinity mapping with natural language understanding (NLU), which was employed to computationally conduct topic modeling and sentiment analysis.

The rationale for collecting multiple data sources, as well as using multiple analysis techniques that blend traditional embodied approaches with computation, is both academic and professional for me. Of course, doing so helps to triangulate and make the research more valid and credible – absolutely a valuable pursuit. But also, from a more practical and professional perspective, it simply helps to expand and deepen my potential understanding of the problem space.

Relatedly, when I use a mixed methods design that synergizes embodied and computational approaches, I always lead with the embodied approach. There may come a time when I feel differently, but at this point, I prefer to augment my decision making rather than automate it. I believe, at least for now, there is no replacement for human creativity and critical thinking despite all of my techno-solutionist leanings. That said, computational tools and methods can be beneficial to spot gaps and, at times, gain some perspective or even reinforcement, especially if you are a research team of one, as I was.

As an example of how a computational approach can be used to reinforce our embodied findings, I compared and contrasted my affinity-mapped themes of the artists and gallery transcripts with the NLU-based approach to topic modeling the same data. While different in the exact wording, the overlap in ideas between my affinity-mapped themes – social connectivity, cultural alliances, equity and inclusion, and livelihood actualization – and the topics displayed in the right-hand sidebar in the below Figure 3.2 of a semantic text network helped to reassure me of the validity and credibility of my insights.

Based on these insights, our team collectively agreed that though the overall art market was sizable, likely with potential for growth both online and off, the mid-market seemed particularly challenged given transparency issues and the lack of credibility of artists and gallerists in this part of the market. Likewise, we thought that the mid-market was a particularly compelling space for change, even if it wasn't the sector that represented the majority of the

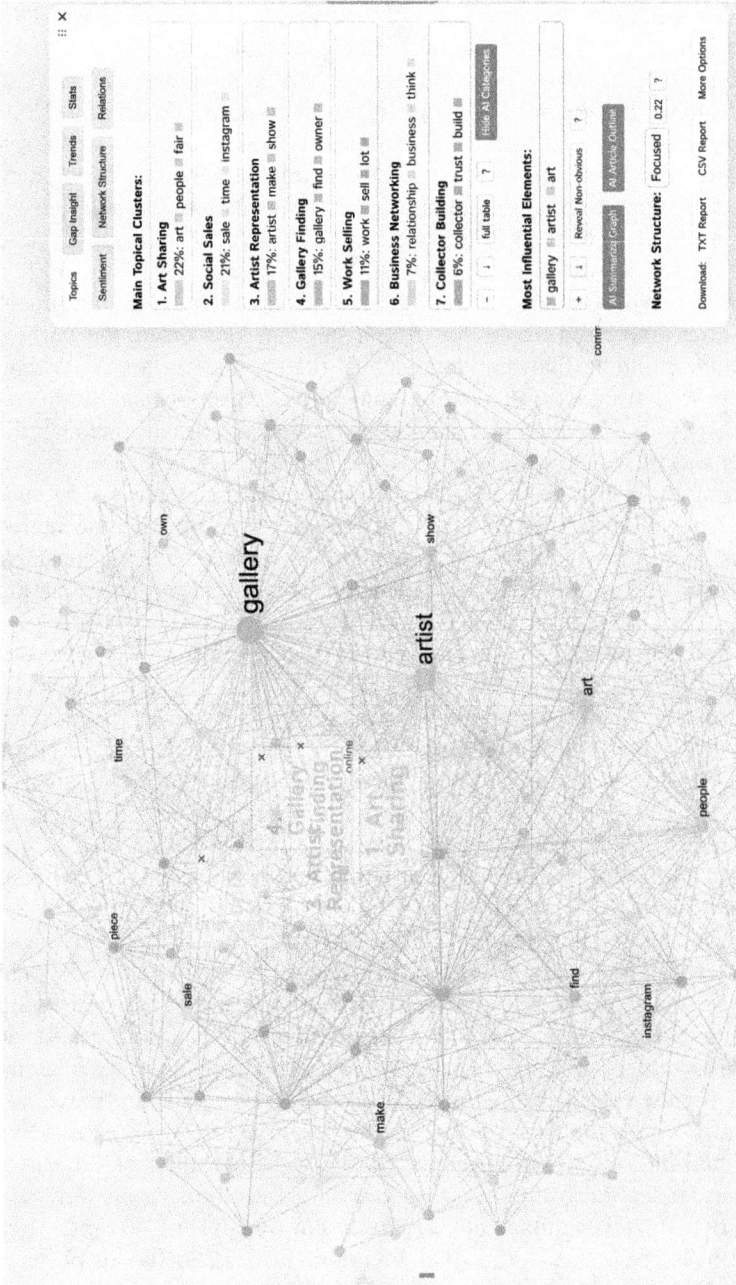

Figure 3.2 Semantic Text Network Graph and Extracted Topics from Interview Transcripts with Artists and Gallerists

money that was exchanged, given the price points and overall sales potential, given the issues associated with the aforementioned U-shaped curve.

Building on this, I reasoned that many of these artists and gallerists lacked the capital – economic, social, and cultural – to help propel them into the higher-end established market, a dilemma that seemed to only be complicated by the broad social inequalities that disproportionately affect disempowered actors, such as females compared to others within the art market. Making matters worse yet, many of these harmful inequities appeared to be amplified by the existing digitalization efforts despite the potential for digital to be a flattener.

Finally, set against this backdrop were a host of other relationship and knowledge-related issues that impacted all actors in one form or another. From the partnership issues between artists and gallerists to the sentiment collectors often expressed about not fitting in. This reinforced the anthropological understanding that markets, such as the art market, are more than mere commercial transactions; instead, they are complex sociocultural systems where power dynamics and capital play critical roles in shaping the experiences and success of its actors.

Considering these insights, we articulated our problem statement: The mid-market presents opportunities for economic growth driven by human-centered innovations; however, it remains burdened by inequalities in relationships, knowledge, and access, and these are not addressed by existing digitalization efforts.

Considering our problem statement, alongside insights from our competitive analysis, we identified a unique niche in the art market. This niche wouldn't necessitate direct competition with well-established, heavily funded companies like Artsy and Saatchi, nor would it involve significant legal or regulatory hurdles. Recognizing that these established platforms already dominated the marketplace with substantial resources, we decided against pursuing similar models. Additionally, we opted out of exploring NFTs, considering the uncertainty as a business model, and also avoided fractional investing and funds, which would involve complex regulatory compliance.

Our focus, therefore, shifted to innovating within a space that was both viable and underserved. Specifically, we decided to focus on the more foundational aspects of relationship building and community engagement and created an initial value proposition – creating relationships with art – to guide our next steps.

From this value proposition, ArtTech was born. Envisioned as a social community for the art market, connecting similar artists, galleries, museums, and collectors within the mid-market, the mobile-first app was conceived as an incremental innovation building of some of the best features of LinkedIn, Spotify, and Tinder. Accordingly, we agreed on a freemium business model, with a plan to match similar counterparties for free. Then, in time, after developing a userbase, we would offer premium services, including phygital experiences that would connect users around curated in-venue activities at galleries, art fairs, and museums, and gamified art education to assist collectors in feeling more comfortable and welcome in the art community.

All of these features, though, would need an accurate recommender system if we were to overcome the challenges identified in the research. Likewise, I began studying the state-of-the-art in recommender systems by reviewing academic papers and patents. As mentioned in the previous section, the trend has been towards hybrid ensembles that are heavily AI-based, with the goal of improving accuracy, fairness, and, increasingly, transparency and explainability – which has become a high-water mark in recent years given the rise of responsible and trustworthy AI initiatives (Deloitte, n.d.).

I knew we couldn't tackle all of those technological challenges, especially not in a minimum viable product (MVP). I also believed that doing so would still not result in an equitable recommender system for ArtTech because our goal was not just accurate recommendations. More so, we wanted fair and transparent recommendations that would help to overcome the issues created by an abundance or absence of capital and its effects on visibility, opportunity, and growth for artists and galleries.

Taking inspiration from Google Search, I envisioned a design for the ArtTech recommender system that equally focused on both producers and consumers. Google, unlike many other platforms, such as Spotify or Netflix, leverages an ensemble of methods to recommend the most relevant content to searchers (consumers), but it also provides website owners (creators) with guidelines for creating content that ranks well in search results. Furthermore, Google equips content creators with visual analytical tools, like Google Analytics and Search Console, to help them understand their performance.

By integrating such an approach into ArtTech, I reasoned, we could empower creators, providing them with clear criteria and insights to increase the chances of their profiles or artworks being recommended. This system would go beyond merely offering accurate recommendations to consumers. It would enable creators in ways that standard recommender systems don't, boosting transparency and allowing all users to visually track how their actions impact the system through a gamified interface. This interface would display their influence level within the system, determined by specific actions they take.

To achieve this, we created the concept of "behavioral capital," which equates to the productive engagement, cooperation, and actions of users within the platform. This concept serves as a democratizing force, ensuring that success in the ArtTech ecosystem is not overly influenced by pre-existing economic, social, or cultural capital but also on the value creators bring through their active participation.

The value this design adds to creators is multifaceted. First, it provides a level playing field where success is not solely determined by pre-existing economic, social, or cultural capital but also by the creator's active participation and contribution to the community. This aligns with the growing demand for more equitable systems in digital spaces, particularly in industries like the art market, where traditional gatekeeping mechanisms often marginalize those who lack access to capital.

Second, the gamified aspect of the system adds an engaging and transparent layer to the process. Creators can clearly see how their behaviors impact their scores and, consequently, their visibility within the platform. This transparency fosters a sense of control and understanding that is often lacking in other recommender systems, where the workings behind content promotion and recommendation are opaque.

Last, the ArtTech model adds value by fostering a sense of community and collaboration. By rewarding behaviors that contribute to the collective good, such as sharing knowledge, supporting fellow artists, and actively participating in the platform, creators not only advance their individual goals but also contribute to a vibrant and supportive ecosystem.

With this design, we aim to establish a more equitable platform where every creator, regardless of background or resources, has a fair chance to be seen and succeed in finding business partners and establishing a sustainable and creative livelihood. We also aim to reimagine what recommender systems can and should be. Our vision extends beyond simply providing accurate recommendations for consumers to also supporting the producers who contribute to these systems.

In essence, we are seeking to create a new model for thinking about transparency and equity in recommender systems. But with efforts to reimagine socio-technical systems comes a great need for responsibility and accountability, and we must grapple with ethical considerations, and so, in the next section, I will argue why anthropologists need to be involved, and why they should get involved earlier in the process, but also, why we need to be humble and open.

The Ethical Contrarian

Throughout this chapter, I have tried to call attention to the ethical considerations of recommender systems, which are many. From the potential biases that impact algorithmic design and decision making to the broader societal impact of socio-technical systems, I have attempted to highlight scenarios that speak to the importance of integrating an ethical perspective. But beware, this is more challenging than it may seem, regardless of our training or codes of ethics.

Though it is true our anthropological understanding of human cultures, social dynamics, power structures, and relativistic ethical norms can and should play a role, we also need to humbly acknowledge our limits. Often, I hear anthropology colleagues argue on social media and at conferences that a product has failed or has a poor design because we weren't involved, with the seemingly implicit underlying assumption that what was missing was an anthropological perspective. In some cases, I am sure that would be true, but it does not have to be true. It also may be the case that even if we were involved, a product could fail or cause harm. There may be many reasons for this, but one of those is the inherent "wickedness" of EmTech, which may produce far-reaching unintended consequences, often with many degrees of separation. Likewise, it is almost inconceivable to think that somewhere in the value chain, some harm won't be done, and if our gold standard is "do no harm," then we are forced to do nothing. That can't be. We must "do some good" (Briody & Meerwarth Pester, 2017).

That is why, in this volume, we have argued for being humble, partnering, seeking allies, and embracing the power of multidisciplinary collaboration. We must recognize that the challenges at the intersection of EmTech and society are too complex to be addressed by any single discipline or individual. Subsequently, to close out this chapter, I will offer my vision for the future.

Going Forward by Looking Back

From the time I was young, I wanted to work in the business and management of tech. Years later, I opted to get a social science degree, not because business and tech were failing me, but because I thought they could do more. I chose anthropology as the specific discipline to help me achieve this goal. Not because I thought anthropology was needed to control those disciplines but more so because I thought together, they could all be more robust. Unfortunately, I don't feel like that is a commonly shared vision.

Too often, I feel that anthropologists are quick to judge disciplines such as engineering and business for being solutionist and at times cynically assume that technology must always result in harm. When I hear this sentiment, I often wonder, what happened to our appreciation for tools (solutions) as well as the holistic and empathetic openness we were taught to have as anthropologists?

Regardless of what may have happened to that openness in the past, I am asking for it now as I share my closing recommendations for rethinking who we are and who we may want to be.

Avoid the Anthropology Halo Effect

As I have tried to communicate throughout this chapter, I genuinely believe anthropology has immense value, but it is not the only discipline capable of contributing to addressing complex problems. In fact, as I've said, it is likely the case that no single discipline is sufficient to address the multifaceted challenges we face in our increasingly VUCA world (Barber, 1992). So, let us all try to avoid falling into the trap of anthropology-centric thinking and be open-minded about what other disciplines can contribute.

Study Other Disciplines

Related, I argue we should immerse ourselves in other ways of thinking beyond anthropology. It is one thing to partner with other disciplines. It is another to embody that discipline. If we have the privilege, we might want to double major, pursue an interdisciplinary graduate degree, obtain non-anthropology certifications, or simply read widely. The most visionary innovations happen at the intersection of diverse perspectives. Bringing an anthropological lens to another field can catalyze breakthroughs in EmTech and beyond.

Break Free from Academic Entrenchment

Academia has its merits, but it also has limits. If we have the privilege to do so, we should at least consider alternate or complimentary career paths where we can apply anthropological thinking in new ways. Working outside academia does not make us a sellout, and many find it rewarding to create positive change through industry roles. In fact, I have never had a guest on my podcasts who has indicated they regret their decision to go alternative academic (alt-ac). Working in industry also does not mean we have to leave the academy entirely. I'm an adjunct, as are others in this volume. So, let us all maintain an open mindset and not let outdated notions of academic purity hold us back.

Adopt a Pragmatic Optimist Mindset

Embracing a pragmatic optimist mindset means balancing our hopeful idealism with grounded realism. It calls for us to address challenges with an understanding of the present yet driven by the belief that deliberate, actionable efforts can foster better futures. Such an orientation calls us to leverage anthropological insights not just for critique but also for constructive intervention.

Be an Anthro-Solutionist

Dedicate yourself to advancing positive change through applied anthropological insights. Avoid knee-jerk rejection of "solutions" – practically all human inventions are solutions to some problem. The need is not less solutions but better ones that thoughtfully address people's values and experiences. Lead the development of ethical, inclusive innovations.

Consider Becoming a Founder-Anthropologist

Founders have immense power to shape the vision, values, and impact of an organization. If you aspire to profoundly influence, explore starting your own company. Whether that is an EmTech company or something else entirely, building your own company will allow you to infuse it with anthropological principles and a human-centered ethos. Embracing the founder-anthropologist path offers us the ability to express our agency and enact the kind of change we wish to see.

So, let's go forward, and create solutions, not problems.

Bibliography

Abdollahpouri, H., Burke, R., and Mobasher, B. 2017. "Controlling Popularity Bias in Learning to Rank Recommendation." In: *The Proceedings of the Eleventh ACM Conference on Recommender Systems* 42–46.

Abdollahpouri, Himan, and Masoud Mansoury. 2019. "The Unfairness of Popularity Bias in Recommendation." *arXiv.* September 19. Accessed September 2021. https://a rxiv.org/pdf/1907.13286.pdf#:~:text=Recommender%20systems%20are%20known% 20to,represented%20in%20the%20recommen%2D%20dations.

Adomavicius, Gediminas, and Alexander Tuzhilin. 2005. "Toward the Next Generation of Recommender Systems: A Survey of the State-of-the-Art and Possible Extensions." *IEEE Transactions on Knowledge and Data Engineering* 17 (6): 734–749. doi:10.1109/ TKDE.2005.99.

Art Basel & UBS. 2019. *The Art Basel and UBS Global Art Market Report 2019.* Market Report, Zurich: Art Basel & UBS.

Art Basel & UBS. 2020. *The Art Basel and UBS Global Art Market Report 2020.* Market Report, Zurich: Art Basel & UBS.

Artz, Matt. 2018. *An Ethnography of Direct-to-Consumer Genomics [DTCG]: Design Anthropology Insights for the Product Management of a Disruptive Innovation.* Denton, TX: University of North Texas.

Artz, Matt. 2022. "Design Anthropology, Algorithmic Bias, Behavioral Capital, and the Creator Economy." *Practicing Anthropology* 44 (2): 33–36.

Artz, Matt. 2024. "The Art and Science of Sandboxing." *Practicing Anthropology.*

Artz, Matt, and Lora Koycheva. 2024. "Introduction." In: *EmTech Anthropology: Careers at the Frontier,* edited by Matt Artz and Lora Koycheva. New York: Routledge.

Artz, Matthew R., and Geoffrey C. Speicher. 2023. *Gamified Participatory Recommender System.* United States Patent US20230046646A1.

Barber, H. F. 1992. "Developing Strategic Leadership: The US Army War College Experience." *Journal of Management Development* 11 (6): 4–12.

Beel, Joeran, Bela Gipp, Stefan Langer, and Corinna Breitinger. 2015. "Research-paper Recommender Systems: A Literature Survey." *International Journal on Digital Libraries* 17: 305–338.

Briody, Elizabeth K., and Tracy Meerwarth Pester. 2017. "Redesigning Anthropology's Ethical Principles to Align with Anthropological Practice." In: *Ethics in the Anthropology of Business,* by Timothy de Waal Malefyt and Robert J. Morais. New York: Routledge.

Brynjolfsson, Erik, Yu (Jeffrey) Hu, and Michael D. Smith. 2006. "From Niches to Riches: Anatomy of the Long Tail." *MIT Sloan Management Review,* July 1.

Callahan, Molly. 2023. *AI & LAW Algorithms Were Supposed to Reduce Bias in Criminal Justice—Do They?*February 23. https://www.bu.edu/articles/2023/do-algo rithms-reduce-bias-in-criminal-justice/.

Danks, David, and Alex John London. 2017. "Algorithmic Bias in Autonomous Systems." In: *Proceedings of the 26th International Joint Conference on Artificial Intelligence (IJCAI 2017) f.*

Deloitte. n.d. *Trustworthy AI^{TM} – Bridging the Ethics Gap Surrounding AI.* Accessed December 28, 2023. https://www2.deloitte.com/us/en/pages/deloitte-analytics/solu tions/ethics-of-ai-framework.html.

Dong, Zhenhua, Zhe Wang, Jun Xu, Ruiming Tang, and Jirong Wen. 2022. "A Brief History of Recommender Systems." *arXiv:2209.01860v1* 1–8.

Fuelarts. 2020. "Fuelarts Art+Tech & NFT Startups Report 2022." Market Report. New York: Fuelarts. https://arttech.org.br/download/Fuelarts_Startups_Report_2022.pdf.

Ge, Y.et al. 2021. "Towards Long-term Fairness in Recommendation." In: *The Proceedings of the 14th ACM International Conference on Web Search and Data Mining* 445–453.

Geyik, Sahin Cem, Stuart Ambler, and Krishnaram Kenthapadi. 2019. "*Fairness-Aware Ranking in Search & Recommendation Systems with Application to LinkedIn Talent Search.*" In: Proceedings of the 25th ACM SIGKDD International Conference on Knowledge Discovery & Data Mining (KDD '19), 2221–2231. doi:10.1145/3292500.3330691.

Goldberg, David, David Nichols, Brian M. Oki, and Douglas Terry. 1992. "Using Collaborative Filtering to Weave an Information Tapestry." *Communications of the ACM* 35 (12): 61–70.

Google. 2021. Introduction | Machine Learning. Accessed 2023. https://developers.google.com/machine-learning/recommendation.

Hale, Kori. 2021. *A.I. Bias Caused 80% Of Black Mortgage Applicants To Be Denied.* September 2. https://www.forbes.com/sites/korihale/2021/09/02/ai-bias-caused-80-of-black-mortgage-applicants-to-be-denied/?sh=16fd61b536fe.

Harper, F. M., and J. Konstan. 2015. "The MovieLens Datasets: History and Context." *ACM Transactions on Interactive Intelligent Systems* 4 (4): 19.

Heaven, Will Douglas. 2020. *Predictive Policing Algorithms are Racist. They Need to be Dismantled.* July 17. https://www.technologyreview.com/2020/07/17/1005396/predictive-policing-algorithms-racist-dismantled-machine-learning-bias-criminal-justice/.

Hensley, C. B. 1963. "Selective Dissemination of Information (SDI): State of the Art in May, 1963." In: *Proceedings of the May 21–23, 1963, Spring Joint Computer Conference, AFIPS '63 (Spring)* 257–262.

Hill, Will, Larry Stead, and Mark Rosenstein. 1995. "Recommending and Evaluating Choices in a Virtual Community of Use." In: *Proceedings of the SIGCHI Conference on Human Factors in Computing Systems* 194–201.

Jordan, Ann T. 2003. *Business Anthropology.* Long Grove: Waveland Press.

Kastrenakes, Jacob. 2021. "Grimes Sold $6 Million Worth of Digital Art as NFTs." *The Verge.* March 1. Accessed November 16, 2023. https://www.theverge.com/2021/3/1/22308075/grimes-nft-6-million-sales-nifty-gateway-warnymph.

Koycheva, Lora. 2020. "Anthropology: An Entrepreneurial Discipline." *EASA2020: New Anthropological Horizons in and Beyond Europe.* Lisbon: European Association of Social Anthropologists.

Koycheva, Lora. 2024. "Anthropology is Good to Build With: From Ethnographic Imagination to Anthropological Speculation in Robotics." In: *EmTech Anthropology: Careers at the Frontier*, edited by Matt Artz and Lora Koycheva. New York: Routledge.

Liu, Yudan, Kaikai Ge, Xu Zhang, and Leyu Lin. 2019. "*Real-time Attention Based Look-alike Model for Recommender System.*" June 12. Accessed September 24, 2021. https://arxiv.org/pdf/1906.05022.pdf.

McKay, Melyn. 2024. "Cargo Cult or Kula Ring? The Battle for Shared Ethos in Web3." In: *EmTech Anthropology: Careers at the Frontier*, edited by Matt Artz and Lora Koycheva. New York: Routledge.

Parker, Erica. 2019. *"LEGO Group Kicks Off Global Program to Inspire the Next Generation of Space Explorers as NASA Celebrates 50 Years of Moon Landing."* July 16. https://theharrispoll.com/briefs/lego-group-kicks-off-global-program-to-inspire-the-next-generation-of-space-explorers-as-nasa-celebrates-50-years-of-moon-landing/.

Paykamian, Brandon. 2021. *"Enrollment Algorithms Raise Equity Concerns in Higher Ed."* November 02. https://www.govtech.com/education/higher-ed/enrollment-algorithms-raise-equity-concerns-in-higher-ed.

Pazzani, Michael, Jack Muramatsu, and Daniel Bill. 1996. "Syskill & webert: Identifying Interesting Web Sites." In: *Proceedings of the Thirteenth National Conference on Artificial Intelligence, AAAI'96* 51–61.

Resnick, Paul, Neophytos Iacovou, Mitesh Suchak, Peter Bergstrom, and John Riedl. 1994. "GroupLens: An Open Architecture for Collaborative Filtering of Netnews." *Research Papers in Economics.*

Ricci, Francesco, Lior Rokach, Bracha Shapira, and Paul B. Kantor. 2011. *Recommender Systems Handbook.* New York: Springer.

Roy, Deepjyoti, and Mala Dutta. 2022. "A Systematic Review and Research Perspective on Recommender Systems." *Journal of Big Data* 9 (59): 1–36. https://doi.org/10.1186/s40537-022-00592-5.

Salton, G., and McGill, M. J. 1986. *Introduction to Modern Information Retrieval.* New York: McGraw-Hill Inc.

Seaver, Nick. 2022. *Computing Taste: Algorithms and the Makers of Music Recommendation.* Chicago: The University of Chicago Press.

Shardanand, Upendra, and Pattie Maes. 1995. "Social Information Filtering: Algorithms for Automating 'word of mouth'." In: *Proceedings of the SIGCHI Conference on Human Factors in Computing Systems* 210–217.

SignalFire. 2021. *SignalFire's Creator Economy Market Map.* Accessed September 25, 2021. https://signalfire.com/blog/creator-economy/.

Singh, Ashudeep, and Thorsten Joachims. *"Fairness of Exposure in Rankings."* In: Proceedings of the 24th ACM SIGKDD International Conference on Knowledge Discovery and Data Mining, London, UK, 2018. arXiv:1802.07281 [cs.IR]. doi:10.1145/3219819.3220088.

Squires, Susan, and Bryan Byrne. 2002. *Creating Breakthrough Ideas: The Collaboration of Anthropologists and Designers in the Product Development Industry.* London: Bloomsbury Publishing.

Steck, Harald. 2011. "Item Popularity and Recommendation Accuracy." In: *The Proceedings of the Fifth ACM Conference on Recommender Systems* 125–132.

Stinson, Catherine. 2022. "Algorithms are Not Neutral." *AI and Ethics* 2: 763–770.

University of Minnesota. n.d. *Fine Tuning the Social Web: John Riedl.* Accessed 2023. https://cse.umn.edu/college/feature-stories/fine-tuning-social-web-john-riedl.

Wasson, Christina. 2000. "Ethnography in the Field of Design." *Human Organization* 59 (4): 377–388.

Wu, Shiwen, Wentao Zhang, Fei Sun, and Bin Cui. 2020. "Graph Neural Networks in Recommender Systems: A Survey." *ACM Computing Surveys* 55 (5): 1–37.

Zhang, Shuai, Lina Yao, Aixin Sun, and Yi Tay. 2019. "Deep Learning Based Recommender System: A Survey and New Perspectives." *ACM Computing Surveys* 52 (1): 1–38doi:10.1145/3285029.

Zhao, X., Niu, Z., & Chen, W. 2013. *"Opinion-based Collaborative Filtering to Solve Popularity Bias in Recommender Systems."* s.l., International Conference on Database and Expert Systems Applications, 426–433.

4 Towards an Anthro-Centric Cybersecurity

Lianne Potter

Introduction

How often do you think about locking your door when you leave your house? For most, it is muscle memory. In placing your key in the door, you are ensuring, barring persistence or skill, that a nefarious person is deterred from entering your property and stealing your things. In the physical world, we are all security experts. Why, then, are we so seemingly cavalier in our digital security – with our cybersecurity?[1]

With this question in mind, this chapter calls for a greater focus on the human factors of cybersecurity. It advocates for developing an anthro-centric approach to understanding the human-centered problems cybersecurity professionals face and driving solutions that enable better security. To accomplish this, I argue the cybersecurity profession should deepen its understanding of both the individuals it seeks to safeguard and the adversaries who pose threats. Incorporating anthropological thinking into the cybersecurity field can help achieve this by uncovering the cultural factors that facilitate the spread of insecure behaviors. The urgency[2] of this call becomes starkly apparent when considering that the global cost of cybercrime is estimated to soar to $13.8 trillion by 2028, a figure that eclipses the current combined net worth of all technology billionaires (Petrosyan, 2023). This is even more salient when we realize that 80% of cybersecurity incidents are ascribed to human error (Chamorro-Premuzic, 2023).

Yet, despite the astronomical costs associated with cybercrime and the frequent media coverage of cybersecurity breaches, insecure behaviors continue to persist, even among cybersecurity professionals (KnowBe4, 2023). This enduring issue raises questions about the efficacy of cybersecurity education and engagement strategies. Specifically, it brings into focus the core messages conveyed by cybersecurity teams,[3] which, despite remaining consistent over the past two to three decades, have failed to stem the tide of insecure behaviors. The persistent failure of these longstanding messages to effect meaningful behavior change suggests that non-technical, culturally mediated factors, discernible through an anthropological lens, may hold the key to devising more effective cybersecurity strategies.

DOI: 10.4324/9781003458555-4

Building on this notion, I argue we must examine the intangibility and sociality of digital threats as contributing factors. Unlike physical security, where threats are often visible and tangible, digital security challenges our abilities to conceptualize risk. This could be attributed to the elusive nature of digital materiality and the subsequent threats that exist behind screens rather than physical barriers. Furthermore, cybersecurity professionals often and unfairly expect the general public to possess an advanced level of cybersecurity knowledge. This expectation extends from identifying malicious online entities, be it a website, download, or phishing email (National Cyber Security Centre, 2023),[4] to the cognitive load of managing intricate and unique passwords across platforms (Rowe, A., 2023).[5] However, individuals often lack the knowledge, education, and technology[6] to assess and combat the risks and likewise face unrealistic expectations to be cybersecurity experts themselves. Meanwhile, security measures defined by cybersecurity professionals frequently overlook human-centered considerations and limitations. Consequently, everyday users are often set up to fail at protecting themselves from cyber threats.

Amidst this context of failed cybersecurity practices and the "wild west" nature of the Internet, universal cyber safety is arguably unfeasible (Pandya, 2019). Nevertheless, victims of cybercrime face undue criticism rather than empathy. They are denigrated as "stupid" (Terranova Security, 2023), "idiots" (CyberSec_Sai, 2023; Ward & Wall, 2018), or the "dumbest" sources of cyber risk (Goodman, 2017). Some even label average users the cybersecurity industry's "greatest" (CIPD, 2023) or "weakest" (Chalico, 2022; Rowe, J., 2023; Dataprise, 2023) links. Of course, negligence occurs at the individual and business levels. However, discussions rarely address the cultural drivers underlying both unintentional (through human error or ignorance) and intentional negligence (via poor practices, risk underestimation, and competing priorities). This is despite people being one of the three pillars of cybersecurity, which emphasizes people, process, and technology (IT Governance 2017).

Notably, technology is listed last, yet it is often *the* emphasized aspect of the pillars over people and people-driven processes (Shackleton, 2021). Organizations often focus on acquiring expensive, complex security tools to safeguard themselves. Properly configured, these tools do provide some defense. However, over-reliance on technology can distract from vital human factors underlying system usage and maintenance.[7] Thus, defenses should account for, and budget proportionally for, the human factors involved.

Therefore, this chapter argues that anthropological perspectives are not only beneficial but are urgently needed to catalyze a vital cultural shift in cybersecurity. To support this argument, I will explain my career journey and why I came to this perspective.

From Wedding Bliss to Digital Divides, then to Develop[er]ing an Interest in Cybersecurity

There is no clear path to becoming a cybersecurity anthropologist. But that is not unlike other applied anthropology careers. Like most anthropologists, specializations often happen through an interest in the field, access to educational programs, and a bit of luck. For example, I started my journey towards cybersecurity while running a wedding photography business. This may seem like an unlikely path, but in photographing at least three weddings a week, every week, for ten years, I developed a deep interest in the cultural significance of weddings. I found myself enamored by the role and importance of ritual and symbolism that surrounded weddings. For this reason, I decided that I would enroll in a distance learning anthropology program to study the concept of ritual.

Given my experience, I initially considered doing my master's dissertation on weddings, but due to the logistics of consent and out of respect for the couples, I decided against it. However, I was still interested in the concept of "the image" and how it related to cultural and community signifiers, especially in light of the increasing popularity of Instagram. Specifically, I was interested in the pursuit of the "perfect" image for the consumption of a mass audience of known and unknown individuals. This interest would unknowingly inform my later thinking about data privacy and prosumer behaviors,[8] but it would also become the basis of my anthropology dissertation titled *The Aestheticism of Fakery and the Commodified Self: Exploring the Impact of the 'Public by Default' Model on Instagram*.

While I enjoyed this field of research, it was during this experience that I had another pivotal moment that would alter my future trajectory. In the course of my research, I learned about the digital divide, which is a social issue that impacts the lives of digital and non-digital natives alike. Pippa Norris, in her 2001 book *Digital Divide: Civic Engagement, Information Poverty, and the Internet Worldwide*, describes the concept of the "digital divide" as an "inequality" of access between the "info-haves and have-nots." Those experiencing the digital divide are often socially excluded, she argues, because of their inability to access vital information and opportunities due to the many of these elements moving to be online only, such as access to medical information, jobs, educational opportunities, and other critical aspects of our lived experience. Digital technologies, therefore, can "unleash new inequalities of power and wealth, reinforcing deeper divisions between the information rich and poor" (Norris, 2001:12).

Quite serendipitously, my discovery of the digital divide happened at the same time as I was moving on from wedding photography to a position as a project manager for a local charity. In this new role, I worked on a project with the open brief of "solve destitution" in the city. Throughout this work, my colleagues and I experienced the digital divide in action. I observed how the very organizations that were there to protect people were letting them down. Charities like the one I worked for had to fill the gaps by completing online forms on their behalf to get them access to their most basic needs. As I would communicate in our quarterly reports to our funders – the greatest barrier to people getting themselves out of destitution was their inability to access online services in a world where "real world" alternatives were quickly disappearing or becoming costly. In other words, the digital divide was the issue, and I decided I wanted to do something about it.

I wanted to use what I had learned about the digital divide and the skills and techniques of anthropology to influence how technology was being created and used for the most vulnerable people in society. But how? I started by looking for digital anthropology jobs. However, searches for "digital anthropologist" on career sites yielded no results. I decided a better tactic would be to learn a technical skill to enable me to be hands-on in the creation of software. So, I decided to teach myself how to code and become a software engineer – I would do "tech for good."

Using only free resources such as FreeCodeCamp.org, CodeAcademy, and YouTube, I spent every waking moment outside of work teaching myself how to code. Taking a ride on the Dunning-Kruger confidence curve, I experienced various emotions while I, from a non-technical background, began learning how to program. Starting from the basic "Hello World" command to eventually build my own, albeit rudimentary, website and applications from scratch, I learned step-by-step. It was exhilarating and empowering but also exasperating when I could not quite understand why my code was throwing out programming errors, only to find I had missed a closing bracket somewhere buried within the code – a literal programming typo!

Though I was at times riddled with impostor syndrome trying to get to grips with a literal new language (the language of code and machines), I was re-energized when I found my "tech tribe," which was vital to my journey because of the reassurance a community of praxis can provide. To know that they, too, had sat in front of a screen for hours on end trying to debug their work and to have them explain concepts with me and troubleshoot my issues brought me great solace that without, I am not sure I would have continued with my journey of code. My learning was also supplemented by the thriving Leeds tech scene, where every night, there were multiple tech meetups for budding technologists like myself to attend to listen to a variety of technology-related topics and tech stacks. Each event enabled me to build up a mental map of what this new-to-me world of technology was ushering in. Simultaneously, I was drawing links between anthropology and software engineering, with a focus on how the digital divide impacts end users and increasingly an interest in its relation to cybersecurity.

My cybersecurity interest bubbled up after attending a cybersecurity talk a few months prior hosted by NHS Digital as part of the Leeds Digital Festival. I was enthralled by what I heard. Fascinated by the threat actors and threat landscape, the tools in their defense arsenal, and the camaraderie of fighting a common enemy and protecting this vitally important institution, the NHS. And so, after five months of intensive learning, I applied for a job in the National Health Service's (NHS) Digital capability, on their software development training scheme.

While I was disappointed to find that they did not have entry or a recent graduate pathway for the cybersecurity team, I was heartened to hear that it would be possible to pivot from software engineering to cybersecurity, and with my background in anthropology, I would be a desirable candidate. Indeed, during the interview, I focused my answers heavily on my experiences of witnessing the digital divide and how I could utilize my anthropological training to ensure that, as a software developer, I would put the human at the center of everything I build and challenge design choices that did not do this. This was a successful approach as I was accepted, began my first placement a few months later, and started my journey working in tech.

As a software developer, I became increasingly fascinated with cybersecurity, and more specifically, with the beliefs, behaviors, and norms of the cybersecurity team. Not surprisingly, they were often viewed disparagingly by the engineering department because they always seemed to be impeding our work, either by blocking our "go live" deadlines with changes or restrictions or forcing us to add on ugly and/or clunky controls that would go against our user research and user experience guidance; that team was the cybersecurity team.

"Security says 'no'" was a common mantra. This contributed to the characterization that the cybersecurity team operated in an "ivory tower," along with the fact that they were also literally separated in another well-secured room, only accessible to those with appropriate security clearance. They were seen as dictating rules and regulations without consideration for their impact. Specifically, the edicts they handed down affected teams developing websites and apps for the NHS. The separation of the cybersecurity function fed perceptions that they were detached and indifferent to challenges faced by other groups. Their frequent rejections of proposals led to feelings they were obstructing progress through inflexible stances.

I would learn later this is a stereotypical characterization of cybersecurity teams in most organizations and a barrier to holistic working and implementing security by design. But at the time, and as an anthropologist, the strangeness of it all immensely piqued my interest. The NHS, as an organization, had strong cultural values aimed at being the most trusted source of information on health in the UK. Contrastingly, however, the cybersecurity team seemed to operate differently from the norm. That is not to say that this team did not share the mission of NHS Digital, but its approach contrasted with the way the rest of the teams functioned. There was less collaboration and transparency, more resistance to working agilely, and innovation was not a goal. I had the urge to find out more and understand why this was the case, but also to see if, using anthropology, I could help make sense of the differences in beliefs and behaviors and bridge the gap between the departments for the betterment of the organization.

It took a year of persistence and additional self-directed learning about technical and non-technical aspects of cybersecurity before I gained access to that closed-off floor and called myself a SOC (Security Operations Centre) analyst. Instantly, I sensed the difference in this business function compared to my other placements within NHS Digital. Perhaps it was the very nature of the work that caused the team culture to be more protective and guarded, with a hint of distrust and paranoia. After all, feeling constantly under attack or spending most of your time imagining the worst will likely influence how you work with others.

Using what I learned in anthropology, I began to develop an understanding of the micro-cultures within the security function. This would later inform my approach to improving team dynamics and fostering an anthro-centric cybersecurity culture. In particular, my learnings enabled me to identify techniques for transforming adversarial relationships between security and other groups. I gained insight into how to break down silos while building greater trust and collaboration across functions. My analysis revealed opportunities for security teams to move from isolation to integration, improving their engagement with diverse stakeholders. In essence, an anthropological lens showed me how security could evolve from dictating policy to collaboratively shaping processes organization-wide.

However, these outcomes did not come easily, given the risk appetite of the team.

A Note on Risk Appetite

Cybersecurity teams often think of "risk" as a dirty word. For most security teams, risk is something to avoid, yet in practice, this is not achievable.

Gone are the days when a Chief Security Information Officer (CISO) could be asked by the board if the organization was "secure" and expect an assured answer of "yes." Today, most security professionals approach the risk of a cyber incident from the perspective of what is known as an "assumed breach." This means that the vast majority of professionals working in the space believe or operate in this environment with the understanding that their systems are already compromised. Even those who are a little more optimistic tout the mantra that a security incident is not a question of "if" but "when." Accordingly, security risk is approached from two perspectives: One, that it has already happened but has not been discovered yet, and two, if it has not already happened yet, it will with a high degree of certainty.

This leads to interesting organizational discussions about risk, but for this chapter's purpose, I want to draw attention to "risk appetite." Risk appetite is how much of a risk an organization is willing to take before it could negatively impact the business. In the case of cybersecurity, it is entirely unrealistic for an organization to say that they have "zero risk appetite" for a cybersecurity incident. They may hope that they will never experience a cybersecurity incident. However, as previously stated, with cybersecurity professionals almost seeing a cybersecurity incident as a foregone conclusion, the likelihood that an organization can put enough controls (whether people, process, or technology) in place to mitigate it entirely is unrealistic for even the most mature and well-funded organizations.

Despite this, when the security team believes that risk can be avoided or miti-gated by saying "no" or controlling their colleagues' work lives with security controls, they forget that their purpose within the organization is to *enable* the business to take risks. Many of modern society's most successful companies and people are risk-takers (Wild, 2016; Carosa, 2020; and Elkins, 2016). Risk can be good. Risk gives you that competitive edge (when done right) and enables innovation. There are many ways the cybersecurity industry can be innovative as a discipline, and a step in that direction is the recollection that innovation thrives when people share ideas and collaborate, which, as this chapter has described, is often not achieved by the security function in organizations.

However, introducing an anthro-centric mindset into cybersecurity offers a potentially powerful model for making sense of the practice. The insights derived from such an approach can uncover how organizational cultures function with divergent understandings of risk and security restrictions. For example, cybersecurity teams, as I have stated, are often risk-averse, and for good reason. Yet other business units may prioritize aims like innovation that require accepting some risks. However, with an anthropological approach, I was able to uncover shared meanings and find a consensus between security-driven risk aversion and business-driven risk appetite.

Based on my experiences at the intersection of cybersecurity and anthro-pology, I have begun to lead the way in this space as one of a handful of anthropologists who specialize in considering the importance of cultural fac-tors in cybersecurity. This work has been supported by my latest role as head of security operations, where I oversee the technical aspects of cybersecurity (technical controls, processes, tooling, etc.) for a major UK supermarket retailer, thereby combining the humanities and the technical to ensure a human-centric approach to the discipline of cybersecurity.

For this work, I have been awarded the Security Leaders of the Year and the Security Specialist of the Year in the Women in Tech Excellence Awards and *Computing Magazine* in 2021. I have also had the pleasure of speaking on this topic around the world at various academic and industry conferences and with my podcast, Compromising Positions.[9] With these talks, I have tried to inspire not only the next generation of cybersecurity anthropologists but also those cybersecurity professionals who are interested in a more holistic approach to enabling good security practices. Similarly, in the following sections, I will fur-ther elaborate on the work of an anthropologist in cybersecurity.

Practical Applications of Anthropology to Cybersecurity

Participant Observation

Throughout my journey from software developer to cybersecurity profes-sional, I did indeed feel like Bronislaw Malinowski (1922, 1979) when he coined the phrase "going native," but it was the only way to thrive and understand this vastly different new culture I had joined.

As a participant observer, it became evident that cybersecurity teams are perceived as blockers because that perception is rooted in either current actions or historical ones. As a relatively new discipline in technology, cybersecurity has had to be self-preservationist. Often, cybersecurity teams are some of the most under-resourced, underfunded, and unloved areas of a business, mostly because of the perception that being secure is a "problem," and most people avoid problems due to complexity and an inherent desire to choose the "happy path." Indeed, figures suggest that for every 100 developers (Irvine, 2021), there is one security person, and that is a well-resourced organization. As a result, this stretched function has historically had to say "no" to more requests to loosen up controls. It is not always an approach a security team wants to take, but it is one of necessity. After all, how can you oversee the security of an entire organization when you do not have the funding or the clout to do so? But understanding the security team's culture is only one, albeit significant, area to understand as to why behaviors and actions, often at the detriment of the organization, proliferate.[10]

Participant observation also enabled me to understand other areas of the business that posed security risk areas, such as customer service, administration (especially executive assistants who are often highly sought-after targets due to their control of high-status individuals, often C-Suite, IT accounts, particularly email), and, of course, other technology functions such as engineering, the creators of said technologies. It is important to note that not everyone in a business disregards security measures except for the security team. In my experience working in various technology companies, I have yet to encounter a software developer who intentionally writes insecure code. However, there are often constraints that hinder their ability to do a perfect job, such as time, resourcing challenges, and competing deadlines. Making matters worse, many security controls put in place by the security teams can impede their work. This is because changes are often made without consulting the people impacted, leading to insecure workarounds. For this reason, the security team needs to take the time to understand the pain points and personas of their customers, step through their user journey, and see how controls put in place can enable bad security practices. Regrettably, this is not a common practice among established security functions.

Next in Line for Confession...

Communication breakdown, in my research, has been a common element that has led to more insecure behaviors. For example, it was not that engineering teams stopped engaging with security from the initial encounter, but after some time with no incentive to engage with them, and usually after years of restrictions, they often started to view security as more of a hindrance than a benefit. Indeed, what is the point of inviting security people to meetings if all they do is shut down progress? Teams are not going to reach out to another team that hinders progress, nor does the security function seem to be forthcoming on their end either, by not being proactive in reaching out to teams well before a scheduled "go-live" date, causing costly delays and potentially impacting morale.

However, participant observation done successfully has led, in my experience, to my role advantageously becoming one of the "security confessors." As a security confessor, I was in a trusted position in which colleagues would willingly reveal their security misdemeanors to me without fear of judgment or retribution. They say "sinners make the best saints" because you need to know the "bad" before you can do good – or you cannot fix what you do not know about, and this indeed has helped me, as a cybersecurity anthropologist, identify blind spots in my security defense that I would not have been aware of.

Reciprocity

In Sahlins' seminal book, *Stone Age Economics* (1972), he describes his typology of reciprocal exchange involving the give-and-take of objects and services to build and confirm social relationships, often described as "gift giving' (see also Mauss, 1954; 2005). He identifies three types of reciprocity: Generalized, balanced, and negative reciprocity. The reciprocal activity received depends on the closeness of that relationship. As social distance increases, relationships become more utilitarian or even confrontational. The knock-on effect is that cultures engaging in more negative reciprocal behaviors lead to increased self-interested attitudes and a disinterest in the well-being and goals of those outside the close-knit group.

Put within the context of cybersecurity culture, security professionals will want to avoid the collective group (their colleagues) being disinterested and self-interested, especially when they need all hands on deck to deal with a security incident. Reciprocal relationships are important to connect people and promote social solidarity. The way they create a sense of obligation can also help the security practitioner achieve their goals. While not apparent at first, it is well within the security practitioner's capabilities to build such relationships from the giving of "gifts." It does not have to be literal gifts, such as a bar of chocolate, every time a good security decision is made by a non-security colleague (although that can help). A gift from the cybersecurity team may take the form of more resource allocation (reducing the cognitive load and skillset barriers and helping people achieve their outcomes securely and in a timely manner), distribution of services, tokens of support, or even the review and loosening of security controls.

The inherent value of the given "gift" is often less significant than the "gift's" effect on building or consolidating solidarity between the giver and receiver. It is through gift-giving that you are offering an invitation to establish a closer in-group relationship, and acceptance of that gift is an unspoken, moral obligation to reciprocate, either immediately or in the future.

There are further gifts a cybersecurity practitioner can give in applying reciprocity: Trust and autonomy. A key complaint security professionals receive is that the function does not trust non-security people to make security decisions within their area of expertise. This, consequently, makes people feel like they lack the autonomy to make decisions that have a direct consequence on how they work and the output of that work, causing further resentment and disengagement. Building trust and autonomy starts with smaller gifts, such as increasing access[11] or the relaxation of controls,[12] making their work seem more frictionless.

To achieve this, start with generalized reciprocity, which is not expecting a return from your gift-giving because you want to begin to establish a strong relationship with your target team, and you do not want to create a sense of obligation at the start. As this relationship develops, you will see your endeavors move towards balanced reciprocity. It is within balanced reciprocity, when done successfully, that the security team may finally begin to receive gifts themselves, and the best gift a security team can be given by others is *accountability.*

Accountability is more than just the "A" on a RACI matrix.[13] Accountability in an organization, when aligned to a process, tool, or risk, is important because it not only clarifies roles but makes individuals responsible for their actions and decisions while accomplishing the expectations of that role. In security, particularly, aiming for accountability outside of the security team should be a priority because there are simply not enough security professionals in an organization to be accountable and because accountability requires a level of proactivity and engagement that helps build positive security cultures and practices.

Thus, we see a pattern emerge; if the security team "gifts" tokens of trust, this leads to people feeling more autonomous in their jobs because they have more control of their situation and/or have more capabilities to respond and react to a situation. This then leads to more accountability, which then leads to improvements in the behaviors needed for accountability. As a result, the power of reciprocity and its impact on security culture should not be underestimated, especially when there is the opportunity to engage in reciprocity in every engagement the cybersecurity team undertakes.

The Tastiest Morsel

When asked why cybersecurity and anthropology make for good bedfellows, I recall an article (Smilyanets, 2021) I read in which security research company Recorded Future spoke to the prolific hacker and ransomware-as-a-service (RaaS)[14] group REvil. In that unprecedented interview, REvil was asked what they thought of the insurance industry, particularly those who offer cybersecurity insurance. REvil described such victims as "The tastiest morsel." When this article came out, I was working in the insurance industry as a security practitioner, and to be in the crosshairs like this was, naturally, very concerning. However, I welcomed the gift in the language they used to describe their targets. "The tastiest morsel" *is* evocative. It triggers something primal and harks back to a time when we were just as likely to be the hunted as we were to be the hunters. I shared this interview with my colleagues in the insurance company and used this narrative to emphasize the seriousness of this singling out of our industry. I explained to them that although we are a target, there are things we can do to protect ourselves; we have a choice, and we are not helpless. We can either make it easy for the cybercriminal and become that "tasty morsel" and lay our data in a tempting buffet style and say "help yourself," or we can make it very difficult to get our "tasty" information, like the honey bees of Nepal (The Guardian, 2014), who make their hives on the steep and inaccessible cliffs of the Himalayas. These honey bees do their best to ensure their honey is as unobtainable as possible; however, that does not mean it is impossible. Indeed, I explained to my colleagues that "Honey Hunters"[15] risk their lives to obtain this tasty morsel. When something is valuable, even the best security controls cannot stop a motivated individual, especially if they have skills and expertise. No matter how much organizations invest in protecting their estate, they will never be completely secure or safe from access attempts. But what matters is that when something does happen, we can collectively face these threats, like the bees who swarm and attack intruders as they get close. It takes one bee to raise the alarm and induce a swarm, and it is the same for alerting cyberattacks. While we would prefer to prevent an attack, what counts when an attack does occur is our ability to stop the spread of it quickly in order to reduce its impact and get our organization back to a "safe" state. If we are united from an organizational culture perspective and have adequate training, processes, and technological defenses in place, this will make us a much less attractive target. That is important because cyber criminals are looking for the greatest return on investment, which is often low-hanging, insecure companies with a poor culture that will allow them to work undetected. If we can make ourselves an unattractive target, in which culture plays a significant part, then the malicious actors will try their luck elsewhere.

A Story of Community

This narrative is one I have used in many organizations to communicate risk; cybersecurity, after all, is just like any other business risk, whether that be natural (a lightning storm taking down all the power in the office, for example) or digital. The "Tastiest Morsel" story not only reminded people of the risks the organization faces but also reminded people of *their* significant part in hardening against these risks. Too often, security professionals play themselves as the sole savior or hero (or even benevolent dictator) in protecting the organization, but effective security works when faced as a collective due to the need for individuals beyond the security and IT team to raise the alarm when something does happen, especially if the technology we place so much stock in, fails to spot it.

However, I'd argue that the stories cybersecurity professionals should tell must be ones of warning, yes, but also of communicating the fact that individuals are not helpless victims. It must be a rallying cry calling on *everyone* to play their part in protecting themselves and others against cyber threats. I see great potential in the effectiveness of these stories if anthropologists can be leveraged to share their understanding of how communities are built and strengthened within this lens.

Storytelling is an effective and often overlooked tool in the cybersecurity toolbox. It is the tool I use most often to create an anthro-centric security culture. This is because human beings are innate storytellers. Our ancestors used storytelling to understand their surroundings, reflecting on the past but also imagining a future that had not yet happened so they could plan and prepare for it, educate, create folklore, and build a thriving community. They used it to entertain, build bonds, and improve recall. Many security professionals, when challenged on why they do things the way they do, will reply to some effect: "Because I said so..." without a proper explanation or reason, despite it being one of the biggest collaboration killers in an organization. As a misconceived rhetorical device, it actually serves to make one's security posture weaker because the problem of cybersecurity is far too nuanced and large to be handled by one department alone. It needs a village, not just a gang.

However, when information is shared, the means of delivery are FUD – Fear, Uncertainty, and Doubt. Fear has been recognized as a motivator to influence a behavior change, but if that is all that is drawn upon, it can cease to be impactful (Curry, 2018) and lead to apathy. As a result, the very people cybersecurity professionals are trying to protect can be fatigued by their interventions, causing them to switch off and turn away from them. The impact of this can be devastating as once an organization loses its ability to face threats as a group; it loses a vital early warning system. This means when something somewhere happens in the organization, it can be disastrous as there is less ability to respond quickly to minimize the impact and spread.

Security (Un)Awareness Training

There is one element of storytelling that is delivered consistently by security professionals: The often-dreaded mandatory security awareness training. Usually provided at the start of employment and mandatory every year after, these teachings are often seen as a chore to avoid or rush through. Indeed, Reeves et al.'s humorously titled research article, *"'Get a red-hot poker and open up my eyes, it's so boring': Employee perceptions of cybersecurity training"*(2021) confirms this perception and suggests that most security professionals either lack the skills or ability to communicate security messages engagingly. That is to their detriment as, by all accounts, when it comes to cybersecurity, this industry has the foundations of excellent narrative stories that would be worthy of any Hollywood blockbuster or Netflix mini-series.

Stories of good versus evil, heroes and villains, and espionage and heists to draw upon, yet, according to Reeves et al., cybersecurity teams bore people instead by getting bogged down in the technological details rather than the human impact. This approach makes learning about security a chore and, according to their research, increases the risk of a cyber-attack.

Furthermore, security awareness and training done poorly have been known to erode trust in the security team[16] and also *encourage* poor security practices through security by obscurity (people not wanting to be shamed or blamed by the security team will often hide their insecure behaviors or circumvent controls put in place by the security team). Organizations should invest in properly trained resources for this area, which can navigate the anthro-centric needs of the awareness program in order to effectively achieve their security goals. The research by Reeves and his colleagues elucidates this point by suggesting that traditional security professionals may not be the best fit for this new role or capability. Therefore, we should consider hiring from non-traditional security backgrounds to create a program that caters to a wider audience than just those highly skilled in security.

Anecdotally, I have noticed a significant increase in job postings related to security awareness functions. This is, of course, a positive development as it shows that organizations are recognizing the need for dedicated resources in this area. However, roles of this kind are still rare, and most organizations are still not hiring staff specifically for this function. Instead, it tends to fall under the additional responsibilities of a security team perpetuating the existing problems.

Therefore, I argue, building upon the findings of Reeves and my personal experience as a security professional, that it is precisely because security professionals fail to understand what it is like for their colleagues to do their job, along with a lack of understanding of the practicalities, politics, and the very culture in which their colleagues operate, that security culture fails to thrive or, indeed, has a negative perception. Subsequently, it is vital to understand the culture, and an anthropological perspective can help cybersecurity professionals appreciate the nuances and adjust their messages and approaches accordingly. While such an argument could be made for all business functions, this is especially important for cybersecurity, which touches all areas of the business in this technology-led world of work.

An Anthro-Centric Security Function

Technical advances to thwart cyber-attacks are being developed by security researchers daily. But regrettably, as quickly as the industry builds something new to deflect or detect intrusion, the cybercriminals seem to be one step ahead, creating something new and complex that can either bypass these interventions or catch the industry completely off-guard. However, as stated previously, the tools for defense, while important and effective when configured correctly, should only be one part of our defense and security-in-depth strategy. To only focus on the technology neglects the very human side of cybercrime, and for the majority of cases, it is the easiest, most cost-effective, and provides the greatest return on investment for the cyber criminals when they start their attacks via the human route. Yet, training and awareness are often the most underfunded element of a security team's defense budget (Aiyer et al., 2022), but this is changing as research year-on-year overwhelmingly demonstrates the need to dedicate budget and resources in this area. The necessity to focus on this area has also been demonstrated in the punitive actions by various compliance and regulatory organizations. Regulatory bodies are responding to this over-reliance on security tooling and issuing costly fines to send a clear message to organizations that are being complacent in their security posture. An example of this is Interserve, a construction company, whom the Information Commissioner's Office (ICO) fined £4.4m not only for failing to keep people's data safe but for (despite having policies that on paper were sound) not ensuring that the right culture was fostered so that employees could follow policies and procedures, and due to inadequate staff training (ICO, 2022). This is a warning all companies with any technological element must heed. It is no longer sufficient to document what "good" security looks like; you must live it. This is an opportunity for the anthropological community to add value in this space as, far from the initial perception that regulation restricts and therefore stifles innovation (Aghion et al., 2021; Eggers & Walsh, 2023), regulation gives organizations the ability to tackle problems and risks in new and creative ways, including the employment of more anthropologists in this space.

Conclusion

This chapter has demonstrated how an anthro-centric approach to cybersecurity can be beneficial, and a rewarding career path. While I am still at the outset of my journey, it is clear to me that anthropologists would be of great benefit to organizations in these roles. In particular, an interesting area of research that I have not yet engaged in would be a study of cybercriminals, how they are organized, and how they interact amongst themselves and with other criminal entities. There is a whole breadth of sophistication when it comes to cybercrime and the criminal undertaking the activity, from script kiddies[17] to hacktivists[18] to nation-state cybercriminals[19] to organized gangs. Perhaps if we understand those attacking us, we might be able to protect ourselves better. However, doing so without an understanding of the cultural underpinnings and psychological motivations of cybercriminals is a failure waiting to happen.

Cybersecurity teams need to do better to create an internal culture that enables all to build resilience against cyber threats. To achieve that, they must cater their processes and training interventions to a wide breadth of expertise, capabilities, experiences, and cultural norms. After all, when you follow the cables, behind every piece of tech is a person, a consumer, a creator, and even a cybercriminal, and we should never lose sight of this.

Notes

1 In this chapter, I will use the terms "cybersecurity" and "security" interchangeably, however, I do have a preference to describe the activities I perform in my current role as "security" related rather than "cybersecurity related."

2 According to estimates, by 2028 the cost of cybercrime worldwide will reach $13.8 trillion. That is more than all of the tech billionaires' current net worth, combined. (Petrosyan, 2023)

3 Have strong, unique passwords for every account, do not click on links you are not expecting, if an email looks too good to be true – it is probably a scam, and avoid downloading programs from untrusted sources, to name a few.

4 "Phishing" is when criminals use scam emails, text messages, or phone calls to trick their victims. The aim is often to make you visit a website, which may download a virus onto your computer, or steal bank details or other personal information.

5 Latest studies suggest that the average user has 100 passwords to remember across various sites.

6 With the use of password managers and multi-factor authentication (also known as MFA or 2FA).

7 Like doors to keep us safe from burglars, we tend to forget that there is a human element involved in the process of turning the key and verifying that the door is locked.

8 An individual who both consumes and produces, in this case, produces and consumes content on social media (see Ritzer, Dean, & Jurgenson, 2012).

9 A podcast that interviews those from non-cybersecurity technology roles and the individuals who specialize in anthropology, psychology, behavioural science, economics, law, philosophy, organizational culture, and design about how cybersecurity teams can better serve the people they are charged with protecting.

10 Such as circumventing security controls using dangerous methods sometimes known as "workarounds," to perform restrictive actions, or fostering a culture that lacks psychological safety so that security events go unreported due to fear of punishment.

11 A touchy subject amongst security professionals, and not without good cause, as poorly implemented Identity and Access Management (IAM) can be disastrous for an organization's security posture. However, many access decisions, especially in more established organizations with legacy teams or technology, can often be reviewed due to them being historic decisions that once protected against a type of threat that is no longer applicable, or can be managed or protected with the introduction of modern security tooling or monitoring.

12 I once worked in an organization where the historic security incumbent took a heavy-handed approach to data exfiltration risks. This took the form of banning all use of Bluetooth connection from endpoint devices. While exfiltration using Bluetooth is possible, the risk is small due to the proximity needed in order to successfully achieve exfiltration, the instability of Bluetooth connections, and also the slowness of exfiltrating data this way would put most threat actors off. I came across the decision to block Bluetooth connections while I was investigating a spike amongst the development teams using Powershell scripts (like a command-line, which is often also blocked from access by the security team) in order to enable Bluetooth. These scripts came from the Internet and their origin and the overall security of these scripts could not be confirmed. Thus, this was an example of the security team implementing controls that resulted in individuals in the organization seeking alternative ways to access, or "workaround" our restrictions, and choosing options that were actually more insecure than what we were trying to prevent. And why did the software developers want to use Bluetooth? So they

could code while listening to music using their Bluetooth headphones. This is a clear case of the security team creating friction in one's day. After this discovery, Bluetooth was enabled and anyone could work and listen to music unimpeded.

13 "A RACI matrix is a document that clarifies which individuals or groups are responsible for a project's successful completion, and the roles that each will play throughout the project. The acronym RACI stands for the different responsibility types: Responsible, Accountable, Consulted, and Informed" (Good, 2023)

14 "Ransomware as a Service (RaaS) is a business model between ransomware operators and affiliates in which affiliates pay to launch ransomware attacks developed by operators. Think of ransomware as a service as a variation of software as a service (SaaS) business model.

   RaaS kits allow affiliates lacking the skill or time to develop their own ransomware variant to be up and running quickly and affordably. They are easy to find on the dark web, where they are advertised in the same way that goods are advertised on the legitimate web. A RaaS kit may include 24/7 support, bundled offers, user reviews, forums and other features identical to those offered by legitimate SaaS providers. The price of RaaS kits ranges from $40 per month to several thousand dollars – trivial amounts, considering that the average ransom demand in 2021 was $6 million. A threat actor doesn't need every attack to be successful in order to become rich" (Baker, 2023).

15 Brave individuals who risk everything by climbing and dangling precariously hundreds of feet off the ground to harvest this precious, hallucinogenic, honey (McConville, 2018).

16 As in the case of West Midlands Trains in which their security team conducted phishing simulations that promised a bonus to its workers during a very stressful time in the organization. The employees at the company felt "tricked" and the security team made national news for its lack of emotional intelligence, which persisted, even after the bad press (Topham, 2021).

17 Usually teenage boys but not always, this term describes a cybercriminal who has little technical skill to undertake these activities and relies on freely available "scripts" (programmes) to execute their attacks. Their motivation is usually for kudos amongst their peers rather than being solely financially motivated.

18 Undertaking attacks for a political cause.

19 Cybercriminals who undertake cybercriminal activities on behalf of governments.

Bibliography

Aghion, P., Bergeaud, A., and Van Reenen, J. 2021. "The Impact of Regulation on Innovation." *London School of Economics*, Accessed 14 September 2023. http://eprints.lse.ac.uk/114352/.

Aiyer, B., Caso, J., Russell, P., and Sorel, M. 2022. "New Survey Reveals $2 Trillion Market Opportunity for Cybersecurity Technology and Service Providers." *McKinsey & Company*, Accessed July 30, 2023.https://www.mckinsey.com/capabilities/risk-and-resilience/our-insights/cybersecurity/new-survey-reveals-2-trillion-dollar-market-opportunity-for-cybersecurity-technology-and-service-providers.

Baker, K. 2023. "Ransomware-as-a-Service." *Crowdstrike*, Accessed July 2, 2023.https://www.crowdstrike.com/cybersecurity-101/ransomware/ransomware-as-a-service-raas/.

Carosa, C. 2020. "Why Successful Entrepreneurs Need to Be Calculated Risk Takers." *Forbes*, Accessed September 10, 2023. https://www.forbes.com/sites/chriscarosa/2020/08/07/why-successful-entrepreneurs-need-to-be-calculated-risk-takers/?sh=37b323162f5b.

Chalico, C. P. 2022. "Your Employees are the Weakest Link in Your Cybersecurity Chain." *EY*, Accessed September 13, 2023. https://www.ey.com/en_ca/cybersecurity/your-employees-are-the-weakest-link-in-your-cybersecurity-chain.

Chamorro-Premuzic, T. 2023. "Human Error Drives Most Cyber Incidents. Could AI Help?" *Harvard Business Review*, Accessed July 29, 2023https://hbr.org/2023/05/human-error-drives-most-cyber-incidents-could-ai-help.

CIPD. 2023. "Cybersecurity – Are your People your Greatest Risk?" *CIPD*, Accessed September 11, 2023. https://www.cipd.org/en/knowledge/podcasts/cybersecurity-people-risk/.

Curry, S. 2018. "Why the Security Industry Should Stop Relying on FUD." *Computer Fraud & Security* 1 (3).

CyberSec_Sai. 2023. "Who are Cyber Idiots? How to Mitigate Risk in Enterprise and Personal Cybersecurity?" *Infosec Write-ups*, Accessed September 10, 2023. https://infosecwriteups.com/who-are-cyber-idiots-how-to-mitigate-risk-in-enterprise-and-personal-cybersecurity-603b718448d1.

Dataprise. 2023. "The 10 Weakest Links in Cyber Security: Top Cyber Security Issues." *Dataprise*, Accessed September 13, 2023. https://www.dataprise.com/resources/blog/ten-weakest-links/.

Eggers, W. D., and Walsh, S. J. 2023. "Regulation that Enables Innovation." *Deloitte*, Accessed September 14, 2023. https://www2.deloitte.com/uk/en/insights/industry/public-sector/government-trends/2023/regulatory-agencies-and-innovation.html.

Elkins, K. 2016. "Mark Zuckerberg Shares the Best Piece of Advice Peter Theil Ever Gave Him." *Make It*, Accessed September 10, 2023. https://www.cnbc.com/2016/08/25/mark-zuckerberg-shares-the-best-piece-of-advice-peter-thiel-ever-gave-him.html.

Good, L. 2023. "What is a RACI Matrix." *Project Management.Com*, Accessed September 10, 2023. https://project-management.com/understanding-responsibility-assignment-matrix-raci-matrix/.

Goodman, M. 2017. "Smart Hackers Rely on Dumb People." *Kordia*, Accessed September 10, 2023. https://www.kordia.co.nz/news-and-views/smart-hackers-rely-on-dumb-people.

ICO. 2022. "'Biggest Cyber Risk is Complacency, Not Hackers' – UK Information Commissioner Issues Warning as Construction Company Fined £4.4 Million." *ICO*, Accessed July 30, 2023.https://ico.org.uk/about-the-ico/media-centre/news-and-blogs/2022/10/biggest-cyber-risk-is-complacency-not-hackers/.

Irvine, T. 2021. "The Ratio." LinkedIn Article, Accessed July 2, 2023.https://www.linkedin.com/pulse/ratio-toby-irvine/.

IT Governance. 2017. "Three Pillars of Cyber Security." *IT Governance*, Accessed September 11, 2023. https://www.itgovernance.co.uk/blog/three-pillars-of-cyber-security.

KnowBe4. 2023. "Over Half of Cybersecurity Professionals Engage in Risky Behaviours at Work." *KnowB4*, Accessed September 13, 2023. https://www.knowbe4.com/press/over-half-of-cybersecurity-professionals-engage-in-risky-behaviours-at-work.

Malinowski, B. 1922; 1979. *Argonauts of the Western Pacific: An Account of Native Enterprise and Adventure in the Archipelagoes of Melanesian New Guinea*. London: Routledge.

Mauss, M. 1954; 2005. *The Gift: The Form and Reason for Exchange in Archaic Societies*. London: Routledge.

McConville, E. 2018. "For a Nepalese Honey Hunter's Last Harvest, Friend and Filmmaker Ben Ayes '99 was there." *Bates*, Accessed July 23, 2023.https://www.bates.edu/news/2018/06/18/for-a-nepalese-honey-hunters-last-harvest-friend-and-filmmaker-ben-ayers-99-was-there/.

National Cyber Security Centre. 2023. "Phishing: Spot and Report Scam Emails, Texts, Websites and Calls." Accessed July 8, 2023.https://www.ncsc.gov.uk/col lection/phishing-scams.

Norris, P. 2001. *Digital Divide: Civic Engagement, Information Poverty, and the Internet Worldwide.* Cambridge: Cambridge University Press.

Pandya, J. 2019. "The Wild West of Cyberspace." *Forbes,* Accessed September 13, 2023. https://www.forbes.com/sites/cognitiveworld/2019/09/24/the-wild-west-of-cyber space/?sh=249bb97eb6b8.

Petrosyan, A. 2023. "Cost of Cybercrime Worldwide 2017–2028." *Statista,* Accessed July 30, 2023. https://www.statista.com/forecasts/1280009/cost-cybercrime-worldwide.

Reeves, A., Calic, D., and Delfabbro, P. 2021. "'Get a red-hot poker and open up my eyes, it's so boring': Employee Perceptions of Cybersecurity Training." *Computers and Security,* 106.

Ritzer, G., Dean, P., and Jurgenson, N. 2012. "The Coming of Age of the Prosumer." *American Behavioural Scientists* 56 (4): 379–398.

Rowe, A. 2023. "Study Reveals Average Person Has 100 Passwords." *Tech.Co,* Accessed July 8, 2023. https://tech.co/password-managers/how-many-passwords-a verage-person.

Rowe, J. 2023. "You are the Weakest Link! (In Cybersecurity)." *Trava,* Accessed September 13, 2023. https://travasecurity.com/learn-with-trava/blog/you-are-the-wea kest-link-in-cybersecurity.

Sahlins, Marshal. 1972; 2017. *Stone Age Economics.* London: Routledge.

Shackleton, T. 2021. "Cybersecurity Budget Trends in 2022." *6DG,* Accessed September 11, 2023. https://www.6dg.co.uk/blog/cyber-security-budget-trends/.

Smilyanets, D. 2021 "'I scrounged through the trash heaps…now I'm a millionaire:' An Interview with REvil's Unknown." *The Record,* Accessed July 2, 2023. https://there cord.media/i-scrounged-through-the-trash-heaps-now-im-a-millionaire-an-interview-with-revils-unknown.

Terranova Security. 2023. "Let's Talk About the 'Stupid User' Myth." *Terranova Security,* Accessed September 10, 2023. https://terranovasecurity.com/stupid-user-myth/.

The Guardian. 2014. "The Ancient Art of Honey Hunting in Nepal – In Pictures." *The Guardian,* Accessed July 2, 2023. https://www.theguardian.com/travel/gallery/2014/feb/27/honey-hunters-nepal-in-pictures.

Topham, G. 2021. "Train Firm's 'Worker Bonus' Email is Actually a Cybersecurity Test." *The Guardian,* Accessed July 31, 2023. https://www.theguardian.com/uk-news/2021/may/10/train-firms-worker-bonus-email-is-actually-cyber-security-test.

Ward, M., and Wall, M. 2018. "How can we Stop being Cyber Idiots?" *BBC NEWS,* Accessed September 10, 2023. https://www.bbc.co.uk/news/technology-45953238.

Wild, A. 2016. "Businesses Who Gamble and Succeeded." *Towergate Insurance,* Accessed September 10, 2023. https://www.towergateinsurance.co.uk/trade-specifi c-insurance/the-risk-takers.

5 Cargo Cult or Kula Ring? The Battle for Shared Ethos in Web3

Melyn McKay

Introduction

The emergence of blockchain technology spawned numerous experiments in alternative governance and value creation. Uniting these was a singular thesis: That decentralized infrastructures for data processing and storage could birth a new, user-operated, and owned Internet upon which more democratic social and economic functions could be built. This vision is what drives the otherwise inchoate collection of actors and activities called "Web3."

When asked to define Web3, the sector's most ardent participants and enthusiastic critics often offer frustratingly diffuse responses. However, both do invariably reference two things: Blockchain and decentralization. More robust explanations quickly veer into the political, providing comment on the state of data ownership (Rouse, 2023; Gartner, n.d.), financial inclusion/exclusion, and Internet openness (Avast, 2022). Some link Web3 indelibly to cryptocurrency (Stackpole, 2022). For others, it's the metaverse, Decentralized Autonomous Organizations (DAOs), or Non-Fungible Tokens (NFTs) (Wassmer, 2022). Critically, to many, Web3 promises a "new" kind of Internet, which evangelists consider a "better" but also "fairer" take on the World Wide Web and the society we've built on top of it[1] – a promise which is not yet fully realized and with which many notable figures take issue (Browne, 2022).

It should not be surprising that a technology espousing decentralization as a founding principle evokes a multiplicity of definitions. However, at its core, blockchain is built on cryptography with the objective to provide a record or "ledger" of tamper-proof transactions. For such a system to work, it must be decentralized so that no single actor or authority can exert undue control over what is included or excluded. This is what sets blockchain apart from the most commonly used data processing and storage technologies today, which are invariably centralized, thereby giving specific actors broad authority to hide, edit, share, or even delete the data they control.

Web3's infancy has been a wobbly one. Despite persistent claims to the contrary, many of its projects were neither new nor novel, a critique that will be familiar to those observers of the broader technology space (Tait, 2019) Indeed, much of Web3 has inherited what anthropologist Anna

DOI: 10.4324/9781003458555-5

Weichselbraun noted is "a basic reliance on liberal ideas of individual rights and private property" (Weichselbraun, 2023).

As a result of this uncritical adoption of Western liberalism, Web3 is at risk of building "innovative" and "alternative" digital spaces, modes of governance, and value systems, which are flattening in their view of human flourishing *despite* the radical capacities supposedly inherent to blockchain technology. Indeed, the sector's fervent enthusiasm for the creation of highly speculative financial services and products seems to suggest a very particular – and familiar – teleology.

In this, anthropology as a field of study is poised to offer a necessary intervention, but only if its members approach Web3 with genuine academic interest. Those of us engaged in the anthropology of ethics, for instance, have in Web3, a perfect site to explore how emergent communities actively and attentively choose between divergent visions for the future. More importantly, engaged anthropologists might guide this nascent sector away from building more technologically complex architectures of Western liberalism and colonial capitalism, directing them instead toward alternatives that bulwark against the most pernicious harms of our time – from climate change to extreme wealth inequality.

Coming to Field

I did not come to blockchain from a background in technology. Rather, I stumbled into Web3 while trying to solve a very real-world problem – how to get international aid funding into Myanmar following the 2021 military coup (Human Rights Watch, 2021). A social anthropologist by training, I've spent the vast majority of my career in the international aid sector. In that time, I helped to design livelihoods and demobilization programs in South Sudan; I evaluated emerging governance structures in Syria during the civil war; and I spent half a decade in Myanmar advising various international non-profits and donor governments on everything from humanitarian access strategies to program implementation.

As a result of my training in anthropology, a significant part of my career has been spent "in the field," speaking to members of communities that are receiving international aid, but also to the local aid delivery partners upon which almost every major aid intervention depends. Following the Myanmar military's ousting of the democratically elected civilian government, two things happened: 1) the military immediately moved to use humanitarian aid access as a means of controlling the international community in Myanmar; 2) the military issued banking restrictions which limited the amount of money that could be withdrawn from accounts on a given day (The Irrawaddy, 2021).

The military has long used humanitarian access in so-called "ethnic" areas, often located at the country's borderlands, to force international actors to recognize the central state's sovereignty in places where it is very much contested (Fortify Rights, 2018). Relatedly, in the years leading up to and after the 2018 Rohingya genocide, in which the Myanmar military violently forced approximately a million people into a series of Internally Displaced Persons (IDP) camps and refugee settlements in Bangladesh, the military regularly refused access to international aid organizations seeking to deliver food aid and shelter (Holmes, 2017). Arguably, the international community's inability – or unwillingness – to navigate these restrictions made them complicit, to a degree, in the military's continued mistreatment of the Rohingya (Mennecke & Stensrud, 2021).

The new junta's manipulation of money movement wasn't just tedious. Though restrictions on accessing funds in-country, including foreign currency (USD), posed an operational challenge to many aid actors, the more concerning risk was physical security. The military has routinely used the banking sector as a means of surveilling and controlling those it deemed a threat to its continued existence – such as artists, activists, and humanitarian aid workers. Receiving a large international bank transfer quickly became a good way to end up being violently interrogated or even detained. This pattern of human rights abuses was familiar to those of us in the aid sector; we'd seen much of the same during the Syrian civil war.

In response, the international aid sector contracted as it struggled to move the money that it had already allocated to various programs in the country. Not only could the international aid actors not easily withdraw money held in-country into cash, but they couldn't transfer funds out of Myanmar or use the money in bank accounts to pay local employees and aid partner organizations. As the Myanmar Kyat tumbled against the US dollar, international aid funds held in-country lost up to 60% of their value (Reuters, 2021).

At the time of the coup, I was working closely with an international aid organization that now struggled to pay its own staff in Myanmar. First, we moved everyone on to Wise, a popular FinTech tool for international banking. This worked for those staff members with passports, the only form of identity documentation Wise accepted to complete its 'Know Your Customer' (KYC) checks, but not for those without (Sullivan & Sur, 2023). The insufficiently functioning postal service made sending ATM cards out nearly impossible, meaning money would have to be transferred into Myanmar bank accounts first in order to access cash. This imperfect solution served our needs for only a few months; following the announcement of targeted US, EU, and UK sanctions, Wise summarily shut down all Myanmar access to their accounts, offering prior users, even those no longer living in-country, limited recourse to reinstating them. In sitting with our team to identify alternative money movement modalities and asking about their security concerns, preferences, and technological capabilities, I was struck by how many raised cryptocurrency as a potential solution.[2]

Anthropologists are not especially known for being great "joiners"; we seem to be epistemologically oriented toward criticism and away from systems that appear to concentrate more power and wealth in the richest 1% (Oxfam, 2023). Likewise, and similar to many in the discipline, I was irritated by and uncomfortable with the fervor surrounding cryptocurrency, largely because the loudest voices in the industry were precisely the types of people I'd spent my career critiquing.

As such, when I started to explore cryptocurrency, I did so from a position of extreme skepticism. It was only when I followed my own tenets of good research and centered the voices and perspectives of marginalized communities that a light bulb lit up. In speaking to Myanmar activists, I began to see how at-risk communities were using cryptocurrency not only to avoid state surveillance but also to develop networks of solidarity with peers in places like Syria. Far from being solely a tool for clandestine organizing, community-based cryptocurrencies were being used as a means of challenging US economic imperialism, finding new ways of generating and sharing value in places where the US dollar standard undermined local sovereignty and wreaked havoc on economies (Medium, 2019). Community-owned data projects, including insurance pools, were being built without the intervention of state governments or even corporations.

It is impossible to talk about the sorts of functions above without touching on NFTs and the smart contracts that underline them. In my research, I discovered smart contracts, automated self-executing "programs" run on blockchains, were being used to arrange agreements amongst large, decentralized groups. These agreements spanned a number of functions, from pooling and redistributing resources (Gitcoin, 2023) to coordinating activities (Barman, 2023). Far from being solely used as a means of extracting wealth via memified ponzi schemes, NFTs were being used for things like protecting doctor's notes in Mexico, providing the medical community there with a new tool for fighting prescription abuse (UNICEF, 2018) Through this research-led process of discovery, I became fully invested in what blockchain could mean for communities around the world, particularly the ability to organize, create, and share value without the risk of that value being co-opted by states and corporations looking to monetize and extract community wealth and work.

Prior to beginning my work in blockchain, my academic focus had been religious nationalism and violence in Myanmar (McKay & Frydenlund, 2022). I had, as such, long been interested in alternatives to state-making (or rather, un-making) and found intellectual purchase in the work of anthropologists David Graeber and James C. Scott. My first encounters with DAOs were thus filtered through the lens provided by works such as Graeber's "Fragments of an Anarchist Anthropology" (Graeber, 2004). Through my academic training, I'd been exposed to anthropological work on value and modes of exchange; these piqued my interest as I encountered various community projects in Web3 that evoked memories of reading Bohannan's work on the Tiv and their spheres of exchange (Bohannan, 1955), Malinowski (and his critics) on Kula rings (Malinowski, 1922), and pub chats with Dr. Cynthia Sear, who's work explores "compers"[3] and the complex relationships that emerge between brands and "consumers" when they are mediated through the joy of uncertainty, cultivated by corporate prizes and raffles (Sear, 2022).

These academic frames have helped me to overcome my own biases. Despite the loudest voices in the room, the actual premise of Web3 and its use in the kinds of communities where I have long worked made me excited about its potential. I hoped to harness the technology to alleviate some of the most challenging pain points experienced by the international aid sector – most notably, in moving more and less restricted aid money directly to local aid partners and the communities they serve.[4] Within the aid sector, this emphasis is known as the 'localization agenda' (European Civil Protection and Humanitarian Aid Operations, 2023).

When I brought my emergent idea to the only Web3 person I knew, I was surprised but excited by how quickly he understood how the technology he'd been building could solve the problems our sector had long faced. Following his introduction to a seasoned blockchain developer, Coala Pay was founded with the mission of building a sustainable last-mile infrastructure for localization in the international aid sector. Using smart contracts, Coala Pay tokenizes local aid organizations' small grant proposals, making it easier for larger international aid agencies and other philanthropic actors to find and directly fund the most impactful projects around the world. Coala Pay's wallet-to-wallet payments mean we couldn't interfere in transactions even if we wanted to. This, and many other features, have been explicitly designed to undermine the legacy of colonial capitalism, embedded as it has been in the international aid sector since its infancy.

Blockchain, in Lay Terms

In the section that follows, I will detail the history of Web3. Throughout, I will reflect on how each phase of innovation shaped the form Coala Pay takes today.

Origins in Cryptography

The origins of blockchain have their roots in the introduction of public-key cryptography. Though cryptography had been a feature of military communications for decades prior, it was not until the 1970s that computer scientists at Stanford University and MIT developed and patented the foundational algorithms enabling secure communication without a pre-shared secret key (O'Reilly, 2023), setting the stage for decentralized systems (Diffie & Hellman, 1976).

At the time, however, the processing power and memory capacity of computers were limited, making complex cryptographic operations time-consuming and resource-intensive (Bhat & Giri, 2023). Advancements in cryptography were primarily driven by academic research and collaboration between experts in the field, not by real-world need or demand, which meant intellectual property issues often complicated the process of adopting standardized protocols. The social and political forces of the 1980s and '90s, especially debates surrounding the control of cryptographic technology by governments, further slowed the pace of innovation as US officials sought legal recourse to ensure that advances in public cryptography would not undermine state surveillance tools (O'Reilly, 2023).

In 1991, Stuart Haber and W. Scott Stornetta unveiled a cryptographically secured chain of data "blocks" designed to timestamp digital documents (Immutable Record, n.d.). This pivotal concept sowed the seeds of blockchain's immutability by introducing "hashing." Each block in the blockchain contains a cryptographic hash, a unique identifier generated from the data within the block. If any data within the block is altered, even by a single character, its hash changes entirely. Since subsequent blocks also include the hash of the previous block, any change in one block cascades and affects all subsequent blocks. This tamper-evident feature makes it extremely difficult for anyone to alter the data in a block without being detected (Bharathan, 2020).

In 2004, a figure by the name of Hal Finney, renowned for his activism in cryptography and his involvement with cypherpunks, introduced a reusable proof-of-work system. The cypherpunks were a group of privacy activists who, in the 1990s, helped establish the use of unregulated digital cryptography within the United States in protest of the government's attempts to throttle the technology (Jarvis, 2022). Finney's concept required the various actors engaged in providing the decentralized computational processing power that makes blockchains run, to solve complex mathematical puzzles in order to verify that a block of data should be recorded on the blockchain ledger.

Then, the world was introduced to an enigmatic persona named Satoshi Nakamoto.[5] Nakamoto's groundbreaking 2008 whitepaper titled "Bitcoin: A Peer-to-Peer Electronic Cash System" married cryptographic techniques, proof-of-work consensus, and a chain of blocks.[6] The resulting amalgamation paved the way for decentralized digital currency transactions and marked the birth of the first-ever blockchain – the backbone of Bitcoin.

Bitcoin allows for peer-to-peer transactions without the need for intermediaries like banks (i.e., "trustless" transactions or those that do not need to rely on trust in a third party like a bank for validation). Its use of proof-of-work consensus addressed the longstanding issue of double-spending (spending the same digital currency unit more than once) in digital currency systems, improving the security of transactions (River Financial, 2022).

Bitcoin's blockchain officially came into existence when its first block, aptly named the "genesis block" or "block 0," was "mined" on January 3, 2009 (Liu, 2014). Mining is the process through which transactions on the Bitcoin network are verified and added to the public ledger (blockchain). When someone initiates a Bitcoin transaction, it is broadcast to the network of actors engaged in the decentralized data processing ("miners") and placed in a pool of unconfirmed transactions. Miners must first solve the cryptographic puzzle required to determine the correct hashing for a block, and the proposed solution must be validated by others in the network before it can be added to the ledger.

Miners are rewarded with a predetermined number of newly created ("minted") bitcoins when they successfully add a block – known as the block reward. The value of each block reward decreases regularly; at the time of writing, the block reward is 6.25 Bitcoins (USD $29,130.90), but this will drop to 3.125 bitcoins per block when the next expected "halving" or block reward decrease takes place in April or May of 2024 (BitPay, 2023). Block rewards incentivize miners to participate in securing the network and validating transactions. In addition to the block reward, miners also collect transaction fees from the transactions included in the block. Transaction fees serve as an incentive for miners to prioritize higher fee transactions and to continue mining even after the block reward diminishes over time.

Once the new block is added to the blockchain, the transactions it contains are considered confirmed and permanently recorded on the public ledger. The miners' work is critical to maintaining the chronological order and immutability of the blockchain. To maintain a consistent block generation time (approximately ten minutes on the Bitcoin network), the mining difficulty is adjusted periodically. The difficulty increases or decreases depending on the total computational power (hash rate) of the network. This adjustment helps maintain the network's stability and security.

Understanding the political challenges that faced early cryptography and the complex computational power required to validate blockchain transactions helps contextualize the modern challenges facing Web3. Global government regulations against cryptocurrencies often appear equally concerned with protecting consumers from financial abuse but also with the nation-state's ability to surveil and control their citizens (Reitman, 2021). "Gas fees," or the fees blockchain users must pay to miners in exchange for their computing power, can be astronomically high when networks are busy. Despite an "open source" ethos, much of the funding for innovation now comes in the form of venture capital, creating IP and ownership issues that stifle collaboration as companies struggle to monetize.

Nevertheless, this basic functionality is what enables Coala Pay's aid funding marketplace to connect donors and local aid organizations directly. We neither intermediary the funds sent between the two users' wallets nor could we intervene in the transactions – most of which settle within a matter of hours.

The Hunt for Scalability

While Bitcoin introduced the concept of a decentralized digital currency, Ethereum played a pivotal role in diversifying the blockchain landscape. Launched in 2015 by Vitalik Buterin, Ethereum quickly became a prominent platform for decentralized applications (DApps). Since 2022, it has leveraged proof-of-stake consensus, introduced in a paper by Sunny King and Scott Nadal in 2012 (King & Nadal, 2012), in an attempt to solve the problem of Bitcoin mining's high energy consumption. Whereas proof-of-work requires miners to utilize computing power in order to solve the cryptographic puzzles required to validate hashing, proof-of-stake requires validators to hold an agreed-upon amount of cryptocurrency, which they "stake" as collateral. Though Ethereum achieved significant improvements in energy consumption compared to Bitcoin, it was still limited by scalability and transaction throughput issues, which prompted the rise of alternative blockchains seeking to improve usability.

For instance, EOS, launched in 2018, sought to improve upon Ethereum's scalability issues by introducing a delegated proof-of-stake consensus mechanism in which holders of the EOS cryptocurrency token voted to make a limited number of elected delegates responsible for validating transactions and creating new blocks on behalf of the community. This design was expected to allow for faster transaction processing and enhanced throughput, enabling developers to build complex DApps with improved efficiency (Volpicelli, 2022). Following what was once the largest initial coin offering (ICO) of all time, a process by which potential blockchain users "fund" or invest in the development of a platform in exchange for tokens representing monetary value and sometimes voting rights, EOS failed to materialize any of its promises (Godsil, 2023). Other attempts have been more successful; Cardano, for instance, utilizes a unique proof-of-stake consensus algorithm called Ouroboros, which selects participants – stake pools, in this case – to create new blocks based on the stake they control in the network (Cardano, 2023).

Some in the blockchain developer community felt improving upon existing technologies would be a faster means of growth than engineering new systems altogether. Layer 2 (L2) solutions, also known as second-layer solutions, refer to off-chain scaling solutions built on top of existing blockchain networks. These solutions aim to enhance the scalability, efficiency, and transaction throughput of the underlying blockchain while minimizing the load on the main blockchain. L2s like Polygon achieve this by processing transactions off-chain and later reconciling them with the main blockchain as needed.[7]

Coala Pay is built on Ethereum because it processes, at the time of writing, the greatest volume of transactions, which creates a degree of security around the chain's future, which is essential to moving aid actors to a new technology. However, its relative costs are a known constraint and one we're working diligently to address through exploratory partnerships with various other L1s and L2s, balancing volume, trust, and cost as we grow.

Records v. Programs

The ability to transact quickly and at volume became especially important with the introduction of smart contracts: In essence, computer programs running on a blockchain. In 2015, Ethereum introduced smart contract technology, first devised by Hungarian programmer Nick Szabo (Szabo, 1996, 1997), to its public blockchain. Smart contracts allow for self-executing agreements with predefined conditions, eliminating the need for intermediaries and enhancing transparency.

While smart contracts facilitate trustless execution within the blockchain, they are limited to data available on the blockchain itself. To interact with external data and real-world events, "oracles" came into play. In 2014, Ethereum introduced the concept of oracles, or data feeds, which enable smart contracts to access data from outside sources (Williams & Peterson, 2019). This integration expanded the potential use cases of smart contracts to encompass real-world data and events. For instance, oracles have been used to enable insurance providers to release pre-agreed insurance payments for certain weather events in anticipation of the crop damage they will cause as soon as they are recorded (Etherisc, 2022). The solution ensures policyholders never need to file a claim, vastly improving the speed with which insurance payments can be made to those affected by emergencies. Coala Pay will pilot its own oracle integration in mid 2024, enabling aid funding to flow more quickly to pre-vetted local aid organizations expected to be affected by flooding and other climate change–related weather events in the Horn of Africa.

Non-Fungible Tokens

The history of Non-Fungible Tokens (NFTs) can be traced back to the early 2010s, but their mainstream popularity and adoption surged in the mid to late 2010s and early 2020s. NFTs are unique digital assets that represent ownership of a specific item or piece of content on a blockchain. Unlike cryptocurrencies such as Bitcoin or Ether (the native token of Ethereum), which are fungible and interchangeable with each other, NFTs are indivisible and have distinct properties that make them valuable for tokenizing digital or physical assets.

The concept of NFTs first emerged on the Bitcoin blockchain through the creation of colored coins. Colored coins were a way of representing assets other than Bitcoin on the Bitcoin blockchain by "coloring" a fraction of a Bitcoin to represent ownership of a specific asset (Bitcoinist, n.d.). However, this implementation had limitations and wasn't widely adopted for tokenizing assets beyond simple experiments. Ethereum's smart contract functionality enabled developers to create programmable tokens, and in late 2017, a protocol called ERC-721 was proposed by Dieter Shirley (Ethereum Improvement Proposals, 2018). This new standard enabled the creation of unique tokens on the Ethereum blockchain, laying the foundation for modern NFTs.

The first NFT on the Ethereum blockchain, called "CryptoPunks," was programmed by Matt Hall and John Watkinson of the software company Larva Labs in June 2017 (Public.com, n.d.). CryptoPunks consisted of 10,000 unique 24 × 24-pixel art characters, each with their own distinct traits. Users could claim ownership of these characters by spending Ether in exchange for owning a unique piece of digital art on the blockchain. Since then, the NFT space has expanded rapidly, with artists, game developers, musicians, and various content creators embracing the technology to tokenize their work and create digital collectibles. Notable NFT marketplaces, such as OpenSea and

Rarible, enable users to buy, sell, and trade NFTs representing a wide range of digital and physical assets, including digital art, virtual real estate, music, videos, virtual goods in games, and more. The NFT market has seen both remarkable successes and occasional controversies, but it continues to evolve as a significant aspect of the broader blockchain and crypto ecosystem – if a poorly understood one.

NFTs have become a lightning rod for popular criticism. Alongside claims NFTs are nothing more than a tool for digital money laundering, rest more nuanced critiques of the art most popular within the collector community – and how quickly many NFT projects lose their value. However, at their core, NFTs represent proof of ownership that rests outside a single nation-state or company. In the aid sector alone, NFTs are being piloted to tackle conflicts surrounding land registration and ownership (Ledger Insights, 2023). Coala Pay uses NFTs to represent the specific set of aid activities a donor has funded, including the number of intended beneficiaries, the location of the intervention, and the type of project. This enables us to "listen" for funding events by monitoring a block exporter or record of all blocks, generating fully automated visual impact dashboards for donor users. This decreases the costs donors otherwise allocate to reporting on their spending, letting more money go directly to local aid workers on the ground. By using NFTs in this way, we're leaving the door open to metaverse tie-ins, too, bringing social impact into spatial computing in new (hopefully) meaningful ways.

Scandals

Several significant blockchain scandals have occurred in the history of cryptocurrencies and blockchain technology. These scandals have had profound impacts on the perception of the industry and highlighted the need for increased security and regulatory measures. For instance, Mt. Gox was one of the earliest and most prominent cryptocurrency exchanges based in Tokyo, Japan. In early 2014, it was handling over 70% of all Bitcoin transactions. However, in February 2014, the exchange suspended trading and filed for bankruptcy, revealing that approximately 850,000 bitcoins, worth over $450 million at the time, had been stolen due to a long-running hack (Baydakova, 2023). This incident remains one of the largest cryptocurrency exchange hacks in history, leading to severe losses for its users and a loss of trust in the industry.

More recently, the Terra scandal, in which a cryptocurrency "pegged" or linked to the value of the US Dollar (UST) via a complicated algorithm involving a second cryptocurrency called "Luna," rapidly disconnected from the dollar and plummeted in value following what was for all intents and purposes a bank run. The sudden loss of value led many to view the incident as outright fraud, or in blockchain terminology, a "rug pull." Similarly, the meteoric crash of FTX, once one of the largest cryptocurrency exchanges, has precipitated significant legislative action. In both instances, the rapid death spiral began with suspicions of mismanagement, which caused a crisis of confidence in Terra and FTX's capacity to act as trusted fiduciary stewards.

Because Coala Pay operates a "do no harm" policy, in keeping with aid sector standards, working at the leading edge of new technology comes with new risks we must continuously monitor and mitigate. In large part, this takes the form of education and advocacy, advising local aid partners to keep their funds in regulated stablecoins on "cold" or hardware-based wallets. While the risks of exploit are very real, so too are the risks posed by fiat-based transactions in the environments in which we work. In many ways, blockchain-based product and service innovations should be driven by users in exactly these kinds of contexts – a reminder anthropologists should be active in providing to Web3's current architects.

Legislation

Governments around the world have rushed to put in place legislation regulating cryptocurrency and NFTs while often lacking the necessary expertise to understand the underlying blockchain technology. Generally passed under the auspices of protecting consumers from potential fraud or stopping illicit activities and payments, from drug sales to money laundering (Hussein, 2023) and "terrorism," the growing body of legislation nevertheless highlights that blockchain has the potential to disintermediary powerful actors, including nation-states. As a result, legislative attacks on blockchain-based activity fall into several "types":

- *Cryptocurrency regulations*: Many countries have introduced or proposed regulations to address cryptocurrencies and digital assets. These regulations often focus on anti-money laundering (AML) and know-your-customer (KYC) requirements, taxation of cryptocurrency transactions, and consumer protection. Some countries have banned or restricted the use of cryptocurrencies altogether, however ineffectively,[8] while others have embraced them as a legitimate form of payment.
- *Security Token Offerings (STOs) regulations*: Security tokens are blockchain-based digital assets that represent ownership or rights to underlying financial assets, like the issuance of company stock. Several countries have introduced regulations for Security Token Offerings (STOs) to ensure compliance with existing securities laws. These regulations are aimed at protecting investors and preventing fraudulent activities in the issuance and trading of security tokens.
- *Data privacy and protection*: Blockchain technology can potentially store sensitive data, raising concerns about data privacy and protection. Some countries have enacted data protection laws that apply to blockchain-based applications, ensuring that user data is handled securely and in compliance with privacy regulations, specifically, the EU's General Data

Protection Regulation (GDPR), which includes a "right to be for-gotten" – a concept complicated by the immutability of blockchain.

- *Smart contract regulations*: Smart contracts have legal implications as they automate contractual agreements. Some jurisdictions have taken steps to clarify the legal status of smart contracts, their enforceability, and liability in case of errors or vulnerabilities in the code.
- *Mining and energy consumption*: The energy-intensive nature of crypto-currency mining has raised concerns about environmental impacts. Some countries have imposed regulations or discussed policies to control or ban cryptocurrency mining operations, especially those relying on fossil fuels.
- *Tokenized securities regulations*: Blockchain technology enables the toke-nization of traditional financial assets, such as stocks, bonds, and real estate. Some countries have introduced regulations to govern the issuance, trading, and custody of tokenized securities to ensure compliance with existing financial laws.

One of the most challenging aspects of blockchain legislation facing Coala Pay is the degree to which we recognize the legal standing of the nation-states involved. For instance, in Afghanistan, local programmers have experimented with building wallets for women disenfranchised by the Taliban – an activity that is technically illegal under the current regime but which one is hard-pressed to justify on any grounds.

Doing the Work

Relevant Anthropological Frameworks for Building in Web3

In my own work, I've found three areas of anthropological study helpful in thinking about Web3. The first two, theories of value and exchange and "gov-ernance" outside of or even contra-the state, are perhaps the most obvious. However, I will argue that the anthropology of ethics also offers fertile ground for developing an engaged – and necessary – anthropology of Web3.

Theories of Value and Exchange

Anthropological theories of value and exchange explore how different socie-ties assign meaning to objects, services, and resources and how they facilitate transactions and social relationships. Notably, many anthropologists have studied the concept of value as it operated in societies without state-sanc-tioned fiat regimes. For instance, the influential anthropologist Bronislaw Malinowski studied the Kula ring exchange among the Trobriand Islanders (1922) (Malinowski, 1922). Malinowski argued that in this system, valuable shell armbands ("Soulava") and necklaces ("Mwali") were exchanged between islands in a ceremonial circuit. Malinowski observed how the Kula ring fostered regional cooperation, strengthened inter-island relationships, and promoted prestige for participants. Notably, objects were not meant to "rest" or be accumulated by individuals – their power was in their exchange. Marcel Mauss noted similar findings in his examination of gift-giving (Mauss, 2011). Mauss argued that gift-giving creates social bonds by engendering a sense of obligatory reciprocity. Simply put, gift-giving creates a forward-looking relationship, with terms that must be honored at a later date, bonding the giver and receiver together in the meantime. The speed with which cryptocurrencies and other digital goods transact on blockchain hints at a potential for collapsing the distance and time that geographically limited these types of exchanges.

In their study of the Tiv people of Nigeria, Laura and Paul Bohannan (1953) highlighted the cultural significance of bridewealth exchanges, emphasizing how these exchanges establish alliances and reinforce kinship ties, suggesting that the Tiv's exchange system reflects social values and obligations rather than mere economic transactions (Bohannan & Bohannan, 1953). Continuing his wife's work, Paul Bohannan's examination of the "sphere of exchange" focused on the categorization of goods and services into distinct social spheres. He observed that the Tiv organized their economic transactions into three spheres: The domestic or household sphere, the sphere of market exchange, and the ceremonial sphere (Bohannan, 1955).

The domestic sphere, Bohannan argued, encompassed everyday economic activities, such as subsistence agriculture and household production. This sphere also involved exchanges within family units and close social networks, where reciprocity and mutual obligations were prevalent. The sphere of market exchange involved transactions with individuals outside of immediate social circles. Market exchanges were governed by more impersonal economic principles, such as price determination and supply and demand. Last, the ceremonial sphere consisted of exchanges conducted during significant rituals and ceremonies. Here, valuable items, like cattle, were exchanged to display prestige and reinforce social status.

Maus and both Bohannans' work highlighted the intricate interplay between economic transactions and social relationships, providing insights into how the movement of goods between people contributes to the cohesion and functioning of society. These anthropological theories demonstrate how the value ascribed to the exchange of certain goods is deeply embedded in social and cultural contexts (Doss, 2014). They emphasize the importance of understanding how this value is shaped by cultural norms, social relationships, and symbolic meaning. More recent anthropological studies have built from and, in some cases, offered corrections to these earlier theories.

For instance, *The Gender of the Gift: Problems with Women and Problems with Society in Melanesia* (1988) has become a germinal text in exploring the complexities of gender relations in non-Western societies (Strathern, 1990). In it, Marilyn Strathern offers significant critiques of traditional anthropological theories, particularly Marxism, which she argues paints women's participation in social "giving" as a form of alienation from their labor and not, as she perceives them to be, a means by which they too engage in social exchange for the purpose of building connections and community.

Annette Weiner's influential work similarly revisits Malinowski's research, providing a critical feminist perspective on the Kula and highlighting the significance of women's roles in exchange – including why their participation has historically been overlooked. Specifically, she argues that Malinowski's own gendered lens, through which he only expected men to be active participants in economic and governance systems, was a survival of his own cultural experience and not an accurate assessment of realities on the ground (Weiner, 1988).

Bill Maurer's work *Mutual Life, Limited: Islamic Banking, Alternative Currencies, Lateral Reason* (2005) examined Islamic banking and alternative financial systems, shedding light on the cultural dimensions of money and finance. Of particular interest to my work is Maurer's examination of alternative currency systems, particularly the Hawala system in the Middle East (Maurer, 2005). Hawala is a system of informal money transfer that relies on trust and personal networks rather than traditional banking channels. The international aid sector is not only deeply dependent upon Hawalas in many areas but also struggles to contend with their extra-legal status (Mohamed, 2023).

In her work on "compers,' or serial entrants of promotional competitions in Australia, Cynthia Sear highlights how women, generally homemakers who have been excluded from traditional financial systems, have been engaged by brands in ways that bring them excitement and joy in the context of otherwise mundane lives (Sear, 2022). She draws attention to the way financial uncertainty is presented as both opportunity and risk, with significant class differences. Certain communities are discouraged from participating in financial risk-taking, while others' financial success is considered a product of their willingness to take risks with bold payouts.

Cryptocurrency, ICOs, and NFTs as Value Created through Exchange

Anthropological work on value and exchange is critical to contesting criticisms of blockchain assets such as cryptocurrencies and NFTs, which frame them strictly as illicit money grabs that threaten to undermine "formal" state economies. Rather, the emphasis anthropological theory has long placed on the social relations created vis-à-vis processes of exchange is critical to understanding why blockchain enthusiasts not only engage but continue to do so even when markets are down.

This is particularly fertile ground to examine through a feminist lens. Just as Strathern argues that Trobriand women are not alienated by the gift process but rather benefit by participating in it as they become encoded into social relations, arguing against seeing exchange as merely a matter of "commodities," we gain insight into why women have recently become some of the most enthusiastic adopters of cryptocurrencies (The Times of India, 2022), and why many have been empowered through the creation and collection of NFTs. As Werner points out, focusing only on "masculine" financial systems (when trying to force Blockchain to fit within this framework) pushes women's participation out of view. Though the phenomenon of the "Crypto Bro," or aggressively and hyper-masculinist enthusiast with little tolerance for reasonable criticism,[9] is very real, to suggest this is all that exists is to undermine the reasons why so many marginalized communities have sought access to blockchain assets as a means of improving their social position, building community, and protecting themselves from certain forms of exploitation.

To that end, Sear provides comments on how to think about blockchain brands creating opportunities for wealth creation through greater engagement. Though these "plays" may seem self-serving and often are, they also offer opportunities to those who may feel left behind by markets. Whether this should be the work brands do, and the degree to which it is self-serving should be understood as part of, not unique to, the opportunities blockchain gives to those in their communities.

Extra-State Relations

One of the most influential anthropological works on "the state" and its monopoly over the economy is James C. Scott's book *Seeing Like a State: How Certain Schemes to Improve the Human Condition Have Failed* (1998). While not exclusively focused on the economy, Scott's work provides valuable insights into how states have historically sought to standardize and control economic activities for the purpose of taxation, resource extraction, and non-consensual governance.

In it, Scott argues that states have imposed simplified, legible, and centralized schemes on their populations to facilitate control. However, these top-down planning efforts often overlook the complexity and context-specific nature of local economies, leading to unintended consequences, social disruptions, and economic inefficiencies. Scott examines historical examples of state-driven projects, such as forced agrarian collectivization, forest management, and urban planning. He highlights how such interventions often disregarded the intricate local knowledge and practices that had evolved over generations, resulting in the degradation of natural resources, loss of community autonomy, and resistance from affected populations.

In the context of the economy, Scott's work underscores the limitations of state-driven attempts to monopolize economic activities and manage production and distribution. He emphasizes the importance of recognizing the diversity and resilience of local economic systems and the need for decentralized, context-sensitive approaches to development and governance.

As an anthropologist with a deep focus on Myanmar, it is impossible to think about the possibilities blockchain offers without reference to Scott's work. Scott, too, drew much of his insight from the Myanmar borderlands, an area which he called "Zomia," where a decades-long struggle to remain outside the Bamar ethnic central state-building project resulted in complex forms of governance, identity, and exchange.

Indeed, following the military coup, Myanmar's representatives of the democratically-elected government formed an entity called the National Unity Government (NUG), which in turn made USDT, a USD-linked stable coin,[10] legal currency (Al Jazeera, 2023). Working closely with various L1s and L2s, the NUG has released its own cryptocurrency payments wallet, and a recently formed Neo Bank called Spring Development Bank, based in Singapore, which has launched accounts that will feature several stable coins as well as fiat deposits, enabling those living in Myanmar to transact entirely outside the view of the new junta (DVB, 2023). This speaks not only to blockchain's ability to protect those who are oppressed by central states but also to the very fact that monopolizing the exchange of value is central to the state-building process – while the NUG is using these tools to undermine the strength of the military junta, in so doing they make a claim, too, asserting themselves as a viable "state" alternative.

Here, it is impossible not to also mention Graeber. Though often known for his work on debt and his influence on the Occupy Wall Street movement, early Graeber explored the intersections of anthropology and anarchism, arguing for a renewed engagement between the two fields. He proposed the idea of "anthropological anarchism" as a way to understand human societies beyond the framework of states and hierarchical structures. As an anthropologist and public intellectual, David Graeber had mixed views on cryptocurrencies (Graeber, 2018). Whilst he supported the idea of creating alternative financial systems that are more equitable and inclusive, he raised concerns about the speculative nature of cryptocurrencies and the risk of creating new forms of financial inequality. He criticized the excessive focus on speculation and profit-making within the cryptocurrency space, arguing that it undermined the original vision of creating a more equitable financial system.

Critically, Graeber questioned the idea that cryptocurrencies would lead to a completely stateless and decentralized world. He argued that, in practice, cryptocurrencies were still subject to regulatory frameworks and were often co-opted by existing financial institutions. Emerging patterns in blockchain legislation would seem to support Graeber's concern; the most successful blockchain companies have been those that submitted to the same degree of regulation as a bank or financial institution.

This does not mean anthropological theories of the state and how to repel it hit a dead end. Both Scott and Graeber's work should be required reading for DAO creators and anyone building in the metaverse. DAOs are a type of organization that operates through rules and code written on a blockchain platform without the need for traditional centralized management.

DAOs are intended to be self-governing and self-executing, following the predefined rules and instructions coded into the smart contracts that form them. The operations and decisions of a DAO are recorded on the blockchain, allowing all participants to view and verify transactions and activities. DAOs are governed by the community of token holders or participants; voting mechanisms in smart contracts enable them to propose and decide on changes to the organization. DAOs often have their own native tokens that represent ownership or voting rights. These tokens allow participants to have a say in decision making and receive rewards for contributions.

DAOs can be used for various purposes, such as crowdfunding, DeFi, content creation, and community-driven projects. They have gained popularity as a way to create decentralized and transparent organizational structures that remove intermediaries and promote direct participation and decision making by members. DAO experiments in governance are not only fascinating to observe but also provide a means of examining how blockchain enables "new" forms of governance that exist outside of states and corporations. Critically, anthropology can provide insight into the otherwise obscured theoretical histories upon which these "new" forms of governance have been constructed. In doing so, anthropologists can help to ensure that DAOs are not operating blind to critical histories and forced to replicate age-old mistakes.

A Personal Anthropology

In my own work, theories of alternative value and exchange have been essential to creating a community of mutual benefit. At the same time, the voices of Scott and Graeber take pride of place in helping me to resist external pressures to "centralize" power on our platform to simplify governance and benefit the distributors of capital.

This has not always been an easy line to walk. For instance, I am quite sure we've lost ecosystem grants distributed by L1s and L2s because we refused to force our local partners to adopt specific tools they were interested in at the time. We have advocated against certain documentation regimes, lobbying exchanges to allow alternative forms of identification so as not to legitimize the Myanmar junta through the process of their own – often thoughtless – bureaucracy.

But most importantly, my work simply "is" anthropologically informed because I am an anthropologist. The way I see the world is indelibly influenced by the lens that education has afforded. I am particularly concerned with the localization agenda because I have seen the operational issues the lack of it causes in the aid sector, but also because I fundamentally hold a critique of colonial capitalism as it is often expressed through the aid sector. Simply put, I believe we would all be better off if the aid sector functioned more like "mutual aid" than like "foreign aid." This is a longstanding and widespread critique of international aid, one which has been frustratingly immune to improvement, at least that which has been predominantly attempted through improved community consultation and engagement. I see the promise of decentralization and alternative modes of value creation and distribution as key to making progress toward a genuine localization of international aid and in such a way as to knit us more closely together without the need for nation-state intermediaries.

In this chapter, I have prioritized the theoretical work of white anthropologists. There is a reason for that: I wanted to bring a new technology into conversation with an old discipline. That discipline, however, has been meaningfully criticized for its own colonial roots. What excites me about the potential of Web3 is that the most important innovations are coming from global majority countries – programmers in places like India, Kenya, and Curaçao, who are putting blockchain to work, solving challenges they face in their own communities. For instance, Kolektivo in Curaçao has leveraged its own social currency to enable the small island economy to resist the Western imperialism snuck in on the back of the dollar standard (Kolektivo, 2023). These are critically important interventions that not only advance the technology but do so in ways that build more just, fairer worlds for those the global banking – and, more broadly, the global information processing – systems have left out, often intentionally.

Anthropology has always been the discipline of counter-hegemonic thinking. If it can be argued that blockchain has the potential to be a counter-hegemonic tool, then anthropologists should be involved in building that tool and shaping it to ensure the ends it achieves are more just. However, these anthropological interventions must elevate diverse community voices in order to be successful. To date, this has been a notable shortcoming in the anthropology of Web3, as it has tended to focus on blockchain as a financial instrument rather than as an alternative value system, exchange, or means of collective organizing.

Critiques such as Graeber's are essential to bring into Web3 because they highlight one of the most significant concerns I and others have – that the current voices most engaged in building these decentralized systems and spaces are those with distinctly hierarchical and extractive aims. Simply put, many see blockchain uniquely as a means of creating new forms of value that exist within or at least adjacent to the so-called "formal economy." Their aim is to maximize their position within this space, which entangles such actors with accumulation and power. As such, their conflict with the state, where it exists, is not an ideological one but rather a frustration with the state's ability to interfere in their extraordinary wealth hoarding and the extreme social stratification created by it.

This is a shame, given the technology's essential qualities, which could create financial inclusion and access in ways that engender new social assemblages that are fairer and more just. If this is the sort of world we want to live in, we need anthropologists (or the anthropologically-informed) involved in the construction of them. Otherwise, the loudest voices in the room may continue to be those such as Bilaj Srinvastin, whose vision of a "networked state" is both blind to the poor but also derived from a desire to have less accountability toward others – not more (Srinivasan, 2022).

Indeed, anthropology is essential to ensuring Web3 brings a diverse set of peoples and practices into view when thinking about blockchain and what it "does" for those who participate in it.

On Risks and Rewards

I initially hesitated to discuss my work in blockchain because I worried it would undermine my legitimacy as a scholar. This is because many anthropologists and other academics have a "knee-jerk," emotive response to blockchain. This is in part because of dominant figures in the space, which echo the masculinist voices of finance – and their societal impact, which anthropologists have long critiqued. However, I would gently suggest that this has also foreclosed genuine and thoughtful engagement with blockchain and its downstream products. The vitriolic response to NFTs and the metaverse is telling in this respect. While gleefully likening these technologies to the Tulip Mania, my fellow anthropologists overlooked what it is these blockchain assets and spaces really do for those building them (Morucci, 2023).

What they end up suggesting is that the people who chose to engage in the space are either blindly greedy or superstitious to the point of being no more than a modern-day "cargo cult" – hanging on to the crumbs of colonial masters dangling wealth and status before them. This, I argue, is an unproductive way to think about this new technology and the people in it. There are destructive forces, to be sure. But there are also builders working to produce a fairer and more just society. These voices are important and tell us something meaningful about the economic and social lives of people around the world and why these alternatives appear so appealing.

To that end, I will acknowledge the joy I've felt in engaging with "building" technology rather than a "dissecting" study and in bringing anthropological knowledge to new audiences. Here, I find a new opportunity for anthropological praxis – to create something that aligns with the understanding of the world I have developed through my work as an anthropologist. This "something" remains inchoate but nevertheless attempts to lessen the worst impacts of colonial capitalism (accepting my own limitations in overturning them completely) while strengthening the positive social impacts of things like gift-giving, exchange, and resurgent modes of inclusive governance that reflect the best of indigenous practices around the world. Moreover, it excites me that Web3 provides a space within which we can appreciate these modes of living absent the strangely "stuck in aspic" element produced by appreciating them as though they were a bygone practice, not the wisdom of living societies.

A Hope for the Future

Through Coala Pay, we hope to create a better means of delivering international aid, one focused more on building communities of solidarity rather than on achieving the soft power goals of "Western" governments. We want local aid actors to receive more and better forms of funding. We want them to determine the activities and services they deliver based on what their communities want - not donor priorities. We want them to be able to receive funds in a way that protects them from various forms of state manipulation, disintermediating the various private and public actors that otherwise take a cut, enabling them to work free from surveillance and violence. Importantly, we want to do this while encouraging international aid donors to think hard about the monitoring regimes they impose based on their own "actuarial" view of risk and its management, given how often this view of risk is misaligned with the risks local organizations face.

More granularly, we're thinking a lot about the value of data and who is remunerated for producing it. In the aid sector, monitoring and evaluation are carried out and produce significant value for foreigners – not the communities producing the knowledge. We want to address that through direct-to-beneficiary surveying that pays participants in remote data top-ups. We want to make this data available to local aid organizations in order to improve intervention design and delivery. We also plan to link this data, via oracle, to our smart contracts – ensuring aid-receiving communities are the ones determining whether a program has been completed well, thereby enabling performance-based milestone payments to move automatically from donor to local partner wallets when agreed outcomes have been met.

We also want to start conversations about art, and particularly NFTs, that emphasize how art, for art's sake, can bring value without needing to be involved in speculative growth. Relatedly, our art is designed to avoid the use of disempowering imagery in non-profit marketing and fundraising materials. We believe international aid should at all times protect the dignity of those receiving it, and this is one intervention in that space that pairs important and impactful work with something long considered to have an aesthetic value. We do this to encourage conversations about a sort of "platonic good" and its meaning in our sector.

In the longer term, we hope Coala Pay's work with local organizations will not only have an impact on the international aid sector but will support the development of locally responsive units of governance that can work autonomously from the state or states to identify, advocate for, and find resources to support locally-led initiatives. In so doing, we hope to encourage other Web3 builders to see these communities as deserving of more complex organizing instruments and tools, encouraging them to engage with these community organizations when building products to ensure they are not only useable for all kinds of people but that the world we are building on blockchain is not merely an echo of colonial capitalism's worst features.

I would encourage all anthropologists to join in these conversations as critics but, more importantly, as contributors. An anthropologically informed Web3 is a more inclusive, counter-hegemonic force in the world, and a space where engaged anthropologists can explore new praxis for co-creation and community making.

Notes

1 Common criticisms of Web2 include users' lack of data ownership, lack of privacy, lack of transparency, and extreme centralization. To the latter point, the world's Internet users spend a combined 422 billion hours on just four sites: Google, YouTube, Facebook, and Twitter. (c.f. https://zyro.com/websites-time).

2 The team's interest in cryptocurrency evolved, as it often does, from necessity. As such, many across Myanmar had come to similar conclusions, just as aid workers and activists in Syria, Sudan, and elsewhere, when facing a similar set of constraints.

3 Sear describes "compers" as those who habitually enter corporate giveaways.

4 Alongside many others in the aid sector, I believe the "quality" of international aid funding can be understood as a factor of its speed in arriving, flexibility in use, sufficiency for actual costs, and appropriateness for the type of intervention most needed and desired by an affected community.

5 The actual identity of Nakamoto has never been confirmed. It is speculated the persona could be an amalgam of several persons.

6 Satoshi Nakamoto, "Bitcoin: A Peer-to-Peer Electronic Cash System."

7 Interoperability between blockchains has been a significant focus in recent years. Projects like Polkadot and Cosmos have sought to facilitate communication and asset transfer between various blockchains. While interoperability is improving, moving assets between blockchains can still be complex and subject to potential security risks. For instance, in the Poly Network Exploit (2021) (see: André Beganski, "Poly Network Attack Conjures Billions of Dollars in Tokens That 'Did Not Exist'," *Decrypt*, July 2, 2023, https://decrypt.co/147059/poly-network-atta ck-conjures-billions-of-dollars-in-tokens-that-did-not-exist), a cross-chain decentralized finance (DeFi) protocol, suffered a massive hack. The hackers exploited a vulnerability in the protocol's code and managed to steal approximately $600 million worth of cryptocurrency. This incident raised concerns about the security of DeFi platforms and blockchain bridges. Nevertheless, cross-chain solutions are essential to preventing silos and a "winner-take-all" mentality.

8 In such contexts it becomes difficult to connect to centralized exchanges to off-ramp to fiat, as the companies behind these exchanges are often unwilling to test local legislation.

9 Others may define this caricature differently, to include outright displays of misogyny and racism. However defined, it is related to the concept of a "tech bro," which tends to emphasize an adherence to the belief that technology is a singularly great pursuit, which bestows those engaged in its development with a social and moral superiority over others, despite a demonstrable lack of capacity in other skills and forms of education, notably the humanities and social sciences, particularly history.

10 Stable coins are created and maintained either via one-to-one deposits, wherein each asset "minted" represents a fiat asset held in the custody of a regulated entity, often a bank or company, or through a complex algorithm which maintains the one-to-one value. Algorithmic models are at constant risk of "depegging" with market fluctuations.

Bibliography

Abouzied, Mohamed. 2023. "The Hawala System: A Risky Alternative to Traditional Banking." *AFC Challenges*, March 10, 2023. https://www.acamstoday.org/the-hawa la-system-a-risky-alternative-to-traditional-banking/.

Al Jazeera. 2023. "Myanmar Shadow Government Approves Crypto as Official Currency." *Al Jazeera*. Accessed December 1, 2023. https://www.aljazeera.com/econom y/2021/12/14/myanmar-shadow-government-approves-crypto-as-official-currency.

Avast. 2022. "What Is Web 3.0? – Avast." Accessed December 29, 2022. https://www.avast.com/c-web-3-0.

Barman, Jyotirmoy. 2023. "A Flexible Design for Funding Public Goods – Quadratic Funding." *DAO Times*, April 17, 2023. https://daotimes.com/a-flexible-design-for-funding-public-goods-quadratic-funding/.

Baydakova, Anna. 2023. "Where the Mt. Gox Money Went: New Details in the BTC-e Exchange Case." *CoinDesk*. Published June 9, 2023. Updated June 13, 2023. https://www.coindesk.com/consensus-magazine/2023/06/09/where-the-mt-gox-money-went-new-details-in-the-btc-e-exchange-case/.

Beganski, André. 2023. "Poly Network Attack Conjures Billions of Dollars in Tokens That 'Did Not Exist'." *Decrypt*, July 2, 2023. https://decrypt.co/147059/poly-network-attack-conjures-billions-of-dollars-in-tokens-that-did-not-exist.

Bharathan, Vipin. 2020. "Blockchain Was Born 20 Years Before Bitcoin." *Forbes*, June 1, 2020. https://www.forbes.com/sites/vipinbharathan/2020/06/01/the-blockchain-was-born-20-years-before-bitcoin/?sh=38930b205d71.

Bhat, Mohd, and Kaiser Giri. 2023. "Impact of Computational Power on Cryptography." In: *Multimedia Security*, edited by Kaiser J. Giri, Shabir Ahmad Parah, Rumaan Bashir, Khan Muhammad. Singapore: Springer. doi:10.1007/978-981-15-8711-5_4.

BitPay. 2023. *"Bitcoin Halving: How the Event Impacts Bitcoin."* Accessed December 1, 2023. https://bitpay.com/blog/bitcoin-halving/#:~:text=As%20of%20mid%2D2023%2C%20the,on%20the%20price%20of%20Bitcoin.

Bohannan, L., & Bohannan, P. 1953. *The Tiv of Central Nigeria: Western Africa Part VIII* (1st ed.). Routledge. https://doi.org/10.4324/9781315295817.

Bohannan, Paul. 1955. "Some Principles of Exchange and Investment among the Tiv." *American Anthropologist* 57 (1): 60–70. http://www.jstor.org/stable/665788.

Browne, Ryan. 2022. "Web Inventor Tim Berners-Lee Wants Us to 'Ignore' Web3: 'Web3 Is Not the Web at All'." *CNBC*. Published November 4, 2022. Updated November 23, 2022. https://www.cnbc.com/2022/11/04/web-inventor-tim-berners-lee-wants-us-to-ignore-web3.html.

"Civil Protection and Humanitarian Aid Operations" *European Civil Protection and Humanitarian Aid Operations*. Accessed December 1, 2023. https://civil-protection-humanitarian-aid.ec.europa.eu/what/humanitarian-aid/localisation_en#:~:text=In%20the%20humanitarian%20sector%2C%20localisation,and%20promote%20long%2Dterm%20sustainability.

"Colored Coins: How They Work on the Bitcoin Blockchain." *Bitcoinist*. Accessed December 29, 2022. https://bitcoinist.com/colored-coins-work-bitcoin-blockchain/.

"The Co-Inventors." *Immutable Record*. Accessed December 1, 2023. https://immutablerecord.com/the-co-inventors/.

"CryptoPunks: A Short History." *Public.com*. Accessed December 1, 2023. https://public.com/learn/cryptopunks-short-history.

Diffie, Whitfield, and Martin E. Hellman. 1976. "New Directions in Cryptography." *IEEE Transactions on Information Theory* 22 (6) (November 1976).

Doss, Cheryl, Gale Summerfield, and Dzodzi Tsikata. 2014. "Land, Gender, and Food Security." *Feminist Economics* 20 (1): 1–23.

"EIP-721: ERC-721 Non-Fungible Token Standard." Ethereum Improvement Proposals. January 24, 2018. https://eips.ethereum.org/EIPS/eip-721.

Etherisc Blog. 2022. "Etherisc Protects Another 7,000 Kenyan Farmers as Part of the Lemonade Crypto Climate Coalition." Accessed December 29, 2022. https://blog.

etherisc.com/etherisc-protects-another-7-000-kenyan-farmers-as-part-of-the-lemona de-crypto-climate-coalition-e169eca3d6bc.

Fortify Rights. 2023. "Myanmar: End Restrictions on Humanitarian Aid in War-torn Kachin State." Accessed December 1, 2023. https://www.fortifyrights.org/mya -inv-2018-08-30/.

Gartner. n.d. "Web 3.0." Accessed December 29, 2022. https://www.gartner.com/en/ information-technology/glossary/web3.

Godsil, Jillian. 2023. "Whatever Happened to EOS? Community Shoots for Unlikely Comeback." *Cointelegraph*, April 27, 2023. https://cointelegraph.com/magazine/wha tever-happened-eos-community-aims-grassroots-comeback/#:~:text=The%20exact% 20reasons%20EOS%20didn,on%20developments%20of%20its%20own.

Gitcoin. 2023. Accessed December 16, 2023. https://www.gitcoin.co/.

Graeber, David. 2004. *Fragments of an Anarchist Anthropology.* Chicago: Prickly Paradigm Press.

Graeber, David. 2018. Twitter Post. April 30, 2018, 12:27 PM. https://twitter.com/da vidgraeber/status/990857460176089088?lang=en.

Holmes, Oliver. 2017. "Myanmar Blocks All UN Aid to Civilians at Heart of Rohin-gya Crisis." *The Guardian*, September 4, 2017. https://www.theguardian.com/world/ 2017/sep/04/myanmar-blocks-all-un-aid-to-civilians-at-heart-of-rohingya-crisis.

Human Rights Watch. 2021. "Myanmar: Junta Blocks Lifesaving Aid." *Human Rights Watch*, December 13, 2021. https://www.hrw.org/news/2021/12/13/myanmar-junta -blocks-lifesaving-aid.

Hussein, Fatima. 2023. "Founders of Crypto Mixer Arrested, Sanctioned After U.S. Cracks Down on Tornado Cash." *CTV News.* Published August 23, 2023. Updated August 23, 2023. https://www.ctvnews.ca/business/founders-of-crypto-mixer-arres ted-sanctioned-after-u-s-cracks-down-on-tornado-cash-1.6531485.

Jarvis, Craig. 2022. "Cypherpunk Ideology: Objectives, Profiles, and Influences (1992– 1998)." *Internet Histories* 6 (3): 315–342. doi:10.1080/24701475.2021.1935547.

King, Sunny, and Scott Nadal. 2012. "PPCoin: Peer-to-Peer Crypto-Currency with Proof-of-Stake." August 19, 2012. https://decred.org/research/king2012.pdf.

Kolektivo. 2023. Accessed January 1, 2023. https://www.kolektivo.cw/.

Ledger Insights. "IDB and Blockchain Company ChromaWay to Build Land Reg-istry." Published January 31, 2023. https://www.ledgerinsights.com/idb-blockchain-p roperty-registry-chromaway/.

"Legal Restrictions on Cryptography." *O'Reilly.* Accessed December 1, 2023. https:// www.oreilly.com/library/view/web-security-privacy/0596000456/ch04s04.html.

Liu, Alec. 2014. "Turning Five: A Timeline of Bitcoin's Greatest Milestones." *VICE*, January 5, 2014. https://www.vice.com/en/article/kbzq99/turning-five-a-timeli ne-of-bitcoins-greatest-milestones.

Malinowski, Bronislaw. 1922. *Argonauts of the Western Pacific: An Account of Native Enterprise and Adventure in the Archipelagoes of Melanesian New Guinea.* London: Routledge & Kegan Paul.

Maurer, Bill. 2005. *Mutual Life, Limited: Islamic Banking, Alternative Currencies, Lateral Reason.* Princeton University Press. http://www.jstor.org/stable/j.ctt7sj0p.

Mauss, Marcel. 2011. *The Gift: Forms and Functions of Exchange in Archaic Societies.* Chicago: University of Chicago Press.

McKay, Melyn, and Iselin Frydenlund. 2022. "Buddhist 'Radicalism': A Vehicle for Female Empowerment?" In: *Laughter, Creativity, and Perseverance: Female Agency in Buddhism and Hinduism*, edited by Ute Hüsken, pp. 94–119. Oxford University Press. https://doi.org/10.1093/oso/9780197603727.003.0005.

Medium. 2019. "The First Ever DAO in Curaçao: Curadao." July 8, 2019. https://m edium.com/caribbean-blockchain-network/the-first-ever-dao-in-cura%C3%A7ao-cura dao-da7d34e03267.

Mennecke, Martin, and Ellen E. Stensrud. 2021. "The Failure of the International Community to Apply R2P and Atrocity Prevention in Myanmar." *Global Responsibility to Protect* 13 (2–3): 111–130. https://doi.org/10.1163/1875-984X-13020013.

Morucci, Mick. 2023. "Why Anthropologists Are More Interested in Bitcoin Than Economists." *Bitcoin Magazine*. Updated April 25, 2023. Original publication May 9, 2021. https://bitcoinmagazine.com/culture/anthropologists-are-interested-in-bitcoin.

"Myanmar Central Bank Limits ATM Transactions, Account Withdrawals." *The Irrawaddy*. March 1, 2021. https://www.irrawaddy.com/news/burma/myanmar-centra l-bank-limits-atm-transactions-account-withdrawals.html.

Nakamoto, Satoshi. 2008. "Bitcoin: A Peer-to-Peer Electronic Cash System." \t "_blank"http://dx.doi.org/10.2139/ssrn.3440802.

Oxfam. 2023. "Richest 1% Bag Nearly Twice as Much Wealth as the Rest of the World Put Together Over the Past Two Years." January 16, 2023. https://www. oxfam.org/en/press-releases/richest-1-bag-nearly-twice-much-wealth-rest-world-p ut-together-over-past-two-years#:~:text=The%20report%20shows%20that%20while, December%202019%20and%20December%202021.

"Ouroboros - Cardano." *Cardano*. Accessed December 1, 2023. https://cardano.org/ ouroboros/.

Reitman, Rainey. 2021. "Cryptocurrency Surveillance Provision Buried in Infrastructure Bill Is a Disaster for Digital Privacy." *Electronic Frontier Foundation (EFF)*, August 2, 2021. https://www.eff.org/deeplinks/2021/08/cryptocurrency-surveillance-provision-buried-infrastructure-bill-disaster-digital.

Reuters. 2021. "Myanmar Currency Drops 60% in Weeks as Economy Tanks Since February Coup." September 29, 2021. https://www.reuters.com/world/asia-pacific/m yanmars-junta-powerless-currency-drops-60-four-weeks-economy-ta nks-2021-09-29/#:~:text=Myanmar%20currency%20drops%2060%25%20in% 20weeks%20as%20economy%20tanks%20since%20February%20coup,-Reuters& text=Sept%2029%20(Reuters)%20%2D%20Myanmar's,military%20coup%20eight% 20months%20ago.

River Financial. 2022. "How Bitcoin Solves the Double Spend Problem." Accessed December 29, 2022. https://river.com/learn/how-bitcoin-solves-the-double-spend-p roblem.

Rouse, Margaret. 2023. "Web 3.0." *Techopedia*. Last updated June 27, 2023. https:// www.techopedia.com/definition/4923/web-30.

Scott, James C. 1998. *Seeing Like a State: How Certain Schemes to Improve the Human Condition Have Failed*. New Haven, CT: Yale University Press.

Sear, Cynthia. 2022. "On Becoming Unstuck: Teleoaffective Tactics, Thrills, and the Serial Entrants of Promotional Competitions in Australia." *Ethnos* (2022): 1–23. doi:10.1080/00141844.2022.2114517.

"Spring Development Bank Is Open for Business." *Democratic Voice of Burma (DVB)*. Written August 18, 2023. https://english.dvb.no/spring-development-ba nk-is-open-for-business/.

Srinivasan, Balaji. 2022. *The Network State: How To Start a New Country*. Kindle edition. July 4, 2022.

Stackpole, Thomas. 2022. "What Is Web3? Your Guide to (What Could Be) the Future of the Internet." *Harvard Business Review*, May 10, 2022. https://hbr.org/2022/05/what-is-web3.

Strathern, Marilyn. 1990. *The Gender of the Gift (Studies in Melanesian Anthropology)*. First Edition. Los Angeles: University of California Press.

Sullivan, Daniel P., and Priyali Sur. 2023. "Separated and Detained: Will Biden and Modi Discuss the Plight of Rohingya Refugees in India?" *The Wire*, June 21, 2023. https://www.refugeesinternational.org/the-wire-separated-and-detained-will-biden-and-modi-discuss-the-plight-of-rohingya-refugees-in-india/#:~:text=The%20Rohingyas%20are%20a%20persecuted,crossed%20international%20borders%20without%20visas.

Szabo, N. 1996. "Smart Contracts: Building Blocks for Digital Markets." http://www.fon.hum.uva.nl/rob/Courses/InformationInSpeech/CDROM/Literature/LOTwinterschool2006/szabo.best.vwh.net/smart_contracts_2.html.

Szabo, N. 1997. "Formalizing and Securing Relationships on Public Networks." *FIRST MONDAY* (Sept. 1, 1997). http://firstmonday.org/ojs/index.php/fm/article/view/548/469. Tait, Amelia. 2019. "Why Do We Keep Praising Silicon Valley for Reinventing the Wheel?" *The Guardian*, January 14, 2019. https://www.theguardian.com/commentisfree/2019/jan/14/silicon-valley-marketing-student-loan.

"The Co-Inventors." *Immutable Record*. Accessed December 1, 2023. https://immutablerecord.com/the-co-inventors/.

"The Exact Reasons EOS Did Not Deliver on Its Promises Remain Unclear, with Blame Destined to Be Pointed in Multiple Directions: at Its Founders, Who Have since Moved on to Developments of Its Own." *Cointelegraph Magazine*. April 27, 2023. https://cointelegraph.com/magazine/whatever-happened-eos-community-aims-grassroots-comeback/#:~:text=The%20exact%20reasons%20EOS%20didn,on%20developments%20of%20its%20own.

The Times of India. "Every Third Crypto Investor a Woman on Buyucoin Platform." *The Times of India*. Last updated March 7, 2022. https://economictimes.indiatimes.com/markets/cryptocurrency/every-third-crypto-investor-a-woman-on-buyucoin-platform/articleshow/90047933.cms?utm_source=contentofinterest&utm_medium=text&utm_campaign=cppst.

UNICEF. 2018. "Prescrypto: Making Sensitive Clinical Data Portable, Safe, and Private." December 9, 2018. https://www.unicef.org/innovation/stories/prescrypto-making-sensitive-clinical-data-portable-safe-and-private.

Volpicelli, Gian M. 2022. "Why the EOS Blockchain Is Getting Bullish." *Wired*, May 10, 2022. https://www.wired.com/story/eos-bullish-blockone-blockchain/.

Wassmer, Scott. 2022. "Web3: More Than Just The Metaverse." *Forbes Business Council*, September 26, 2022. https://www.forbes.com/sites/forbesbusinesscouncil/2022/09/26/web3-more-than-just-the-metaverse/?sh=504ee12279ab.

"Web Security & Privacy: Chapter 4. Web Security." *O'Reilly*. Accessed December 1, 2023. https://www.oreilly.com/library/view/web-security-privacy/0596000456/ch04s04.html.

Weichselbraun, Anna. 2023. *"What's Governing Web3?"* Presentation given at USC Berggruen Fellows Brown Bag Lecture Series, February 1, 2023.

Weiner, Annette B. 1988. *The Trobrianders of Papua New Guinea*. New York: Holt, Rinehart and Winston.

Williams, Austin K., and Jack Peterson. 2019. "Decentralized Common Knowledge Oracles." *Ledger* 4 (2019): 1–23. https://doi.org/10.5195/ledger.2019.166. https://ledger.pitt.edu/ojs/ledger/article/view/166.

6 Anthropology is Good to Build With

From Ethnographic Imagination to Anthropological Speculation in Robotics

Lora Koycheva

> "The ultimate, hidden truth of the world is that it is something that we make and could just as easily make differently."
> David Graeber, *The Utopia of Rules: On Technology, Stupidity, and the Secret Joys of Bureaucracy*

The development of robotic technologies has been enjoying accelerated growth in recent years. Spurred on by advancements in adjacent, hardware-enabling industries and technologies such as cloud computing, advanced sensors, 5G connectivity, AI, and additive manufacturing, robots hold a host of yet-unfulfilled promises – either to disrupt and upend human lives through displacing humans and creating unemployment havoc or, conversely, to create new infrastructures through which human beings can conceive of, conduct, and experience their lives. The potential application of robots is near endless – from how people consume content to how they overcome distance; from how education and healthcare are delivered to how deliveries are made, and mobility is reconfigured; from how housing is produced to how household energy is produced and managed. Yet this potential is hardly ever imagined, seen, and understood, let alone realized. Whenever robots are mentioned, the mind's eye typically invokes the proverbial evil, metal humanoid of Hollywood blockbusters. Distrust of robots is, by now, a default cultural schemata.

Against this limited imagination and popular distrust of robots, in this chapter I share how they captured my own anthropologist's fancy and why I believe that they are an emerging technology full of promise for society in times of existential peril – a promise too valuable to be left primarily in the hands of business people and engineers. In sharing insights from my journey into the world of robotics through laying the foundations of a venture whose vision is to rebuild the human condition with robots, I want to make a case that anthropologists can – and should – cross the chasm between the ethnographic imagination as we know it and, instead, operationalize it for an anthropological speculation as a form of intervention into the world. My immediate purpose here is not to offer a concrete framework or flesh out the conceptual precedents that allow this. My purpose is to show how I think about speculation as a valuable vector to bring otherwise inaccessible

DOI: 10.4324/9781003458555-6

ethnographic theory into the world of business, innovation, and emerging technologies – and, in my case, to help build robots.

In what follows, I will describe some elements of how I am developing a hybrid practice: One foot in academia and one foot in industry. Such a practice is largely determined by the realities of the technology: Robotics are a demanding, complex, slow, largely research-based field, which can exist either as an innovation endeavor within wealthy corporate multinationals – such as X, the moonshot factory (owned by Google) or the robotics arm of Amazon – or within the safe harbors of academic departments, where extraordinary engineering developments are pursued for the sake of scholarly research without much thought, opportunity, or indeed will to make the jump into becoming products. The relatively few startups that pursue this path independently suffer notoriously high failure rates. How, then, to rebuild the human condition with robots if the robotics sector is itself barely holding together compared to software products, for example? My answer has been to start laying the foundations of an organization at the intersection of academia and industry.

As I delve into a necessarily brief overview of the world of hardware, I invite you to imagine: How would you make the world differently with this emerging technology? How and why I am going about it is what this chapter is focused on.

Unexpected Enchantments: An Anthropologist Walks into a Robotics Lab

I did not discover robotics; robotics found me. This highly complex technology, the cultures that shape it, the people who move it forward, and the worlds it will enact and help shape were never on my radar when I was working on a variety of other topics after I graduated. They were most certainly not even a remote interest when I was starting out my education. In those days, I had the luxury of being able to dabble in many disciplines – from literature and creative writing to broadcast journalism, law, and cultural studies. I was encouraged to pursue anthropology by two of my undergraduate mentors, themselves anthropologists, who thought (generously) that I would make a good anthropologist. The discipline, as it turned out, was not only all those things in which I had previously dabbled taken together but so much more.

Robotics was most certainly not on my radar in graduate school, where my primary research interests were political and urban anthropology, linguistic anthropology, and questions of agency, normalcy, and normativity in Eastern Europe. I obtained my doctorate in 2012, at the height of the socioeconomic fallout of the 2008 global crisis, when the hiring freeze was pervasive in universities worldwide. Still thinking that I would pursue the academic career I was trained for, I was very lucky to be selected for the prestigious Andrew Mellon Postdoctoral Research Fellowship at the School of Slavonic Studies at

University College London on a project about area studies, a largely qualitative interdisciplinary field, remaining relevant with regards to quantitative thinking – what would soon enough become popularly known as Big Data.

That postdoc had limited success. I was miserable in England. I was also disoriented in my work because making the most of multidisciplinary environments is not something that comes intuitively to the majority of anthropology graduates, at least as they were minted back in the 2000s. I was trained as an anthropologist and prepared to work in an anthropology department because that was the hallmark of all top programs in the US back then. Nor was it easy to figure out how to balance research with the administrative load of work so often placed on temporary staff. It took a lot of trial and error before I could realize that such a training is invaluable, but it needs to be vectorized differently. For me, this happened later on during my second (also academic) postdoc while I was researching entrepreneurship cultures within the academic sector (Koycheva, 2022).

There, I was exposed to a myriad of very intelligent people from business and engineering backgrounds, caring very honestly and earnestly about bringing change and improvement in the world but going about it through creating technologies and businesses which would shape the everyday lives of millions – if not hundreds of millions – of people. In doing participant observations with them on how universities can foster more research-based startups, it was becoming clear that if the pathways they have to bringing change are equally uncertain, at least they are more creative. What is more, it was becoming abundantly clear to me that there are opportunities for classic anthropological theories and methods to enable, supercharge – and why not even lead, as I am attempting to achieve with my own venture – the technologies needed for social change. What was equally clear was that the task should not be left to the engineers alone and that getting involved late in the process – as is often the case even in the most successful example of business anthropology – is not only the only way to do this but, more arguably perhaps, even not the best way to do this.

The pivotal moment, when things went click for me, came at a hackathon, when a 20-something software engineer working on a novel humanoid robotic system almost off-handedly mentioned to me that he often wonders if "we are not actually creating the next slave race." Needless to say, a principled speculation like this works quite a bit like catnip to someone trained in political anthropology and interested in innovation, revolution, and social change, so while I continued to research on my original mandate of research-based entrepreneurship and teams, in my free time I also started reading a lot more on the hardware technology itself so that I could understand it better on its own terms.

What soon became apparent was the most fascinating world of building next generation machines which has been poorly understood in the popular imagination and discourse around their building and implications. It also became apparent that the potential of robotic technology is often hampered by dominant market logic and innovation paradigms, classically rooted in the problem-solution dyads, which stipulate that venture capital funds products which solve problems and do so fast and at scale. This crowds the innovation space with incrementally innovative products which, despite their profitability, do not actually address fundamental, existential areas of the human condition, all of which are very often infrastructural in nature and requiring a radical imagination. I was struck by the fact that robots could – if only enabled and built with an anthropology-first approach rather than technology-first approach– "make the world differently," in the immortal insight of David Graeber (2015) – and very radically so. Therefore, I did what anthropologists do for a living: I had many curious, honest "help-me-understand" conversations with robotics engineers about how they see their work, their ideals, what they care for, and why they chose hardware in the first place. This was not a formal kind of ethnography. It was an ethnographer making sense of a new world not out of a scientific interest but of an existential one.

It has been through the influence of the profound, stimulating intellectual friendships with roboticists that my journey towards founding an initiative in this technological space was slowly but surely being shaped. I was soon very lucky to have the help of one of them in being not only my partner in thinking and dreaming about how such an initiative would take shape but in challenging my thinking, encouraging me to pursue it by making introductions and working with me on initial founding documents (the dreaded pitch decks); and helping me navigate the transitory spaces of thinking like a scholar but acting like a founder. Eventually, we articulated a foundational document: Part white paper, part manifesto. The executive summary read as follows:

> Robotics technology is proliferating exponentially, driven by advances in adjacent enabling technologies, such as 3D printing, sensors technologies, cloud computing, and 5G.
>
> Cultural adaptation to such cyber-physical systems has been slower, fragmented, and heterogeneous, given that cultural understandings and popular attitudes vary and are a function of preexisting underlying cultural principles and mora. Although there exist initiatives which are focused on the future, very few exist which focus on robotics specifically as one of the exponential technologies which are most resisted for very different cultural reasons across societies. These initiatives are also very limited in scope and focus either on a specific contextual application (robots for work in factories) or a philosophical dimension (ethics of robotics). Combined together, these two existing dynamics spell out a lack of sociocultural framework to keep thinking and implementing robotics from society's perspective, and this prevents a holistic view on a topic in which impact can only be seen in retrospect but not worked towards purposefully in an applied manner. It also allows impact to become solely the sometimes purposeful, sometimes incidental, but always fragmented and uncoordinated by-product of the commercial

realities that shape robotics companies. At the same time, as human societies are going through epochal times of collective ecological, economic, biotic, and ideational crises, questions of whether and how we can build, steer, and harness the potential of technology for the continuous survival and thriving of the species in an advanced equitable and meaningful manner loom large. Climate change and justice, whether social, intergenerational, or economic, loom large as social priorities. Parallax is a new generation of interventional initiative, co-founded by a social and business anthropologist and a roboticist and CEO, as an answer to these hitherto poorly integrated global phenomena. It aims to change how we view the role of robots and robotics in the world; to enable the better building and deployment of robotics businesses with a view of the social and the cultural impact in mind; and to harness the power of existing and emergent robotics technologies for the future of humans.

Polyfocal and multi-level and built on participation-first principles, Parallax's vision is to prepare society for living with, and eventually as, robots through shifting our collective thinking away from the "robots-as-tools" paradigm towards a more systemic and holistic view of "robotics-as-paradigm," thus creating value for society and business value for robotics companies.

We did a very quiet and limited launch of our concept to potential allies from both the robotics and the social sciences and design worlds. The roboticists were intrigued, and some loved it. The rest dismissed it as pie in the sky largely because they thought it too ambitious – feedback which we ourselves decided to dismiss. This is how, in April of 2021, Parallax (as *Robots, actually!* was then called) took its first step. Since then, the initiative died several times, but returned to life again and again, evolving as it survived: An ideal and a work of conviction too hard to ignore, despite a near-biblical list of difficulties. At present, *Robots, actually!* – although not yet public facing – is actively working towards funding several main areas of interest and piloting a number of programs through creative, research, and business partnerships across three main domains. *Work with a Robot* aims to intervene into what the future of work will look like, in working with and alongside robotics technologies. *Green like a Robot* aims to intervene into how robotic technology can help mitigate climate change effects. *The Gender of the Robot* explores questions of transhumanist import and focuses specifically on embodied humanoid robotics (such as bionics). All the programs leverage the wealth of anthropological insight about life forms and meaning. In other words, *Robots, actually!* is not only "speaking for the social" (Knox & John, 2022) but is a moonshot for the social: Anthropology-first but powered by robotics and based on supercharging robotic development through offering an alternative innovation model for hardware in society.

To sum up, if I had stumbled on this technology by chance, concluding that this can be where my life's work should be located was a combination of both realization and deliberation. Like most anthropologists, I have an idealistic streak about the world, and I would like to change it for the better. Unlike most anthropologists, and perhaps precisely because I started as an ethnographer of political and social change in the (post)socialist sphere, the sphere of my own childhood, I do not equate this impetus with the nearly automatic anti-capitalist Marxist critique of the status quo which often characterizes significant parts of anthropological work. I became disenchanted with politics very quickly, and my first realization was that if I wanted my work as an anthropologist to benefit humanity, it would not be through politics and politically informed activism but through products creating benefit at scale.

The four initial drivers behind *Robots, actually!* therefore are as follows. 1. There are increasing existential risks to societies, especially climate change 2. The answer to such risks cannot be left in the hands of market logic alone in dictating how robots are made. 3. The response to such existential changes is necessarily infrastructural – and as far as technology can play a part in infrastructure, robotics will have the biggest impact and holds the biggest promise because of the robots' versatility. 4. For me personally, as a political anthropologist, politics is too slow in making a change. So, if I wanted to make a change, I had to go into product. To that, as of late 2022 and early 2023, the leaps made by various iterations of AI – from predictive to generative – will supercharge the otherwise painstakingly slow development of embodied robots. Against this backdrop, to paraphrase a favorite of my Marxist political anthropologist colleagues, "what is to be done?" if one is an anthropologist?

What Is to be Done? But First, a Message on Theory – and the Ethnographic Imagination

Theory takes pride of place in anthropology – the very heart of the anthropological enterprise, and it continues to be the central objective of the discipline and the training of its specialists. What is important for my purposes here is also that it is in many ways indelible from, and co-terminous with, the ethnographic imagination. "At its core, anthropology demands an imaginative leap by comparatively challenging the naturalness of one's own cultural world," noted Catherine Trundle (quoted in Gibson, 2014, 3). Similarly, in a masterful rereading of major anthropological staples, such as Malinowski and Weber, Huon Wardle asserts that the work of anthropology is that of the anthropological imagination in that "the ability to recognize the lives of others as on a par with my own is an imaginative ability" (2015, 291). In that sense, making anthropological theory is an endeavor of the imagination, and anthropology is a fundamentally creative practice.

But anthropologists need to transition from being the makers *of* theory – "How does the way we practice ethnography inform theory-making?" recently asked the incoming editors of HAU (Ferme, Costa, & Durham, 2019, 8) – to being makers *with* theory. "We do not beat upon, or beat up on, composers or painters or sculptors to declare their theories before we allow them to proceed with their works," wryly notes Harry Wolcott in discussing the art of conceptualizing in anthropological fieldwork (2005, 171). What good is theory for in the world from which it originates? The need to make this switch has largely been with me, implicitly and explicitly, in all that I do for my venture. I remain committed to demonstrate by example to non-anthropologists that "there is nothing as practical as a good theory" (Greenword & Lewin 1998, 4, quoted in Yorks, 2005) and to inspire anthropologists that the "theory-practice apartheid" (Baba, 2005) was always a shackle of our own choosing which is as limiting as it is illusionary.

If theory is the purpose of ethnography and anthropology, then it is precisely theory – which I consider to be equivalent to the ethnographic imagination – that needs to be re-evaluated and re-purposed in the ways that anthropology approaches emerging technologies in novel ways that hold not only explanatory but also transformational and interventional potential. In this and the next sections, therefore, I briefly overview how anthropological theory currently lives in the world of robotics (very much in the spirit of the ethnographic imagination) and how reworking it in a speculative vein can open up new levels of engagement with both business and robotics.

The Robot in the Ethnographic Imagination and Engineering Practice

As far as being emergent, robots are perhaps the oldest and longest-in-the-making emerging technology. As an idea, automatons have captured the human imagination for millennia (Mayor, 2018; see also Riskin, 2016; Wood, 2003). Famously, and perhaps predictably, Leonardo DaVinci also tried his hand at robotics (Rosheim, 2006). What we commonly refer to – and imagine as – robots today is largely imprinted on the idea of the mechanical slave race of Czech playwright Karel Capek's 1920 play *R.U.R.*, which quickly toured the world and put robots into the limelight in the UK, the USA, and Japan, among others (Robertson, 2018). Robots – and the field of robotics as a multidisciplinary endeavor involving insights and cross-functional teams of software, mechanical, and electrical engineers, designers, and the rare social scientist – are more than the popular "tin man" trope. In fact, just like anthropology, robotics is often popularly misunderstood, very complex, and indeed slow to deliver on its final product. In what follows, necessarily cursory due to the space constraints of a single chapter, I will try to give a bird's eye overview of both robotics and the way ethnography has approached this fascinating and often terrifying technology. The section that follows will go into a little bit further detail of one of our programs – Green Like a Robot – and discuss one specific case: Robots in forest fire prevention and mitigation.

Anthropology in and of Robotics in 2023

To be sure, anthropology – with its propensity to make an object of study out of the most ordinary and extraordinary objects alike – has not missed the opportunity to engage robotics and mechatronic engineering. Roughly two main modes of engagement can be immediately recognized.

The first one is through tracing how ethnography or (more often than not) – to channel Tim Ingold (2014) – what passes for ethnography in engineering contexts, informs UX research on human-robot interaction, from system development to deployment in specific contexts such as the hospital and elderly care sector, in households, and, more rarely, in public environments. A cursory look at one of the most prestigious conferences on robotic development, the ACE/IEEE International Conference on Human-Robot Interaction, might reassure that ethnography – as a method, if not as a more-than-a-method ethos of research and being in the world – is alive and well in engineering and consumer product development. Vacuum cleaners (e.g. Fink et al., 2013; Forlizzi, 2007) and elderly care robots (e.g. Sabelli et al., 2011) are only some of the examples of work which has tapped into the ethnographic repertoire in validating various aspects of robotic systems.

For the more academically and theoretically inclined, the anthropological treatment of robots and automation will not have gone unnoticed in paradigmatic works which have redefined how to think about machines in social and cultural terms, such as that of Donna Haraway's (1991) paradigmatic thought. Sarah Pink and her collaborators at the Monash Emerging Technologies Lab have mounted a prolific and significant body of scholarship which sits at the intersection of applied and theoretical anthropology in innovating with method and in advancing the ethnographic study of human-machine worlds (e.g. Pink, 2022a; Pink, 2022b).

Careful ethnographies of the ways in which robots come to be and become embedded in the social and cultural fabric of societies, are richly detailed and carefully theorized in the work of Kathleen Richardson (2015; 2018), Jennifer Robertson (2018), and more recently James Wright (2023). Those accounts masterfully deploy the classic ethnographic scrutiny and critique to examine the robot as a social and cultural phenomenon in various contexts – from robotics labs in the UK to elderly care facilities in Japan.

However, despite being paradigmatically attentive and detail-oriented, such ethnographic imagination has been far outpaced by the engineering imagination – and its shorter path to action and to building machines. As a result, anthropology is yet to fully capture creatively the vast spectrum of the kinds of robots which exist and are about to change how we experience social, natural, and cultural realities, as well as to establish a position in robotics as having more to offer than simply one method of the many available to validate a system or a part thereof.

The State of the Art in Robotics in 2023

Although it is notoriously difficult to define what a robot is, and even roboticists disagree and even resist a single definition (Darling, 2021; Robertson, 2018), such systems, as I already suggested, come in various shapes and sizes; and for various domains and purposes. The most famous are the ones of Hollywood blockbusters and recent scandals: Humanoids and autonomous vehicles. Humanoids are perhaps the easiest to envisage whenever the word robot is spoken, not only because of early modern efforts to create a mechanical man – such as in DaVinci's knight – but also especially due to Hollywood blockbusters, such as *Ex-Machina* or *M3gan*. Contemporary real-life humanoids abound – and are, importantly for the classic ethnographic imagination – female for the most part. Ameca, Nadine, Sophia to name just a few, are easily recognized the world over as mechanical reproductions of various forms and ideas of womanhood – an element of robotics and smart machines carefully explained by, for example, Kathleen Richardson and Charlotta Odlind (2022) in their work on sex robots. Similarly, a strong critique was recently expanded to include the feminization of ostensibly subservient smart home machines (also femininely named, like Amazon's Alexa) by Yolande Strengers and Jenny Kennedy (2021).

In turn, autonomously driven cars will be popular from the many ways in which various companies have attempted (and largely failed) to bring them into existence, much to the social platform-enabled *Schadenfreude* of commentators with largely social scientific backgrounds (often anthropologists). Unlike with the humanoids, self-driving cars have already become the center of attention and regulatory action through the high-profile accidents they have been involved in.

Beyond these well-known examples, however, robotic technology proliferates in many shapes and forms, somewhat too broadly grouped by the IRF as either industrial or service robots. The more granular reality is that robots can be seen in any domain which can accommodate a machine of any kind – in the confines of private homes and gardens; in hospitals and care facilities; in farms and in warehouses; on conveyor belts; and in entertainment.

Manufacturing robots – such as arms or forklifts – are the most widely deployed worldwide, and some of the oldest robotic technology rolled out on factory floors, where they were meant to take over the proverbial dirty, dangerous, and dull jobs – as most industrial robots generally are not meant to come in contact with humans. Cobots – short for collaborative robots, designed specifically for human-robot interaction in industrial contexts without the need for a protective cage around them – are being deployed with increasing frequency. Mobility and automobility are being increasingly robotized or built as a robot from scratch. In the delivery sector, both wheeled bots and drones are being tested in various national contexts to make deliveries from pizza to plasma. Autonomously driving cars and trucks remain a moonshot, although one which has been aggressively capitalized in the late 2010s, only to lead to a number of high-profile bankruptcies. Humanoids – robots which have a human shape and form and often visage and characteristics – once the most popular in public and least capitalized robotic space, are making a comeback with well publicized funding rounds in 2023 in the pursuit of a general-purpose humanoid – a robot which can be deployed for a wide variety of tasks. Teleoperated robotic systems – whether morphologically in the human form or more readily resembling machines – allow the manipulation of the robot by a human agent for various purposes from a great distance, often thousands of miles away. Medical robots perform surgeries, swim in nano-form in the human body, or provide bionic replacements and exoskeletal support.

It is worth mentioning robots are very biomimetic in their designs. They are inspired from various natural life forms – the human arm; the swarm of the bee; the wing of the bird; the slithering of the snake; and the gait of the quadrupeds are only some of the ways in which what constitutes a robotic technology is far more than the banality of the *Terminator* and *M3gan* variety.

Finally, lest this non-exhaustive list of kinds of robots might seem like the robot revolution is upon us already, it is worth taking the perspective which anthropologists are not too eager to take. A quantitative examination of the state of robotics in the world in 2023 will show that there are roughly 3.5 million robots currently deployed – most of them industrial and more than half of them in China, according to the most recent report of the International Robotics Federation (2022). This is a fraction compared to the numbers of the rest of the machines currently in circulation, such as washing machines, laptops, cell phones, and cars (Hostettler, 2023). If ideationally, there is nothing emergent about the robot, quantitatively, the robot is yet to fully emerge as a normalized technology.

The point here is very much one driver behind *Robots, actually!*. The applicability of robots in such a plethora of contexts and for so many purposes is underpinned by their morphological versatility – their many shapes and forms, as seen in the non-exhaustive examples I have mentioned. What is more, with the latest developments within AI, although still largely speculative as of 2023, this applicability – and consequently market opportunities and, therefore, social impact – will increase steadily and quickly. For anthropology to make substantial early inroads into this rapidly evolving and growing industry, it would have to avail itself to more than the trademark descriptive, explanatory tools it has at its disposal. It will have to posture itself and its entire apparatus in an appropriately speculative and open-to-experimentation, boldly imaginative way.

Green Like a Robot: From Ethnographic Imagination to Building with Anthropological Speculation

What if…?

Consider the automobile. In the relatively short time it has been around as an invention, the impact it has had on the lives of the overwhelming majority of people on the planet has been fundamental. It has melded itself to how notions of masculinity around the world are experienced (e.g. Morgan, 2009). It can become a symbol not only of nations and countries but also of entire political economic systems (e.g., Berdahl, 2000). More significantly still, the car has the power to create what Catherine Lutz has termed "the car-made city" (e.g. Lutz, 2014). For a complex mechatronic technology that emerged and scaled early in the 20th century, the car has done so much more than help to get from A to B faster. The car has, unarguably, shaped the modern world as much as geopolitics and culture have, in what Daniel Miller has called "the humanity of the car" (Miller, 2001).

Now consider all the grievances which are popularly held against cars today, especially where cities are concerned. Most cars continue to be major polluters. They create noise and congestion – which pollutes even more. They take up precious urban space because they are typically big. They require parking lots, which take up even more space – the space for parks, playgrounds, housing. When improperly used, they kill people, and sometimes, they do so when properly used. Mention a major urban blight, and chances are, one way or another, you can link it to the pervasiveness of automobiles. Many large urban centers are now looking for innovative solutions to mitigate against the effects of automobility – from banning cars altogether from large swaths of city centers, like in Berlin,[1] to the polemic 15-minute city model – which Paris recently has looked into adopting.[2] Despite all their harms, however, cars will be very difficult (not to say impossible) to get rid of – especially given how embedded the automobile industry is in economies and politics.

I believe that robots will be in the next century (if not in this one already) what cars have been in the 20th century. I make the above equivalence often when I pitch, formally or informally, *Robots, actually!* to various potential partners, collaborators, and funders. I often ask my interlocutors in those instances, "if humanity knew then about cars, what we know now is their effects on our lives, how would we go about building cars and the worlds which cars create?" I never get a concrete answer – although, importantly, nobody has ever argued to ban cars in the same way the bankruptcy of robotic companies is met with *Schadenfreude* in the public space.

In my current work to leverage in the world of robotics the breadth and wealth of ethnographic accounts and theories about the myriads of iterations of human experience, that question (although in part unfair) is already a step towards shifting from the ethnographic imagination towards building with anthropologically-informed speculation. One such area of work which I am currently developing is Green Like a Robot – a platform for exploring how robots can be used in creating resilient communities and mitigate the effects of climate change. In what follows, I will briefly introduce the platform, a pilot project currently in early stages of development, what anthropological theories can be relevant for it, and above all – how I approach them in a speculative vein.

Green Like a Robot: Robots for Climate Change Mitigation

Green Like a Robot is conceptualized as a platform within *Robots, actually!* and is dedicated to championing, developing, and experimenting with robots which help mitigate against climate change, regardless of its contexts. It aims to connect various stakeholders in the research, development, and exploration of hardware solutions to climate change. The creation of this platform draws inspiration and energy from the confluence of several aspects of contemporary approaches to climate change and makes use of the ethnographic imagination by putting it to speculative use in several ways.

Where climate change is concerned, the overwhelming focus of effort of governing bodies, political actors, as well as various initiatives has been to focus on regulation and promoting behavioral change. Emerging technologies hold a lot of promise within the space, but they are yet to become the go-to solution at scale, including – but perhaps especially so – robotics.

Cyber-physical systems and their morphological diversity of form and function can lend itself productively to a number of applications for climate change detection, management, and intervention. There are robots harnessing the energy of ocean waves and cleaning riverbeds. Robots are increasingly playing a role in waste management collection and recycling plants. They are also deployed to regulate traffic in large cities as a means of air pollution management.

At first, it might seem counterintuitive for anthropology to intervene, outside of the ways in which I have already alluded to – via UX or acting as a critical "checks and balances agent" to business and engineering via its trademark critique – and the critical ethnographic imagination. The impetus for this program ignited when I read Michael Taussig's *Mastery of Non-Mastery in the Age of Meltdown* (2020). In discussing humanity's mimetic appropriations of nature, he asks, "But if a bird's wing is a gift to civilization, what does the bird get in return?" (Taussig, 2020, 6). This struck a chord with me. So many robots are bio-inspired – either bio-mimetic or bio-plausible, in that they crawl, fly, swarm. One of the most original existing propositions on how we can start adapting to living with robots is Kate Darling's call to look at our relationships with animals (2021). Yet this pithy and characteristically anthropological question in that it thinks about equivalences and relations (Strathern, 2020) is the one which nobody (else) is asking – and complicates Darling's suggestion in that humans have not been good to other species. This inspired me to think: What if there is a way for the bird – and everything it stands for in Taussig's question – to get something back in return? Why would anyone give back robots, for that matter? What role would anthropological theory play in this, from behind the walled garden of its complexity?

Software continues to dominate the currently available technological answers to how to mitigate climate change, largely due to the well-known venture capitalist preference of funding software rather than hardware.[3] Such software-based solutions usually revolve around sophisticated data capture, management, and predictive analytics for automated and semi-automated decision making in domains as varied as regulating traffic to industrial carbon accounting. These are already important advancements towards helping the world cope with climate change.

My interpretation of the situation is, however, slightly different – and very much informed by the recent "infrastructural" (e.g. Furlong, 2014; Larkin, 2008, 2013; Anand, Gupta, & Appel, 2018; Hetherington, 2019) turn in anthropology. Specifically, a foundational posit in Green Like a Robot is that climate change is an infrastructural condition – where infrastructure is composed of a plethora of elements which "articulate social relations to make a variety of social, institutional, and material things (im)possible" (Anand, Gupta, & Appel, 2018, 4; see Larkin for a foundational overview) and indelible from environmental change not only in the sense that "the environment is the infrastructure of infrastructure (and that) carbon is the infrastructure of the infrastructure of carbon" (Heatherington, 2019, 6).

Infrastructure is largely invisible, expensive, complex, mechanical, physical, and material, as well as enmeshed with local and global politics, which often deter from real change and make it difficult to adapt and respond to the uncertainties brought forth by climate change – so complex and large scale that conceptualizing it requires thinking in scenarios, as the reports from IPCC suggest (Lee et al., 2021). It would follow that to properly address and mitigate for such an infrastructural condition, an infrastructural response is necessary – and a complex, mechanical, physical, material responsive system *is* a robot. In this, *Robots, actually!* actually, has a definition of robot.

The present moment in anthropological theory, therefore, informs a lens through which to connect the dots differently on how emerging hardware technologies address climate change through a translation of the most recent ethnographic imaginations of the ruination of the climate and life in such ruins (e.g. Tsing et al., 2017). More fortuitously still, developments in the methodological repertoire of anthropology are supercharging this move to bring ethnographic theory in application (rather than conversation) with engineering and business.

Until very recently, inquiring into the future, let alone intervening in it, would be off-limits for the anthropological method. Yet there has been a gathering tide of methodological advancements in social science and design, without which a platform like Green Like a Robot would not be possible. Anthropology interfacing with design science has been one such advancement, and the work of Sarah Pink (e.g., Pink et al., 2022b), Chris Miller (2018), Keith Murphy (2016), and Wendy Gunn (Gunn, Otto, & Smith, 2013; Gunn & Donovan, 2016) offers a wealth of approaches which can be quickly applied in various hardware experimentations. Also applicable are developments from anticipatory ethnographies (Lindley et al., 2014) and the adoption of prototyping as a method for social scientific inquiry (e.g., O'Connor & Peck, 2017; Corsín Jiménez & Estalella, 2017), especially as pioneered in the open urbanism sphere (e.g., Corsín Jiménez, 2014). From researching emerging worlds (Salazar et al., 2017: Pink, 2022b) and creating lexicons for phenomena "yet-unseen" (e.g., Howe & Pandian, 2020 for the Anthropocene in specific) to establishing radical activist anthropologies as a paradigm for decolonizing design (Escobar, 2018; Tunstall, 2020) there has never been a better, and indeed easier, time to create a project of speculative import and with an interventionist, applied potential of making the Anthropocene live-able – for human and non-human species and agents alike. What is more, the exceptional wealth of insights from urban and environmental anthropology provides a contextualized understanding of the structures and processes of living in urban and suburban environments.

Finally, the question to ask here is: Ok, but how – how does one turn the imagination into speculation? The conceptual and methodological precedents of this are the subject of ongoing work (Koycheva, n.d.) For the purposes of this chapter however, there are four elements I want to suggest as a teaser, especially as they relate to founding one's own venture.

Turning the ethnographic imagination into an applied anthropological spec-ulation requires several re-orientations in the anthropologist's thinking. One requirement is a shift in temporal thinking. It is important for the discipline to start normalizing a forward-looking outlook which asks questions about how the phenomena it studies are expected to develop next and to what end. Tra-ditional anthropological education demands of anthropologists to answer a "So what?" question. To that, it needs to start adding "and what next?".

Because of that, and even more importantly, a second shift required is to think about phenomena not only as objects to be theorized but as opportu-nities to be developed – as full of prospective value for someone, something, somewhere. For me, this is one of the most speculative and applied moves anthropology has not yet made.

Finally, a third shift should be a re-balancing of our commitments to ethics versus that prospective value – what Matt Artz has recently called "the value-ethics paradox" in anthropology (Artz, 2023). No single object is ever purely good. One way or another, anthropology will have to come to terms that, despite ethical risks and problems with emerging technologies, they can and regularly do offer a lot of value to consumers and users of these products.

So, What can a Bird Get in Return? The Cyborg Forests of the RoBosco Project

I want to exemplify this kind of thinking with a short snapshot of a pilot project which is currently in its initial stages of development. The RoBosco project aims to create robots for forest fire prevention by positing that forests are cyborg in themselves, and their cyborg properties should be enabled in making them resilient to forest fires. The problem of forest fires has, in recent years, become front and center in the news in many areas of the world. From Australia to California, from Siberia to Spain and Greece – in the past few years, we have seen the world, quite literally, burning. The phenomenon is expected to increase, with the UN predicting that the incidence of forest fires could rise by 50% by 2100,[4] with governments poorly prepared to deal with this infrastructural issue. Already, the economic losses of recent wildfires are costing hundreds of billions of dollars in the US alone due to insurance pay-outs, job losses, and property damage. What is more, wildfires are caught in a vicious loop of carbon emissions. When forests – the best available infra-structure the world has for storing and cleaning carbon dioxide – burn, they release all the stored carbon into the atmosphere, in addition to producing more carbon through the burn. This is especially the case with the Amazon as well as the boreal forests of the global Arctic.

The strategies for dealing with wildfires are extremely diverse yet increas-ingly inadequate given the scale of the phenomenon. Some come across as near suicidal – methods still practiced in Russia's north and northeast where so-called "smokejumpers" dive directly into the burning woods from air-planes.[5] Others rely on machines: For example, dedicated fleets of aerial vehicles – airplanes and helicopters. These, however, have always had their inefficiencies. High winds sometimes make it impossible for the airplanes to fly, whereas dumping water on fires is a very imprecise and increasingly unsustainable approach in a context of increasing water scarcity. Within the tech space, the response to this "global problem" (in the parlance of innova-tion) has been appropriately diverse. One line of response is to develop soft-ware-based, AI-enabled early-warning sensing technologies. Another has been to develop infrared imaging, which allows firefighters to see through other-wise dim environments. Yet another is to deploy teleoperated robotic systems covered in extreme heat-resistant materials.

The ethnographic imagination would look at this problem space and approach it from a variety of potential angles. It might theorize wildfires as boundary objects (Star & Griesemer, 1989; see also Gluesing 2018 for a business perspective) and look at them in an ANT and STS perspective: Noting, for example, the distributed agencies of human and non-human spe-cies. Biopolitics and governmentality over life and emergency would be an especially fruitful lens – these disasters do not happen outside of local and global regulatory regimes, which directly or indirectly affect how life is gov-erned and stewarded (e.g. Petryna, 2013). Given that the impact of a forest fire continues years after the flames are put out, they can also be seen as anthropocenic hyperobjects, in Timothy Morton's terms (2013) – as phenom-ena of enormous temporal and spatial dimensions which fundamentally defy what a thing is in the first place. Finally, the ontological turn in anthropology, in its push for ethnography beyond the ethnos and the human (Kohn, 2013; Rees, 2018), are also immediately relevant when thinking of burning forests.

The point here, however, is not to do only this and to advance each of these theories. The point of building with these anthropological theories is to go one step further and to ask that "what next will be of value" question to which I alluded above – of value to the birds, of value to the trees, of value to those who live close to forests, and of value also to the insurance companies (among many other potential companies affected). What opportunity does the ontological turn in anthropology spell out for the forest?

The RoBosco project aims to bring the insights of all of these anthropological theories together and to explore how it can decolonize design (Tunstall, 2020; Escobar, 2018) in its most fundamental level by treating Nature like a stakeholder and a user of the technology and not a passive recipient and a resource to be extracted from. A key interest in the project is how it can help design *with* forests, not for forests; how it can treat forests as infrastructure but also leverage cyber-physical systems as an infrastructure which enables faster and more environmentally-attuned responses. It will explore how forest fires can be mitigated if the cyborg potential of the forest is put central in the design process. Key work which will take place in 2024–2026 is to develop an open-access library called "Translating the Anthropocene for Engineers, Innovators, and Funders," in which the otherwise inaccessible thought of the environmental humanities and social sciences will be translated and offered as a toolkit to engineers so they can build with it the next generation of cyber-physical systems. Simply put, engineers will not come to anthropology to read *How Forests Think* (Kohn, 2013). Anthropologists must go to the engineers with a translation. I see such a translation, which would make the critique understandable, as the first step in establishing the ethical creation of robots.

The Ethics of Robots

The topic of ethics in robotics – whether software or hardware – is profound and by now also prolific enough to merit not only its own chapter but a full-blown book. The failings, failures, and scandals involving robotics technologies have been well publicized in the popular media and have been also well discussed in scholarly and in applied circles. Within the realm of mobility, autonomously driven vehicles have resulted in collisions and death.[6] Vacuum cleaners have been known to collect swaths of audio-visual data without a person's consent.[7] Drones have been known to shut down airports.[8]

Beyond those contexts, hardware is also being actively developed for military applications, which open up a host of questions and concerns at the interface of the government's ability to enforce law and order internally and protect the body politic externally. There have already been numerous debates around the well-publicized attempts to weaponize robot dogs[9] and using robots to police and patrol in certain cases. In the increasingly globally hostile geopolitical climate since 2022, dual use funding – investing into technology which can serve both civilian and military purposes and application – is becoming more frequent and sought after.[10] For a cash-strapped, chronically underfunded sector in comparison to software, the implications for how hardware will be developed in the future loom large and difficult to answer. Most roboticists I know have always been adamantly against collaborating with the military, yet how this will change in the future is an educated (and, likely, pessimistic) guess.

Additionally, the making of robots continues to be a dismally male domain, and, in the Anglophone-dominated Occident at least, remains also dismally white. Once again, here, there are important initiatives that are making strides into redressing this, such as DAIR, but they tend to be on the scholarly or activist side, and – until 2023 at least – the focus falls on artificial intelligence and large language models (LLMs).

My take on all this is this. Robots are here to stay – and proliferate (I am, in fact, committed to their proliferation). The conditions under which that will happen is entirely within our own collective making. Robots will have their inconveniences, downsides, and dangers – just like any other product on the market. Yet if humans are to adapt their lives to them and accommodate them, then the benefits of robots had better be worth the detriments – and then some! The next generation of hardware must be built better. To that end, my own way of doing ethics has been profoundly anthropological. I am trying to build new relations – between humans and machines; between nature and machines; between humans and nature; and humans and humans through machines. In this, the founding *Robots, actually!* is an effort in applied anthropological ethics.

Do! Advice for Getting into Robotics

When I read advice of venture worn-out founders, even of organizations less complex than *Robots, actually!*, it often starts with "Don't do it." I beg to differ. By all means, do it! This is not to say it will be easy, sane, healthy, or successful (likely all four to the contrary). The reality is that the work is slow, difficult, and often misunderstood.

Building a hybrid practice, especially in hardware, is not for the faint hearted, and I should acknowledge the political economic realities of this kind of pathway straight away. If you are a sole breadwinner or a single parent, this kind of risk is probably very difficult to assume in practical terms, even if conceivable. There are large (and frequent) periods of precarious employment and lack of finances. Due to the nature of the work – especially the speed and complexity of aligning so many stakeholders and integrating a wide variety of opinions, frameworks, and organizational remits and realities – the advisable thing to do is to start your journey in this as a parallel project to something more immediately economically viable. Pursuing a hybrid practice is a logical and advisable thing to do. All this said, should robots appear appealing to venture into, in whatever capacity, then the advice I have is this.

First off, when you get lost, it's ok – so make the most of it. Throughout the years, what has struck me is that anthropology has forgotten its art of getting lost. Much earlier in the discipline's history, to be an anthropologist often arose from situations of being lost quite literally and of coming in contact with the unfamiliar. As the world kept getting more and more familiar, anthropology had to work to, as the beloved adage goes, "make the familiar unfamiliar," and it has excelled at this. This is an important skill and an attitude which will help you along the way, but I would urge you to not forget how to get lost – in people, ideas, topics.

One such way of getting lost is to not be afraid to "go native." This is an example of anthropology's self-inflicted hyperventilation which I never quite understood. This is a strange idea – moralistic at best and epistemologically suspect at worst. There is no one unitary way of "being native," so how could anyone else "go native" at all? Then, "being native" is a moving signpost because change happens to everyone, everywhere. Finally, it's an accusation which assumes not only a lack of reflexivity on the part of the anthropologist (the irony!) but also, above all, a lack of rational choice. It is very easy to say that I have gone native in the world of robotics which I started studying for different reasons. This misses the point that I chose the world of robotics and that I choose it every single day, despite the significant hurdles of being a social scientist, female, foreign, largely seen as academic, not MBA educated. I choose it for very specific rational reasons and not because I naïvely fell victim to its charms and could not somehow self-reflect.

The second way of getting lost is in exploring the world of technological expertise of the emerging technology. If you want to do this, do not read only the anthropology journals and go only to the ethnography conferences (however applied). Go to the engineering events and the business conferences. Read the engineering journals, and try to build an understanding of the engineering at face value and on its own, and not through the lens of thinking about it like an anthropologist. This comes anyway. But getting lost means paying heightened attention, and that is a crucial first step. To give an example from my own desk, I read not only "Robots Won't Save Japan" (Wright, 2023) I read also "Wax-actuated adaptive tiles radically cut heating and cooling energy."[11] I try to learn the proverbial language.

In that vein is my second piece of advice: Learn to code – but read ethnographies. While you have to get lost enough in the tech logic, tech practice, and tech speak, you cannot afford to get unmoored from what makes the discipline what it is. Nor should you dismiss classical ethnographic work as useless. I was flabbergasted at an event when I heard a business anthropologist argue that there is no need to read Claude Levy-Strauss if you want to be an anthropologist today and that you have to be able to code. Yet code is code, whether in symbols or bits and to sacrifice ethnography to coding is as short-sighted as not equipping code with ethnography and ethnography with code. It's not a question of swapping but a practice of complementarity and recombination.

My third piece of advice is: Do the literal math. Anthropologists pride themselves on understanding complexity, but to grapple with complexity means necessarily grappling with scale, and that means to also learn to think in numbers. I do not mean here of being able to apply mixed methods, although this helps. What I mean is to be calculative about phenomena because technology is dictated largely by market players who think in numbers.

My fourth piece of advice is: Forgive. For all our relativism, anthropologists can often end up being a very uncompromising bunch. The inability to deploy relativism with the people with whom one disagrees is often the paradoxical case with anthropologists. I am still learning – admittedly the hard way – that forgiveness is relativism applied. I am learning to forgive the capitalists for being capitalist and the Marxists for being Marxists. Nor am I keen on changing them. What I am keen on doing is trying to find where they can work together to get stuff done for the betterment of society.

My fifth piece advice is: Your tools are not your destiny, so don't make them out to be so. Recognize and use the heuristics at your disposal – relativism, culture, empathy, ideology, vocabulary, representation, Marxism, constructivism, bias, reflexivity, etc. – for what they are: Tools, each of which has a specific purpose for a specific context, and an appropriateness of use. Be relativist when you have to be and a Marxist when you must. Do not chain your entire thought, work, and journey to a single heuristic once and for all.

And once you do all that, my final advice is: Act. Do! To all the mentorly advice which I carry with me in my career, with which I have peppered this chapter, I wish to add the nagging of my partner in the early days of our collaboration: "Where is your call to action at the end?" he'd say. So, my call to all who read this and who would like to imagine the world differently and with robots: Let's! Email me with your ideas, thoughts, and questions about anthropology and robots at lk@robotsactually.com.

Notes

1 Frearson, 2022.
2 Gongadze & Maassen, 2023.
3 HIIG, 2014.
4 https://www.who.int/health-topics/wildfires#tab=tab_1
5 https://www.nationalgeographic.com/environment/article/russian-smokejumpers
6 https://www.npr.org/2022/06/15/1105252793/nearly-400-car-crashes-in-11-month s-involved-automated-tech-companies-tell-regul
7 https://www.technologyreview.com/2022/12/19/1065306/roomba-irobot-robot-va cuums-artificial-intelligence-training-data-privacy/
8 https://www.euronews.com/2020/03/02/flights-grounded-at-frankfurt-airport-after-drone-activity
9 https://www.theverge.com/2021/10/14/22726111/robot-dogs-with-guns-sword-international-ghost-robotics
10 https://www.euractiv.com/section/defence-and-security/news/embargo-9am-eu-invest ment-fund-launches-e175-risk-investment-programmes-in-defence-start-ups-smes/
11 https://newatlas.com/technology/wax-motor-adaptive-roof-tiles/

Bibliography

Anand, Nikhil, Akhil Gupta, and Hannah Appel, eds. 2018. *The promise of infrastructure*. Durham, NC: Duke University Press.

Artz, Matt. 2023. "Consumer DNA Tests and the Value Ethics Paradox" https://econa nthro.org/publications/the-exchange/consumer-dna-tests-and-the-value-ethics-paradox/. December 7, 2023.

Baba, Marietta. 2005. "To The End Of Theory-Practice 'Apartheid': Encountering The World." In: *Ethnographic Praxis in Industry Conference Proceedings* 2005 (1): pp. 205–217. Oxford, UK: Blackwell Publishing Ltd. https://doi.org/10.1111/j. 1559-8918.2005.tb00023.x. (Appears online in 2009).

Berdahl, Daphne. 2000. "'Go, Trabi, Go!': Reflections on a Car and Its Symbolization over Time." *Anthropology and Humanism* 25 (2): 131–141. https://doi.org/10.1525/a hu.2000.25.2.131.

Corsín Jiménez, Alberto. 2014. "The Right to Infrastructure: A Prototype for Open Source Urbanism." *Environment and Planning D: Society and Space* 32 (2): 342–362. https://doi.org/10.1068/d13077p.

Corsín Jiménez, Alberto, and Adolfo Estalella. 2017. "Ethnography: A Prototype." *Ethnos* 82 (5): 846–866. https://doi.org/10.1080/00141844.2015.1133688.

Darling, Kate. 2021. *The New Breed: How to Think about Robots.* Penguin UK.

Escobar, Arturo. 2018. *Designs for the Pluriverse: Radical Interdependence, Autonomy, and the Making of Worlds.* Durham, NC: Duke University Press.

Ferme, Mariane C., Luiz Costa, and Deborah Durham. 2019. "Future Orientations." *HAU: Journal of Ethnographic Theory* 9 (1): 6–9. https://doi.org/10.1086/704170.

Fink, Julia, Valérie Bauwens, Frédéric Kaplan, and Pierre Dillenbourg. 2013. "Living With a Vacuum Cleaning Robot: A 6-month Ethnographic Study." *International Journal of Social Robotics* 5: 389–408.

Forlizzi, Jodi. 2007. "How Robotic Products become Social Products: An Ethnographic Study of Cleaning in the Home." In: *Proceedings of the ACM/IEEE International Conference on Human-robot Interaction*, pp. 129–136.

Frearson, Amy. 2022. "Berlin Citizens Propose Law to Ban Cars from the City Center." *Dezeen*. Janaury 28, 2022. https://www.dezeen.com/2022/01/28/car-free-berlin-autofrei/.

Furlong, Kathryn. 2014. "STS Beyond the 'modern infrastructure ideal': Extending Theory by Engaging with Infrastructure Challenges in the South." *Technology in Society* 38: 139–147. https://doi.org/10.1016/j.techsoc.2014.04.001.

Gibson, Lorena. 2014. "Guest Editorial: Anthropology and Imagination." *Sites: A Journal of Social Anthropology and Cultural Studies* 11 (1): 3–14. https://doi.org/10. 11157/sites-vol11iss1id275.

Gluesing, Julia C. 2018. "Using Boundary Objects to Facilitate Culture Change and Integrate a Global Top Management Team." *Journal of Business Anthropology* 7 (1): 32–50. https://doi.org/10.22439/jba.v7i1.5491.

Gongadze, Salome and Anne Maassen. 2023. "Paris' Vision for a 15-minute City Sparks a Global Movement." *World Resource Institute Insights.* January 25, 2023. https://www.wri.org/insights/paris-15-minute-city.

Graeber, David. 2015. *The Utopia of Rules: On Technology, Stupidity, and the Secret Joys of Bureaucracy.* London/Brooklyn: Melville House.

Gunn, Wendy, and Jared Donovan, eds. 2016. *Design and Anthropology.* Routledge.

Gunn, Wendy, Ton Otto, and Rachel Charlotte Smith, eds. 2013. *Design Anthropology: Theory and Practice.* Taylor & Francis.

Haraway, Donna. 1991. *Simians, Cyborgs, and Women: The Reinvention of Nature.* Free Association Books.

Hetherington, Kregg, ed. 2018. *Infrastructure, Environment, and Life in the Anthropocene*. Durham, NC: Duke University Press.

Hostettler, Rafael. 2023. *"The Industry to Learn From – And Why."* Blog. https://www.devanthro.com/the-industry-to-learn-from-and-why/ Last accessed January 24, 2024.

Howe, Cymene, and Anand Pandian, eds. 2020. *Anthropocene Unseen: A Lexicon.* Santa Barbara, CA: punctum books.

Ingold, Tim. 2014. "That's Enough about Ethnography!" *HAU: Journal of Ethnographic Theory* 4 (1): 383–395. https://doi.org/10.14318/hau4.1.021.

International Robot Federation. 2022. *World Robotics Industrial Robots Report 2022.* https://ifr.org/downloads/press2018/2022_WR_extended_version.pdf Last accessed January 24.

Knox, Hannah, and Gemma John. 2022. *Speaking for the Social: A Catalog of Methods.* Santa Barbara, CA: punctum books.

Kohn, Eduardo. 2013. *How Forests Think: Toward an Anthropology Beyond the Human.* University of California Press.

Koycheva, Lora. n.d. "Specualtive Anthropology: Concepts, Methods, Theories, and the Way Forward." Working paper.

Koycheva, Lora. 2022. "Of Sciences and Startups: An Anthropological Perspective on Academic Venturing." In: *Anthropology and Entrepreneurship – The Current State of Research and Practice.* Edited by Edward Liebow and Janine Chiappa McKenna. Arlington, VA: American Anthropological Association.

Larkin, Brian. "The politics and poetics of infrastructure." *Annual review of anthropology* 42 (2013): 327–343.

Larkin, Brian. *Signal and noise: Media, infrastructure, and urban culture in Nigeria.* Duke University Press, 2008.

Lee, J.-Y., et al. 2021. "Future Global Climate: Scenario-Based Projections and Near-Term Information". In: *Climate Change 2021: The Physical Science Basis. Contribution of Working Group I to the Sixth Assessment Report of the Intergovernmental Panel on Climate Change* Edited by Masson-Delmotte, V., P. Zhai, A. Pirani, S. L. Connors, C. Péan, S. Berger, N. Caud, Y. Chen, L. Goldfarb, M. I. Gomis, M. Huang, K. Leitzell, E. Lonnoy, J. B. R. Matthews, T. K. Maycock, T. Waterfield, O. Yelekçi, R. Yu, and B. Zhou. pp. 553–672. Cambridge, UK/New York, NY: Cambridge University Press. doi:10.1017/9781009157896.006.

Lindley, Joseph, Dhruv Sharma, and Robert Potts. 2014. "Anticipatory Ethnography: Design Fiction as an Input to Design Ethnography." In: *Ethnographic Praxis in Industry Conference Proceedings,* 2014 (1): 237–253.

Lutz, Catherine. 2014. "Cars and Transport: The Car-Made City." In *A Companion to Urban Anthropology.* Edited by Donald M. Nonini, pp. 142–153.

Mayor, Adrienne. 2018. *Gods and Robots: Myths, Machines, and Ancient Dreams of Technology.* Princeton, NJ: Princeton University Press.

Miller, Christine. 2018. *Design + Anthropology: Converging Pathways in Anthropology and Design.* Routledge.

Miller, Daniel, ed. 2001. *Car Cultures.* Berg.

Morgan, Wendy M. 2009. "Gender on Wheels: Cars as Symbols of American Masculinity." *Semiotics.* Edited by Farouk Y. Seif, 513–520.

Morton, Timothy. 2013. *Hyperobjects: Philosophy and Ecology after the End of the World.* University of Minnesota Press.

Murphy, Keith M. 2016. "Design and Anthropology." *Annual Review of Anthropology* 45: 433–449. https://doi.org/10.1146/annurev-anthro-102215-100224.

O'Connor, Erin, and Peck, Suzanne. 2017. "The Prototype: Problem Work in the Relationship between Designer, Artist, and Gaffer in Glassblowing." In: *Craftwork as Problem Solving: Ethnographic Studies of Design and Making*. Ed. Trevor Marchland. London and New York: Routledge.

Petryna, Adriana. 2013. *Life Exposed: Biological Citizens after Chernobyl*. Princeton University Press.

Pink, Sarah. 2022a. "Trust in Automation." In: *Everyday Automation*, edited by Sarah Pinket al. London: Routledge.

Pink, Sarah. 2022b. "Design Anthropological Filmmaking for Automated Futures." *Qualitative Inquiry* 28 (7): 781–797. https://doi.org/10.1177/10778004221097060.

Pink, Sarah, Kaspar Raats, Thomas Lindgren, Katalin Osz, and Vaike Fors. 2022. "An Interventional Design Anthropology of Emerging Technologies: Working Through an Interdisciplinary Field: Design." In: *The Palgrave Handbook of the Anthropology of Technology*. pp. 183–200. Singapore: Springer Nature.

Pink, Sarah, Minna Ruckenstein, Martin Berg, and Deborah Lupton. 2022. *Everyday Automation: Setting a Research Agenda*. pp. 1–19. Routledge.

Rees, Tobias. 2018. *After Ethnos*. Durham, NC: Duke University Press.

Richardson, Kathleen. 2015. *An Anthropology of Robots and AI: Annihilation Anxiety and Machines*. London: Routledge.

Richardson, Kathleen. 2018. *Challenging Sociality: An Anthropology of Robots, Autism, and Attachment*. Springer.

Richardson, Kathleen, and Charlotta Odlind. 2022. *Man-Made Women: The Sexual Politics of Sex Dolls and Sex Robots.*. Springer.

Riskin, Jessica. 2016. *The Restless Clock: A History of the Centuries-Long Argument over What Makes Living Things Tick*. Chicago: University of Chicago Press.

Robertson, Jennifer. 2018. *Robo Sapiens Japanicus: Robots, Gender, Family, and the Japanese Nation*. University of California Press.

Rosheim, Mark. 2006. *Leonardo's Lost Robots*. Springer Science & Business Media.

Sabelli, A. M., Kanda, T., and Hagita, N. (2011, March). "A Conversational Robot in an Elderly Care Center: An Ethnographic Study. In: *Proceedings of the 6th International Conference on Human-Robot Interaction* pp. 37–44.

Salazar, Juan Francisco, Sarah Pink, Andrew Irving, and Johannes Sjöberg, eds. 2017. *Anthropologies and Futures: Researching Emerging and Uncertain Worlds*. London: Bloomsbury Publishing.

Star, Susan Leigh, and James R. Griesemer. 1989. "Institutional Ecology, 'Translations' and Boundary Objects: Amateurs and Professionals in Berkeley's Museum of Vertebrate Zoology, 1907–39." *Social Studies of Science* 19 (3): 387–420. https://doi.org/10.1177/030631289019003001.

Strathern, Marilyn. 2020. *Relations: An Anthropological Account*. Durham, NC: Duke University Press.

Strengers, Yolande, and Jenny Kennedy. 2021. *The Smart Wife: Why Siri, Alexa, and other Smart Home Devices need a Feminist Reboot*. Cambridge, MA: MIT Press.

Taussig, Michael. 2020. *The Mastery of Non-mastery in the Age of Meltdown*. University of Chicago Press.

Tsing, Anna Lowenhaupt, Nils Bubandt, Elaine Gan, and Heather Anne Swanson, eds. 2017. *Arts of Living on a Damaged Planet: Ghosts and Monsters of the Anthropocene*. University of Minnesota Press.

Tunstall, Elizabeth Dori. 2020. "Decolonizing Design Innovation: Design Anthropology, Critical Anthropology, and Indigenous Knowledge." In: *Design Anthropology*. pp. 232–250. London: Routledge.

Wardle, Huon. 2015. "Afterword: An end to Imagining?" In: *Reflections on Imagination: Human Capacity and Ethnographic Method*, edited by Mark Harris and Nigel Rapport, pp. 275–294. London: Routledge.

Wolcott, Harry F. 2005. *The Art of Fieldwork*. Rowman Altamira.

Wood, Gaby. *Edison's Eve: A Magical History of the Quest for Mechanical Life*. New York, NY: Penguin Random House.

Wright, James. 2023. *Robots Won't Save Japan: An Ethnography of Eldercare Automation*. Cornell University Press.

Yorks, Lyle. 2005. "Nothing so Practical as a Good Theory." *Human Resource Development Review* 4 (2): 111–113. doi:10.1177/1534484305276176.

7 Latin American NewSpace

Anthropological Collaborations and Critiques

Anne W. Johnson

Introduction

In the last decade, the private sector has come to dominate human activities in outer space, leading to a new philosophy of space exploration based on commercial rather than scientific or governmental interests. NewSpace, as this orientation and its associated practices have collectively been called, largely revolves around the United States-based companies SpaceX and Blue Origin. However, recent years have seen the emergence of countless global government and entrepreneurial projects that look to capitalize on this emerging technoeconomic sector, characterized by increasing private sector investment, a series of technological innovations, and what has been termed the "democratization of outer space."[1] Although the idea of an anthropology of outer space may seem counterintuitive, given the discipline's emphasis on "being there" as the foundation of ethnographic fieldwork, in the context of the recent space boom, anthropological approaches to the knowledge, practices, discourses, objects, and meanings that surround humans' relations to outer space has become increasingly relevant. One of anthropology's most valuable contributions is its focus on the experiences of populations that have often been rendered invisible or marginalized.

For this reason, I discuss in this chapter the possibilities of anthropological encounters with actors who participate in the Latin American space industry, which, although modeled on its United States counterpart, incorporates a series of elements derived from particularities of the region's historical, sociocultural, and geopolitical experiences. I am particularly interested in how young "space people," as many call themselves, attempt to innovate technology and business practices in Latin America, a region whose resistance to the imposition of Western notions of progress often complicates the simple replication of NewSpace models. After a brief description of how I came to study and work alongside the NewSpace movement as an anthropologist, I summarize the history of the space sector in Latin America, paying particular attention to recent socio-technological developments.

Using a recent engagement with the South American chapter of the Space Generation Advisory Council, an international organization for students and

DOI: 10.4324/9781003458555-7

young professionals in the space sector, as a case study, I reflect on the methodological choices I have made and their consequences both for my individual research and more collaborative activities. After a discussion of the importance of establishing "para-sites," or spaces of dialogue with "experts" from a variety of fields, and the epistemic potential of speculation, I conclude with a discussion of the possibilities of anthropological insights for a critical understanding of these processes, but also for the implementation of strategies for creatively negotiating their underlying tensions, both from an applied and academic perspective.

Becoming a Space Anthropologist

Except for wanting to be an astronaut for about five minutes when I was eight, I have never been that interested in outer space. I do enjoy looking at the stars, and I appreciate a dark night sky, but I don't love science fiction (*Star Wars*, they tell me, is more of a space opera than true science fiction). I don't want to live on Mars, and I don't even like flying in an airplane. Until recently, I didn't follow rocket launches or read up on space policy or NASA's latest projects. But as my work with "space people" progresses, I find myself more and more captivated by and, at the same time, more and more critical of human activity in space. This double movement of engagement and critique is a hallmark, I think, of all anthropological endeavors.

During most of my training and professional life as an anthropologist, I have been interested in expressive culture, as I came to anthropology as an undergraduate using theater studies after taking a class on "non-western performance." I ended up graduating with a dual degree in theater and anthropology and a thesis on Mexican-American popular performance. As a graduate student, I wanted to continue to research masking and performance traditions, this time in southern Mexico, so I moved to the state of Guerrero in 1999 to undertake fieldwork. My dissertation topic had to do with how inhabitants of the state's northern region commemorate local heroes of Mexico's war for Independence from Spain, and I became familiar with most of these figures, many of whom gave their names to local towns or municipalities. But one day, someone mentioned the town of Zumpango de Neri, and I didn't recognize the name "Neri." When I asked, I was told, "Neri! Yes, Guerrero has been to outer space."[2] Rodolfo Neri Vela, Mexico's first astronaut (and only astronaut, according to many), orbited the Earth aboard the shuttle Atlantis as a payload specialist for a little over a week in 1985, accompanying the launch of Mexico's first satellite system. But at the time, my interests lay elsewhere, so I mentally filed this information away.

In 2018, having settled permanently in Mexico, I accompanied my daughter to a talk by a Mexican astrophysicist about dark matter at the National Autonomous University (UNAM) in Mexico City. The speaker, whose name I no longer remember, alluded to an experiment designed at the UNAM that had been sent to the International Space Station. "The UNAM has been to outer space," he said proudly, echoing the words I had heard in Guerrero some years before. At the time, I was reading Lisa Messeri's work on U.S. place-making practices in outer space (Messeri, 2016), and I was inspired to think about whether or not outer space might also be a Mexican place and, if so, how Mexicans imagined themselves in space in the past, the present, and the future.

A couple of months after the talk, I emailed several people and institutions who I thought might help me think about this question. Three hours after sending out my query, I received a reply from an official of the Mexican Space Agency (AEM) interested in my project and the possibility of increasing the Mexican public's knowledge about outer space and the agency's mission to promote space technology. "We need to create a Mexican culture of outer space," he told me, appealing to my training as an anthropologist. Thanks to the networking possibilities provided by my connection to the AEM, I came to know, directly or indirectly, almost all the sites and social actors that have come to define what has become a five-year project on Mexican imaginaries of outer space. These include a space instrumentation laboratory at the UNAM, a space technology start-up, national and international student organizations, cultural and artistic collectives, and a rural community that promotes astrotourism activities.

Although the topic seems exotic to many of my colleagues in anthropology (less so to collaborators in the space industry, who more readily accept that "space" should be a topic of interest to everyone), I have found many parallels between my current project and the more "traditionally anthropological" objects of study that I researched earlier in my career. Although I have certainly had to learn new information about science and technology and become more fluent in the language specific to the space milieu, a surprising number of topics have transferred seamlessly from one project to the other. In Guerrero, for example, I was interested in how narrative constructions of the past inform actions in the present. In the space imaginaries project, I find myself questioning how historical national identities inform dreams of a technological future. In my previous research, tensions between the periphery (Guerrero) and the center (Mexico City) were constantly highlighted. In my current research, those same tensions are also evident, although at a larger scale, as Mexico, a peripheral player in the space industry, engages with the United States and other hegemonic space centers. Anthropologists would recognize the importance of rumor, symbolism, ritual, and material culture in both contexts. For example, gossip played an important part in how I came to understand the inner workings of the local community in Guerrero as well as the space sector: What projects get chosen and why, how power and influence are distributed, and what attitudes are expressed toward specific actors and institutions. Collective memory, especially about past "successes" (famous insurgents and victories in battle in the case of Guerrero; astronauts and satellite launches for the space sector), continues to be celebrated in commemorative events. Additionally, nationalist iconography appears both in the discourses of regional history and space-centered discourse: Devil masks in Guerrero include pre-Hispanic Eagle and Jaguar warriors, while satellites are called Quetzal-Sat and AzTech-Sat. Finally, structural realities, such as the need to immigrate for economic, academic, or professional reasons, inform the experiences of artisans and space engineers alike.

Methodologically, too, some things have not changed. Ethnography, now multi-sited rather than spatially bound, continues to inform my approach to working in the field of outer space. Empathy, collaboration, and dialogue remain fundamental pillars of my professional practice. In Guerrero, I collaborated with government actors several times on projects having to do with public policy around gender violence, culture, and health. These experiences have helped me in my current collaborations with the AEM, which forms part of the federal Secretary of Communications and Transportation (SCT), both in terms of understanding how government institutions work and communicating effectively with government actors whose interests may not always coincide with mine.

I am still an academic professor and researcher based in an anthropology graduate program in Mexico City, but through immersion in the field of space studies, I have increasingly embraced a scholar-practitioner position as I engage in public anthropological activities, such as outreach and consulting. In a later section, I will discuss how my methodology has expanded to include more innovative forms of collaboration with actors in the space sector.

From Old Space to New Space in Mexico

The mid-twentieth century was meant to mark the dawn of a new "space age," the beginning of the process of human expansion into the cosmos, whose material benefits would be felt by human populations living on Earth. This phase of the space age revolved around attempts by the United States and the Soviet Union to advance space technology and its applications, both civil and military, and was marked by events like the launch of Sputnik (1957), the flight of Yuri Gagarin (1961), and the Moon landing (1969). The end of the "space race" came about as the U.S. and the Soviet Union began to concentrate on collaborative projects in outer space rather than competition, eventually resulting in the construction of the joint International Space Station. Political support for, and public interest in, space exploration declined after the end of the Cold War, and space-age dreams of human occupation of the solar system went largely unfulfilled (Neufeld, 2018, 63).

However, this dream has had a resurgence in the twenty-first century, in large part because of private sector investment in the space industry. Companies such as SpaceX, Blue Origin, and Virgin Galactic have come to constitute what has come to be called New Space, dominating not only human activities in outer space but also public conversations about what these activities should include. The new era has also been referred to as "the billionaire space race" (Jackson, 2021), which, while continuing Silicon Valley attitudes that include faith in the power of technology to make the world a better place and belief in a capitalist free market as the best economic structure for generating innovation and development (English-Lueck, 2017, 9), are centered around the idea that human expansion into space is a necessary step in preserving the human species. The space sector – while still engaging in scientific exploration – now promotes activities such as innovation in rocket and rocket fuel technology, space infrastructure, space mining, space delivery services, and space tourism (Valentine, 2012, 1047). Given the troublesome social, economic, and ecological consequences of their belief in endless expansion, especially for already marginalized populations, it is difficult to put aside the problematic concentration of resources and decision-making capability in the hands of a few technophilic billionaires. But, from an anthropological perspective, listening harder to hear quieter voices can be a way of imagining unexpected strategies, innovative projects, and unexplored paths.

Although there are commonalities between the histories of the space sector in the Latin American region, the development of the space industry in each country has followed a distinct trajectory.[3] Because it is the context I know best, I will mention a few key moments in the history of the Mexican space sector as an example of the development of the industry in Latin America as a whole. Looking at outer space from this region, rather than from the United States and Europe, provides a window into the ways in which U.S. and Eurocentric models and ideologies are appropriated in the "global south," but also the kinds of alternative futures that might be promised by dreams of outer space from the margin.

One lineage tracing Mexican activities in space dates to pre-Hispanic cosmological knowledge: The classical Mayans and other ancient populations developed impressive methods for observing the sky and adjusting their terrestrial activities accordingly, and even today, this perceived heritage plays a part in nationalist discourse around outer space activities (Johnson, 2020). A more recent lineage can be considered the emergence of Mexican aeronautics as an important force in the economic sector (Soland, 2019). But in many ways, the history of modern Mexico in space begins with the International Geophysical Year. The IGY, 1957–1958, was one of the most important moments in the history of space exploration, but also for global collaboration and international relations. Sixty-seven countries, including Mexico, and nearly 80,000 scientists participated in this international project to study the Earth as part of a much larger cosmic system. This renewed interest in astronomic and astronautical activity provided the impetus for investment in researchers and research facilities in Mexico (Urrutia Fucugauchi 1999, 128).

Important advances were made in December of 1957 when, two months after the launch of Sputnik, a team of scientists from the Autonomous University of San Luis Potosí (UASLP) successfully launched the first Mexican rocket into the atmosphere from a desert region, baptized by journalists as "Cabo Tuna" or Cape Cactus Fruit, in a tongue-in-cheek reference to Florida's Cape Kennedy. In 1962, President Alfredo López Mateos created the

National Commission for Outer Space (CONEE), the first governmental space organization in Mexico, whose objective was to provide support for research on rockets, telecommunications, and atmospheric studies. The commission's advisory committee included representatives from the National Autonomous University (UNAM), the National Polytechnical Institute (IPN), the Secretary of Communication and Transportation (SCT), and the Secretary of Foreign Relations (SRE). Two years after the first launch from San Luis, the CONEE's rocketry team also began to build and launch rockets. Other programs sponsored by the CONEE included the creation of a program of atmospheric balloon probes, the acquisition of meteorological and remote sensing data from U.S. satellites, research into space medicine, and participation in international debates around space law (Gall & Álvarez, 1987, 111–114). However, internal tensions, as well as the economic crisis of 1976 and the creation of other state agencies that duplicated the CONEE's functions, contributed to López Portillo's decision to dissolve the commission in 1977.[4]

Satellite communications became increasingly important in the 1960s and 1970s. In 1968, Mexico became the second country to transmit the Olympic Games by satellite and in color. The Mexican government had affiliated with the global satellite network INTELSAT so that the games might be broadcast to the public. The SCT also built Mexico's first satellite tracking station in Tulancingo, Hidalgo (at the time, the largest satellite antenna in the world). For many years, Mexico had been buying images produced by NASA's Landsat system, the first series of satellites designed to monitor natural resources through visual data production. However, renting communication satellites and buying Landsat images from NASA for the purposes of Earth observation proved to be a short-term solution, given the increasing importance of satellite data from the latter half of the twentieth century as well as increasing fears over the uses of data gathered in Mexico by foreign satellites. Eventually, the Mexican government negotiated the obtention of two geostationary satellite positions in 1979.

Three years later, at a cost of 92 million U.S. dollars, Mexico's Secretariat of Communication and Transport (SCT) hired Hughes Space and Communications (later Boeing), to construct Mexico's first satellite system, consisting of two satellites, Morelos 1 and 2, and a ground control center in the Iztapalapa area of Mexico City. The state-run company TELECOMM would take charge of the satellites' operation, but the design and delivery of the new technology, as well as training and maintenance, would be undertaken by international experts. This strategy was the object of critique by some, as it meant that Mexico would continue to be technologically dependent on the United States instead of moving toward national sovereignty and autonomy, unlike countries such as Brazil and India, which invested in the longer-term strategy of consolidating national human and technological resources (Borrego & Mody, 1989). In 1985, through an agreement with NASA, the Mexican government put its two satellites in orbit and sent Mexican citizen Rodolfo Neri Vela into space on board the space shuttle Atlantis. In 1993, the

Morelos satellite system was replaced by the Solidaridad system, also constructed by Hughes, for 300 million dollars. The telecommunications industry was privatized in 1997, and its satellite systems came under the control of the Mexican company SATMEX, later acquired by the transnational company Eutelsat for 831 million dollars (in addition to the 311-million-dollar debt that had to be paid).

The Mexican Space Agency (AEM) began its operations in 2013. For decades, only the United States and the Soviet Union had governmental space programs, but by 2018, that list had grown to more than 70 national space agencies. In addition to the "big six" (the United States, the Russian Federation, Europe, China, India, and Japan), more than 70 other countries have space agencies. As is the case for Mexico, most of these do not have launch capabilities but depend on international cooperation with larger agencies to access, develop, build, and launch space instruments. Mexico's (re)entry into the space industry is part of a wider trend of what space enthusiasts might (optimistically) term "the democratization of outer space," made possible by the decreasing costs of acquiring, producing, and launching space infrastructure. Private investment has been key to this development, but so has the miniaturization of technology – the development of smaller and smaller satellites and robots, for example – and the increase in space actors with whom to collaborate. These actors include commercial companies and international organizations, but also governmental institutions of the nearly 80 countries that now have national space agencies. In 2021, Mexico and Argentina signed an agreement establishing the creation of the Latin American and Caribbean Space Agency (ALCE). To date, 19 countries have joined the project, although so far, the regional agency continues to exist only on paper.[5]

In 2016, the International Astronautical Federation held its annual congress in the Mexican city of Guadalajara, called "the Latin-American Silicon Valley."[6] Notably, Elon Musk gave the keynote speech, "Making Humans a Multiplanetary Species,"[7] in which the founder of SpaceX announced his plans for the colonization of Mars, inspiring thousands of young people in Mexico to imagine their own futures in the space sector. In many ways, the 2016 IAC also marked a transition in Mexico from "Old Space" (the age of giant telecommunication satellites) to a Latin American New Space: The age of CubeSats, the commercialization of data obtained through earth observation, start-ups, and regional and global collaborations. The slogan "Space is for all" was heard repeatedly at the IAC, and the "space generation" in Mexico and other Latin American countries took it to heart and took advantage of the relative accessibility of innovative space technology and its promise for a better future.

Collaborating with Space People

Although there is more conceptual and contextual overlap than one might think, in practical terms, researching the space sector is quite different from working in a relatively small, centralized community. Actors in the space sector may refer to themselves as "space people," a "space community," the "space industry," or participants in the "space field," or they may use more specific terms depending on their discipline or affiliation. But whatever the terminology, my interlocutors are widely distributed across geographical locations and institutions, a situation that requires a methodological approach that focuses on networked actors rather than territorialized populations.

Social scientists have developed several structured methods applicable to the analysis of distributed networks. Social network analysis (SNA), for example, focuses on the connections between individuals and provides a way for researchers to map these relations and extract qualitative and quantitative information about them using social analysis software (Wasserman & Faust, 1994). The study of communities of practice (CoPs) also centers on social relations but is focused more on the production and transmission of shared occupational knowledge and identity (Wenger, 1998). While "epistemic cultures" refer to the systems and processes of scientific knowledge production: "those amalgams of arrangements and mechanisms—bounded through affinity, necessity, and historical coincidence—which, in a given field, make up how we know what we know" (Knorr Cetina, 1999, p. 1). I find all three perspectives useful for thinking about the kinds of relationships that shape the space sector in Mexico; however, I must admit that my approach has been more iterative, following the organic emergence of connections that arise from my interactions with diverse actors who may or may not be part of communities of practice or epistemic cultures, given that the "space people" population in Mexico constitutes a looser network than either of these terms imply. This approach is akin to the classic "snowball" technique in social research in which a first contact with an "expert" or "key informant" leads to other contacts, and so on and so forth. In this way, I have accumulated a wide network of interlocutors whose relations could probably be charted on a graph but also may only be connected through their shared passion for outer space. These include engineers at telecommunications companies, officials at the space agency, researchers at space instrumentation laboratories, artists and cultural collectives, student astronomy clubs, international astronautical organizations, community leaders who promote astrotourism, space start-up entrepreneurs, analog astronauts, and visitors to science museums and planetariums.

My work practice is flexible, mobile, and multi-sited by necessity and participatory and collaborative by design. Some of my research has been done in permanent "sites" – the Mexican Space Agency, the UNAM's Space Instrumentation Laboratory (LINX), the co-working space of the start-up Dereum Labs, the community center of a planned Dark Sky park – but because of the nature of the field, most of my ethnography is multisited (Marcus, 1995). It involves interviews in offices and coffee shops and attending and/or participating in space events, especially industry and academic conferences, and fairs, but also space contests, cultural festivals, and science outreach workshops. Instead of the traditional extended fieldwork in one site, my research includes attendance at major national and international events throughout the year, in which the most interesting encounters come about while drinking coffee after the structured talks. In between events, my research time is spent having informal conversations with established interlocutors, conducting formal interviews with new interlocutors both in person and online, observing scientific and technical processes in laboratories, and attending industry and cultural workshops, either as a participant or facilitator. The timing of these activities depends on the availability of the people in my network, the event calendar, and my own writing deadlines and is not limited to a structured fieldwork period. My notes tend to be collages of interview transcripts, PowerPoint slides, descriptive fieldnotes, links to YouTube videos, photographs, space-related memes passed around on social media, children's drawings, and testimonies of UFO sightings, in addition to annotated academic texts, government documents, electronic newspaper clippings, and industry whitepapers.

Aside from the temporal and spatial flexibility this research demands, I find that the most productive way of engaging with the space sector is through collaboration. In this I follow one of the models set forth by Dominic Boyer and George Marcus, in which collaboration "decenters the conventional ethnographer-informant relation through para-ethnographic epistemic partnership with expert interlocutors or by involving audiences in projects of media and knowledge making" (Boyer & Marcus, 2020, 13). Ethnography in this case, involves an active co-creation of knowledge by "experts"; that is, by subjects who possess a body of knowledge that they are willing to share and have a stake in the outcome of the research, "moderately-empowered counterparts" rather than "marginalized others" (Marcus, 2000, 2). This work is carried out in what Marcus has called "para-sites," spaces of reflection, that allow dialogue to "truly do its work" and "facilitate alternative thinking by subjects who are deeply complicit with and implicated in powerful institutional processes in times of heightened consciousness of great social transformation" (Marcus, 2000, 5). In these para-sites, knowledge is co-created, subjects partially align, and processes of distance and engagement allow for sometimes surprising outcomes. A kind of reciprocity is generated, although not necessarily in the classical anthropological sense of "I extract information from you and your community, and in return, I..." serve as godparent to your child, write a historical chronicle for the town, sponsor an event, etc. For me, the reciprocity involved in work in para-sites is along the lines of "I learn from you and write about my experience, and, at the same time, I contribute my knowledge and experience to the creation of something new in which you are also interested." So far, these collaborative exchanges have been well-received, especially as they are perceived to contribute to the consolidation of what many interlocutors call a "space culture" in Latin America.

One of the most important tools I have employed in these collaborations has been the facilitating of encounters of collective speculation. Once the province of literary and filmic science fiction, speculation has become a potent strategy in industry, design, and business for tracing social and economic trends, as well as projecting possible futures. Some of my interlocutors engage in speculation as part of their work: One of the directors at the AEM, for example, has published speculative texts as a way of motivating his readers to think about how Mexico can participate in an outer-space economy through space mining (Duarte, 2022). The anthropological use of speculation, however, adds a critical edge to these projects by calling for speculative fiction to "become not only a resource for imagining alternative worlds but also a medium for remaking our presence in the world" (Anderson et al., 2018). I have facilitated various speculative sessions, including workshops with STEM students that help them think about the social consequences of the development of outer space technology and infrastructure. Especially for participants in STEM fields, anthropological speculation becomes a way of thinking beyond "human factors" in technology, gesturing toward the role of culture viewed more broadly for understanding how technology impacts human populations. Speculation becomes not only a way of imagining far-off futures but also rethinking life on Earth in the present. In either case, speculation from Latin America decenters the futures imagined by global technoscientific centers.

To make this discussion of methodology clearer, I will describe a recent applied engagement I had with the South American branch of the Space Generation Advisory Council (SGAC), an international non-profit organization that calls itself "THE global network for students and young professionals interested in the space industry" and declares its mission "to enable and empower the young generation in advancing humanity through the peaceful uses of outer space."[8] The SGAC is allied with both the United Nations Program on Space Applications and the International Astronautical Federation and has more than 25,000 members in 165 countries, organized, following the U.N. model, into regional groups, which are meant to foster diversity with respect to "the three G's: geography, generation, and gender." In the summer of 2023, I participated as an "expert" in the SGAC South American regional workshop[9] held in Bogotá, Colombia. I had met Oscar, Colombia's SGAC "point of contact" through Twitter the year before, and after a few interviews and conversations held during a space-centered reading group, he invited me to contribute to the SGAC event he was organizing. I was to give a talk on space anthropology, participate in panels on the future of the Latin American space sector and space science outreach strategies, and lead a working group around the theme of space culture, a topic that would be included for the first time at a SGAC regional workshop.

The event began with a welcome message from Oscar to the attending public, comprised of students and professionals in the field of space from South American countries, all under the age of 35. The encounter was meant to be a means of "strengthening Latin American space ecosystems" so that, eventually, "no one need leave their country to study or work in their chosen field."[10] Speakers gave short talks about the social, economic, and political challenges of developing space ecosystems in Latin America, the technical challenges for developing space infrastructure, and possible strategies for overcoming these obstacles. They spoke about the history of space programs in their own countries, the importance of international collaboration, the need for clearer laws and regulations around space activities, and the role of the SGAC in creating networks and mentorships. Other speakers gave presentations about their own work in specific fields of the space industry, as experts included Latin-American–born engineers at NASA, research universities, and other organizations. Among other issues, panels addressed the benefits of space analogs, the problem of gender inequality in the space sector, and strategies for fomenting space outreach activities. Informal conversations also revealed other tensions and anxieties about the SGAC as an international organization, about the frustrations felt by space enthusiasts who had few opportunities to study or advance their careers in their own countries, and about the barriers faced by Latin Americans who must emigrate if they want to pursue their space dreams.

I discussed Latin American "space cultures" with examples from my work in Mexico, and I shared my thoughts on the importance of incorporating multiple knowledges and projects for the future, cautioning against a passive acceptance of Silicon Valley-style discourse. As far as I could tell from their responses, audience members seemed to agree with the basic premise of developing a critical attitude toward "imported" models and concepts, although some still lamented the absence in Latin America of what they referred to as a Californian "culture of innovation."

In my working group, which was very well-attended (although not as well-attended as the more spectacular working group on developing space missions led by a NASA engineer with experience collaborating on Mars and asteroid avoidance projects), we talked about the concept of culture and taking up the notion of "astroculture" coined by space historian Alexander Geppert to refer to "a heterogeneous array of images and artifacts, media and practices that all aim to ascribe meaning to outer Space while stirring both the individual and the collective imagination" (Geppert, 2018, 8). We started speculatively, imagining what a Colombian astroculture might look like. Participants shared their own stories about how they came to be interested in space and their hopes for Colombia's future. I presented some information about indigenous cosmology as a means of introducing some reflection about the potential for decolonizing space technology (although much more work needs to be done in this respect), and we invented an outreach project that would function as an exchange of knowledge between people in the space industry and inhabitants of rural communities. I was excited by the level of interest in the social and humanistic aspects of outer space, especially as most participants were students and young professionals in STEM fields, particularly engineering. For me, the event provided an embarrassment of ethnographic riches as well as an opportunity to learn from other experts in technical and scientific fields while, as I mentioned above, generating a dialogue around what my interlocutors called the "human factors" in outer space activities. In fact, the productive friction between my use of the term "culture" and my interlocutors' preferred term "human factors" became a common point of interest, as did the use of the term "ecosystem" in the context of the space industry.

As a result of this event, I was invited to collaborate on further projects, such as participating in an analog mission at a newly constructed habitat outside of Bogotá, giving talks at a workshop on space culture in isolated Colombian communities, engaging in informal conversations about space and cultural outreach with employees of the Colombian Air Force,[11] and co-authoring a paper on SGAC with a Brazilian engineer at NASA. Though it proved to be especially meaningful and productive, my experience in Bogotá is not unique; I have had equally profound exchanges with members of other groups in para-sitic situations, including a rocket club contest and convention in Acapulco, a futures workshop convened by a space tech start-up at the headquarters of the AEM, a festival centered on Saturn in a rural community developing astrotourism activities, and a series of workshops in different Mexico City neighborhoods organized by a cultural collective that imagines Mexican futures on Mars.[12]

Anthropology and Space Ethics

It is easy to be seduced by the passion of "space people" for the possibilities of cosmic exploration and their firm belief in the power of space technology to make the world a better place. Underdog narratives of Mexicans who, despite all odds, have carved out places in the space industry through technological innovation are particularly compelling. However, the impacts of space technology must be viewed with a critical eye, as sending objects into space has environmental consequences. Rocket launches, for example, which have tripled over the past decades, are the only source of pollution above the troposphere. The exhaust produced by solid-fueled rockets contains hazardous chemicals that contaminate soil and water, while even the "eco-friendlier" hydrocarbon-fueled rocket engines emit exhaust that contains black carbon directly into the ozone layer.[13] Furthermore, the debris comprised of "non-operational satellites, spent rocket stages, and other bits and pieces created during the launch and operation of satellites" forms a giant cloud of "space junk" around the Earth and represents significant collision risks for rockets taking off as well as and orbiting satellites. The 100 trillion bits of debris in orbit, only 23,000 of which are tracked because of their size, mean that:

> There is enough human-generated space debris concentrated in the critical region in LEO between 700 and 900 kilometers to create more debris even if no new satellites were launched....The growth of debris will increase the risks—and thus the associated costs—of operating satellites in critical regions such as LEO....These rising costs will likely hinder commercial development of space and will place additional pressure on

government budgets, potentially resulting in the loss of some of the benefits currently derived from space, or preventing discovery of new benefits.
(Masson-Zwaan, 2017, 35)

On the other hand, statements such as "Guadalajara (where the 2016 IAC
was held) is Mexico's Silicon Valley" hides a problematic acceptance of what
has been termed "the California model" of technological and economic
development, and an overly optimistic belief that if you "build a research
park, they will come" (O'Mara, 2011). The transplantation of this Californian fantasy ignores the historical and cultural context that made Silicon
Valley entrepreneurs successful: "a combination of national military spending
and suburban infrastructure investment" as well as "the presence of powerful
research institutions...and an unusually risk-tolerant business culture that
welcomed and nurtured iconoclasts and dreamers" (ibid.). It also hides the
structural violence that made the economic development of Silicon Valley
possible, whose victims were, in large part, the region's Latino communities
(Pitti, 2004). The promise of "infinite growth" implicit in the Californian
economic model and extended into space by promotors of resource mining on
the Moon and asteroids has a dark side: Climate change, pollution, and the
intensification of social and economic inequalities, for example.

Elon Musk, who may be considered one of Silicon Valley's most recogniz-
able representatives, inspired Mexicans in 2016, but he is not the only voice
that should be heard when making plans for the future. Looking at the space
sector from an anthropological perspective and from its Latin American
margins allows for the visibilization of alternative futures in outer space and
on Earth. "Space is for everyone" should be a reality, not merely a marketing
slogan. Taking the phrase seriously implies including Latin American voices
in the discussion but also assuring that, as Latin American countries become
"members of the space club," their space activities do not contribute to the
silencing of other voices in their own communities, but rather promote radical
inclusion of marginalized groups in STEM fields, including women, members
of the LGBTQ+ community, people with disabilities, indigenous, rural, and
Afro-Latino populations.

But critiquing the space industry is not enough. In my work, I position
anthropology as a disciplinary partner in the establishment of spaces of dialogue with actors in the industry – para-sites – that allow for an exchange of
perspectives. Like any dialogic relation with diverse publics, especially those
whose interests may be perceived as aligned with socioeconomic systems and
political structures that anthropologists tend to want to subvert, collaborating
with actors in the space industry can be fraught with tensions. For this
reason, at one point in my research, I attempted to separate my approach to
the project into two levels, one critical and the other collaborative. However, I
have come to understand my relationship with my topic and with my interlocutors as a more complex intertwining of public and academic anthropology and to see both approaches as critical strategies of engagement.

As a response to my work with Latin American actors with varying degrees of power, agency, and critical reflexivity, I have tried to move away from a binary division between the powerful and the powerless, the West and the rest, market forces, and cultural critique. I consider my practice with the space sector to engage a form of "public anthropology," like that called for by Robert Borofsky and Thomas Hylland Eriksen, among others (Borofsky, 2010; Eriksen, 2006). While I do produce work meant to be read by other anthropologists or social scientists interested in outer space and/or Latin America, I am also interested in the ways in which anthropological work can contribute to a public discussion on the consequences of outer space activities more generally. At the same time, I try to attend to my interlocutors in the space sector, who are often more interested in specific issues related to their field, like how to create a "space culture" in a country or region and how to "harness culture" to strengthen a space ecosystem. I try to be open and responsive while resisting simple answers to complex questions. Empirical contextualization and nuanced arguments are part of an anthropological toolkit that adds to the conversation and the development of an industry.

Space Anthropology

As a result of what has been an unexpected thematic shift in my professional life, I have learned a few things, which is not to say that I am not still learning and being continually surprised by what emerges from my research and interactions.

The first thing I have learned is the importance of collaboration, inter-disciplinarity, and the value of clear and timely communication. "Doing things in space" requires the employment of a wide variety of knowledges and abilities, and while disciplines such as physics, engineering, chemistry, biology, and computer science are clearly fundamental, so are design, psychology, law, medicine, sociology, literature, media studies and, increasingly, anthropology. This work has allowed me to learn other languages (at least partially): Those of the disciplines with which I interact and that of non-academic communication. Knowing how to talk about anthropological concepts and insights without resorting to academic jargon has been the key to establishing a productive dialogue with my partners. This was certainly the case for my work in Bogotá with the members of the Space Generation Advisory Council, as well as with participants in other futures workshops. Instead of lecturing on the social and environmental consequences of space exploration, I try to frame these workshops ludically, allowing participants to think critically about what a future in outer space might mean, which objects, people, and ideas they would like to take with them, and which they would leave behind. Learning how to respond to emerging events and dialogues quickly has been part of this process. Applied work in NewSpace moves quickly. This has meant that, in order for my anthropological perspective to be taken into account, I have had to participate in round tables about "the future of Latin America in space" with less preparation than my past work, write brief summaries of dialogues that occur in space workshops right after they occur, and give immediate feedback on the social impact of technological projects. I should note that immediacy and pithiness are skills that are not typically imparted in academic anthropology programs, but are crucial to succeeding in this line of work.

The second lesson that I have learned is the value of saying "yes" to opportunities that seem a little out of left field. The best "para-sites" are the ones that emerge organically and often unexpectedly from shared encounters and not necessarily the ones that are intentionally organized. It would never have occurred to me to take into account the imaginative possibilities of rocketry clubs, for example, had it not been for a chance meeting at a conference that led to an invitation to evaluate experimental rocketry projects for their social and environmental impact.

The last thing I have learned that I would like to share here is that space is fun. The enthusiasm of space people, as I have said, is contagious, and, in my experience, space enthusiasts are most generous about sharing their experiences with an anthropologist. As a result of our interactions, I get to speculate about life on one of Saturn's moons, marvel at the technological and scientific complexity of rockets and robots, and listen as engineers wax poetic about satellites as human prostheses in the vastness of the cosmos. Feet firmly on the ground, rooted in ethnographic critique and participant observation, I am becoming a space person, too.

Notes

1 See (Valentine, 2012) for an anthropologically informed discussion of NewSpace and its associated practices, ideologies, and imaginaries.
2 As it turned out, Zumpango de Neri was named after Eduardo Neri, a noted nineteenth-century jurist, and not Neri Vela. But, as the astronaut himself told me years later, "there are many branches of Neri's." And the fact that inhabitants of Guerrero connected Zumpango to Neri Vela is evidence of his importance in the national imaginary.
3 Argentina was the first country in Latin America to develop a space program followed by Brazil, then Mexico. Today, the only countries to have official space programs and to have launched satellites are Argentina, Bolivia, Brazil, Chile, Colombia, Ecuador, Mexico, Peru, Uruguay, and Venezuela. Eighty-five of the more than 3,000 satellites currently in orbit are operated by Latin American countries. The region's combined space budget is a fraction of the budget allocated by the U.S. government to NASA for outer space activities (Guzmán, 2021, 201).
4 Another important space initiative in Mexico was the construction of a ground tracking station in Guaymas, Sonora, which was used from 1961–1963 in support of NASA's Project Mercury, and later Project Gemini.
5 See https://www.gob.mx/sre/prensa/mexico-sera-sede-de-la-agencia-latinoamericana -y-caribena-del-espacio?state=published, consulted August 18, 2023.
6 See video of the complete inauguration of the 2016 IAC at https://www.youtube. com/watch?v=jDwVZL-CGnQ, consulted August 11, 2023.
7 https://www.youtube.com/watch?v=H7Uyfqi_TE8, consulted August 11, 2023.

8 https://spacegeneration.org/, consulted August 15, 2023.
9 Mexico is included in the North American, Central American, and Caribbean region, a division which has both supporters and detractors.
10 Message from convener Oscar Ojeda to attendees of the South American Space Generation Workshop, Bogotá, June 2023.
11 As Colombia has no governmental space agency, the Air Force has become the de-facto institution for space activities, and a site in which many students and young professionals undertake internships. I recognize, of course, the complicated historical relationship between anthropology and the military and the ethical challenges that arise from academic-military collaborations. My interactions consisted of a pair of conversations with a young woman working for the Air Force who had been charged with developing space science outreach programs for diverse populations. During our dialogue, I stressed the importance of learning from these populations and taking seriously their pre-existing ways of knowing outer space.
12 Marsarchive.org. For more on this collective, see their eponymous website: marsarchive.org.
13 https://www.space.com/rocket-launches-environmental-impact, consulted August 16, 2023.

Bibliography

Álvarez, Román. 1987. "La estación rastreadora de Guaymas." In: *Las actividades espaciales en México: Una revisión crítica*, pp. 117–120. Mexico City, Mexico: Fondo de Cultura Económica.

Anderson, Ryan B., Emma Louise Backe, Taylor Nelms, Elizabeth Reddy, and Jeremy Trombley. 2018. "Speculative Anthropologies." *Fieldsites*, Theorizing the Contemporary, December 18. https://culanth.org/fieldsites/series/speculative-anthropologies

Borofsky, R. 2010. *Why a Public Anthropology?* Center for a Public Anthropology, Hawaii Pacific University. https://books.google.com.mx/books?id=neo7twAACAAJ.

Borrego, Jorge, and Bella Mody. 1989. "The Morelos Satellite System in Mexico," *Telecommunications* 13 (3): 265–276.

Boyer, Dominic, and George E. Marcus. 2020. "Introduction." In: *Collaborative Anthropology Today: A Collection of Exceptions*, edited by Dominic Boyer and George E. Marcus, pp. 1–21. Ithaca [New York]: Cornell University Press.

Duarte, Carlos. 2022. "Minería espacial: Más cerca de lo que imaginamos." *Hacia el Espacio* (blog). October 2, 2022. https://haciaelespacio.aem.gob.mx/revistadigital/articul.php?interior=1197.

English-Lueck, J. A. 2017. *Cultures@SiliconValley*. 2nd edition. Stanford, California: Stanford University Press.

Eriksen, Thomas Hylland. 2006. *Engaging Anthropology: The Case for a Public Presence*. Oxford/New York: Berg.

Gall, Ruth, and Román Álvarez. 1987. "La Comisión Nacional Del Espacio Exterior En México, Evaluación de Sus Actividades." In: *Las Actividades Espaciales En México: Una Revisión Crítica*, edited by Ruth Gall, Román Álvarez, Liga María Fadul, Fátima Fernández, Hector Schmucler, and José Castro Villalobos, pp. 108–116. Mexico: Fondo de Cultura Económica.

Geppert, Alexander, ed. 2018. *Imagining Outer Space*. New York, NY: Springer Berlin Heidelberg.

Guzmán, Joseph. 2021. "Space Programs in Latin America: History, Current Operations, and Future Cooperation." *USAF Journal of the Americas* 3 (3): 200–219.

Jackson, Tim. 2021. "Billionaire Space Race: The Ultimate Symbol of Capitalism's Flawed Obsession with Growth." Online magazine. *The Conversation.* July 20, 2021. https://theconversation.com/billionaire-space-race-the-ultimate-symbol-of-cap italisms-flawed-obsession-with-growth-164511.

Johnson, Anne W. 2020. "Space Cultures and Space Imaginaries in Mexico: Anthropological Dialogues with the Mexican Space Agency." *Acta Astronautica* 177 (December): 398–404. https://doi.org/10.1016/j.actaastro.2020.08.002.

Knorr Cetina, Karin. 1999. *Epistemic Cultures: How the Sciences Make Knowledge.* Cambridge, MA: Harvard University Press.

Marcus, George E. 1995. "Ethnography in/of the World System: The Emergence of Multi-Sited Ethnography." *Annual Review of Anthropology* 24: 95–117.

Marcus, George E. 2000. "Introduction." In: *Para-Sites: A Casebook against Cynical Reason*, edited by George E. Marcus, pp. 1–14. Late Editions 7. Chicago: University of Chicago Press.

Masson-Zwaan, Tanja. 2017. "The International Framework for Space Activities." In: *Handbook for New Actors in Space*, edited by Christopher D. Johnson, 2017 edition, pp. 2–53. Broomfield, Colorado: Secure World Foundation.

Messeri, Lisa. 2016. *Placing Outer Space: An Earthly Ethnography of Other Worlds.* Experimental Futures. Durham, NC: Duke University Press.

Neufeld, Michael J. 2018. *Spaceflight: A Concise History.* Boston, MA: MIT Press.

O'Mara, Margaret. 2011. "Sillicon Valleys." *Boom*, 2011. https://boomcalifornia.org/2011/06/16/silicon-valleys/.

Pitti, Stephen J. 2004. *The Devil in Silicon Valley: Northern California, Race, and Mexican Americans.* Princeton, NJ: Princeton University Press.

Soland, Peter. 2019. "The Miracle (and Mirage) of Mexican Flight: Aviation Development in Mexico, during and after the Second World War." *The Journal of Transport History* 40 (1): 25–43. https://doi.org/10.1177/0022526618823931.

Urrutia Fucugauchi, Jaime. 1999. "El Año Geofísico Internacional 1957–1958 y los Programas de Investigación Interdisciplinaria en el Inicio del Siglo XXI." *GEOS*, June 1999.

Valentine, David. 2012. "Exit Strategy: Profit, Cosmology, and the Future of Humans in Space." *Anthropological Quarterly* 85 (4): 1045–1067.

Wasserman, Stanley, and Katherine Faust. 1994. *Social Network Analysis: Methods and Applications.* Structural Analysis in the Social Sciences 8. Cambridge/New York: Cambridge University Press.

Wenger, Etienne. 1998. *Communities of Practice: Learning, Meaning, and Identity.* 1st ed. Cambridge University Press. https://doi.org/10.1017/CBO9780511803932.

8 Good Ethnography for Good Food

Making Genetic Engineering Palatable to the US Market

Mujtaba Hameed

Introduction

This chapter explores the intersection of anthropology and the emerging field of genetic engineering applied to food production. Through an illustrative case study of a food biotech startup, it highlights the role of anthropological insights in navigating the cultural complexities surrounding the marketing and consumer adoption of genetically modified (GM) foods.

The GM food industry, sometimes known as Foodtech, is a moniker broadly applied to a wide spectrum of innovation within the food and nutrition sector. It is a rapidly evolving field marked by a plethora of challenges. Some of these involve ethical considerations (Stone, 2007; Aistara, 2018); others are related to regulatory compliance and safety (Goldberg, 2001; Conford, 2001); and others are public perception and acceptance (Herring, 2008; Nugent, 2018).

It will not be surprising to say that anthropology, with its wealth of knowledge on food and foodways across cultures, is well positioned to intervene in this milieu of technological developments. It offers unique insights into how an understanding of human societies and culture can drive innovation, help overcome challenges, and facilitate the discovery of new market opportunities.

In this chapter, I share my journey as an anthropologist who became a consultant specializing in foundational research for tech companies, and especially how my expertise, anthropological training, and mindset helped a pioneering Scandinavian startup – which I shall henceforth refer to as Egg 2.0. Specifically, the chapter explores the exact anthropological techniques employed to comprehend and navigate the multifaceted relationship consumers have with food and how this relationship translates into the field of genetically engineered nutrition. From interviewing and semiotic methods to treating my clients like an anthropologist interlocutor in the field – i.e., doing my best to understand their social context as individuals, not just professionals – the chapter details how the anthropological approach proved instrumental in shaping Egg 2.0's product positioning, marketing strategies, and strategic planning. From uncovering changing perceptions around food

DOI: 10.4324/9781003458555-8

to dissecting complex food mindsets, adopting an anthropological perspective helped to unravel the cultural and social underpinnings of food consumption in a way that significantly impacted the company's strategic decisions about how best to grow and become profitable.

In the concluding sections, I cast a forward-looking gaze, contemplating the broader implications of anthropology's role in the food tech industry and potential future directions. I end the chapter with some final reflections highlighting the transformative potential of anthropological approaches within the biotech and food tech sectors, affirming the value of such interdisciplinary collaboration.

In sum, this chapter merges my personal journey with a case study of a consulting project. It highlights how anthropology is employed in a consulting context and how it can innovatively contribute to the food tech industry and beyond, paving the way for culturally-informed strategies that enhance business success and promote broader societal acceptance of responsible, genetically engineered food products. Ultimately, my intention in writing this chapter is two-fold. First, paraphrasing the words of business anthropologists Briody and Meerwarth Pester (2017), I want to show how anthropology can move beyond "doing no harm" and instead actively guide emerging technologies towards positive change. Second, I want to show readers – especially recent anthropology graduates or people contemplating a career switch – an example of a career outside of academia where anthropology is valued. I hope this example will help readers make informed decisions that will result in satisfying professional careers and, in the words of Gillian Tett, show that anthropology can help us "seize the exciting opportunities created by cyber silk roads and innovation" (Tett, 2021, 223).

My Journey into the World of Professional Anthropology

Studying Anthropology and Early Career Experimentation

For my undergraduate degree, I wanted to pick a course that would provide me with a broad understanding of people and culture – to experience something akin to the American style of education, where students can take classes on many different subjects.[1] After some deliberation looking at the various universities offering different social sciences degrees, I decided to apply for a BA in Archaeology & Anthropology at the University of Oxford. I was especially drawn to the flexibility of the course. At the time, the degree structure involved four "core" modules – two on archaeology and two on social anthropology. Students selected three optional courses, any combination of archaeology or anthropology, and wrote a dissertation, which comprised the final module.

This type of course was broad enough to satisfy my wide-ranging curiosity (I was interested in learning about many different societies, past and present, especially their rituals, storytelling, and material culture) while also allowing me to specialize. Pretty soon, I felt that anthropology was more for me, and I chose anthropology classes for all my options. My final dissertation was on linguistic anthropology, which would turn out to be very valuable later in my career, as the case I am offering will demonstrate.

Upon graduating, I had no choice at the time but to enter the workforce – I was not in a financial position where I could have continued my studies. The early stages of my career were varied, as I tried my hand at different fields ranging from software startups to film and theater production. My initial foray into the world of consulting was an entry-level role at a boutique firm in London specializing in marketing innovation – in other words, helping client companies find new ways to speak to their customers. The volatile nature of the industry led to an unexpected cutback, ending my tenure at the firm after only a year, along with half a dozen of my colleagues. However, out of everything I had tried to this point, I found consulting the most interesting. Work was project-based and varied, and I enjoyed the fact that I had been able to work directly with very senior clients (CEOs and CMOs).

I freelanced for a few months after that job ended abruptly, but I was unable to find the kind of consulting opportunities I was hoping for – working with clients and on projects that aligned with my interests in ethical business practices. My bank account dwindled as I struggled to pay rent through short-term gigs. Out of financial necessity, I finally took a full-time business development position offered by a recruiter I had been in touch with previously. While recruiting wasn't my ideal path, I knew the role would provide some much-needed stability.

Surprisingly, in many ways, the job was exactly what I needed at that stage of my career. The experience exposed me to a diverse array of professionals working in fields like design, marketing, startups, and strategy consulting. I visited many different company offices and had in-depth conversations with potential candidates. This allowed me to gain valuable insights into various industries while honing my skills in understanding people's contexts and motivations. Though it was not yet clear to me at the time, this role would eventually connect me with ethical, tech-focused employers – organizations I would not have encountered otherwise. But at that moment, recruiting represented a practical way to stay afloat and build my professional network. It also gave me confidence that the skills I had developed in my undergraduate anthropology degree could provide real value in business settings.

As I saw first-hand how understanding people, culture, and context led to better hiring outcomes, it reaffirmed my belief that anthropological insights had an important role to play in the professional world. This period also put me in a place, both financially and in terms of professional connections, where I could take the next step and pursue a Master's degree in applied anthropology.

Entering the World of Business Anthropology

With my newfound confidence, I chose to enroll for a Master's in Social and Cultural Anthropology at University College London (UCL). This program offered a track called "TEPP" – Teaching Ethnography in Professional

Practice. The TEPP seminars, featuring professionals from different industries, further showcased the practical applications of anthropology in the contemporary world.

After graduating, I was determined to continue fusing my anthropological training with professional practice in a way that could make a positive impact. This led me to an innovation and design consultancy where I carved out an ideal role as a specialist in ethnography. As someone fascinated by understanding humans in their cultural contexts, I was thrilled to gain experience conducting fieldwork across various locales in the US and Europe. I spent the next two invigorating years moving between New York and Amsterdam while employed by this company.

Impact of the Pandemic – The Ethical Turn and Tech Specialization

During the COVID-19 lockdowns, I had ample time for reflection. I had been living an intensely international lifestyle for years – constantly traveling for projects and spending months in New York away from home. Now, grounded in Amsterdam, I found myself working remotely for financial services clients whose projects, while important and lucrative, left me feeling unfulfilled. I realized I wanted my anthropological skills to contribute towards social impact that aligned with my values, improving people's quality of life beyond just the financial.

With this in mind, and remembering the various people I had met during my time as a recruiter, I felt that the tech industry might offer me what I was searching for. Not only was that sector thriving during the pandemic, but I also knew from my MSc about the prevalence of user-centered design within tech (Gunn, Otto, & Smith, 2020) and its overlap with anthropology. I believed I could have more impact working with these types of organizations, knowing that many people in user research positions have social science backgrounds or are sympathetic to anthropological ways of thinking. Furthermore, I was drawn to the idea of working directly with my peers versus those from a more traditional business background, such as marketing or business development. The idea of surrounding myself with like-minded people within a community of practice was an inspiring idea that promised to provide a sense of belonging and purpose. Propelled by this newfound courage to seek out a role that would fulfill my desire to do good, I pivoted to tech – a moment that I like to think of as the "ethical turn" in my career.

After picking up some freelance projects at Google as a strategist and researcher, I joined Stripe Partners, a consulting firm in London focused on technology clients. Their mission to "inspire thoughtful technology" aligned with my goals. One of the partners, Dr. Simon Roberts, is a professional anthropologist and one of the founding members of the EPIC conference and community. During the interview process, I read his book on the importance of the embodied experience of users within business anthropology (Roberts, 2022) and was even further inspired to go into this field. At Stripe Partners, I had found what I had been looking for – a place where I could carry out research using my skills and training from my anthropology MSc, work with clients who understood and valued my educational background call to do good, and a collegiate community of fellow practitioners.

The work was also generally much more rewarding than previous roles because the user-centered approach Stripe Partners thoroughly embraces involves developing deep empathy for users – what customers or consumers are often called in tech – and shaping products to truly suit their needs. As a whole, I found my new experience tremendously fulfilling, but it was a future project that would allow me to focus my anthropological skills on the type of project I had been searching for.

Though I didn't select the project, as is typically the case in consulting, where projects are typically assigned based on staffing resources and availability versus interest, I was presented with the opportunity to work on Egg 2.0, a Scandinavian biotech startup using genetic engineering to drive sustainability. Their social mission resonated with my aim to apply my expertise towards doing good. Even though projects were outside my control, I like to think of this as a gift, calling me to reciprocate and make a difference in the field of genetic engineering, a field with great potential but also challenges that I was confident anthropology could contribute to addressing.

Navigating the Ethics of Genetic Engineering in the Food Industry

GMOs: A Whole New World?

Genetic engineering is defined as "the direct manipulation of an organism's genes using biotechnology" (National Human Genome Research Institute, 2020). Proponents of genetic engineering in the food industry argue that it promises higher yields, pest resistance, and nutritional and flavor enhancement. Beyond these immediate benefits, genetically modified organisms (GMOs) have the potential to address some of the pressing challenges of our time, such as sustainability and climate change. For instance, drought-resistant crops can help farmers maintain yields in areas increasingly affected by water scarcity (Gómez-Barbero, Berbel, & Rodríguez-Cerezo, 2008). Similarly, salt-tolerant GMOs can be cultivated in areas with saline soils, expanding the arable land available and potentially reducing the need for deforestation (Roy et al., 2014).

The Flavr Savr tomato, introduced in 1994, was one of the first GMOs to reach the US market and one that proponents still point to when discussing the benefits (Bruening & Lyons, 2000). Since then, the use of genetic engineering in food production has expanded, with key crops like soybeans, corn, and canola being heavily modified. Monsanto, now a subsidiary of Bayer, has been a central figure in the expansion of GMOs. While they have introduced genetically modified (GM) seeds that have revolutionized many agricultural settings, such as their Roundup Ready soybeans designed for glyphosate resistance (Charles, 2001), they have also been a focal point of controversies.

These controversies revolve around issues of seed patenting, farmer lawsuits, and concerns over biodiversity loss.

Controversies and Setbacks

Public protests against Monsanto have been widespread, with activists and concerned citizens organizing marches and campaigns to highlight the company's perceived monopolistic practices and the potential environmental and health risks of GMOs. These movements gained momentum, especially during the late 2000s and early 2010s, culminating in global events like the "March Against Monsanto" (*The Guardian*, 2015). On the legal front, Monsanto has faced numerous lawsuits. Some farmers challenged the company's strict patent enforcement (Howard, 2009), while others, along with non-farming plaintiffs, claimed health damages from glyphosate exposure, a key ingredient in Monsanto's Roundup herbicide (Gillam, 2017). Critics argue that Monsanto's practices prioritized profits over ecological sustainability and farmer autonomy, deepening the societal rift on the ethical dimensions of GMOs in the food industry.

The Monsanto example is not isolated. Despite its technological advancements, genetic engineering in food has often been met with skepticism and controversy (Burke, 2012). Another prominent example is the Starlink corn incident in 2000 (not to be confused with the Starlink brand for communications technology by Elon Musk), where a genetically engineered corn variety, approved only for animal consumption, was found in human food products (Bucchini & Goldman, 2002). The incident fueled public concern over potential allergenicity and the regulatory system's efficacy.

Other controversies include the labeling of GMOs. Consumer advocacy groups such as the Non-GMO Project and the Center for Food Safety have long argued for transparency and the right to know what is in their food (Klümper & Qaim, 2014). In many countries, including much of Europe, mandatory GMO labeling is in place, reflecting public demand and policy responsiveness (Fernandez-Cornejo et al., 2014). Cultural perceptions of "naturalness" also play a significant role in public distrust. Genetic modification, for some, is seen as an unnatural intervention in the food supply, challenging deep-seated beliefs about what is considered "natural" food (Frewer et al., 2013). Studies, such as the one by Scott, Inbar, and Rozin (2016), have shown a segment of the population to be "Absolutists" who are totally against genetic engineering of any kind. Such individuals often ground their objections in a mix of ethical, religious, and cultural reasons.

The Anthropological Perspective on GMO Ethics

Anthropologists and other social scientists have long played a role in contributing to this debate. Often drawing on biomedical anthropology, they have offered a unique perspective on the field. Studies have ranged from focused studies on the development of specific new technologies, such as PCR, by luminaries like Paul Rabinow (1996) to wider critiques on the impact of bio-technologies on society.

From an anthropological perspective, the ethics surrounding GMOs in food intertwine with cultural norms, traditional agricultural practices, and social values. Glenn Davis Stone's ethnographic work (2007) illustrates the complex relationship between local farming practices and the introduction of GMOs. Stone's fieldwork in Warangal, India, documents how the advent of geneti-cally modified cotton profoundly altered traditional farming methods, chal-lenging the ethical frameworks that farmers operated within. He raises questions about technological dependency, the displacement of local knowl-edge, and the resulting socio-economic rifts.

Similarly, Aistara (2018) explores the ethics of GMOs within the context of organic farming sovereignty. Through her study, she reveals how GMOs dis-rupt traditional forms of biodiversity conservation and seed sovereignty, which are deeply embedded in cultural heritage and ethical practices. She argues that the push for GMOs often ignores the ecological ethics practiced for generations, threatening not just the environment but also the cultural fabric that supports sustainable farming practices.

These anthropological insights suggest that the ethical challenges of GMOs are not just about safety and scientific integrity but are also about the pro-tection of cultural diversity and the rights of small-scale farmers. Such ethical considerations ask us to ponder who benefits from GMOs and at what cost to our collective heritage and future food security.

When viewed more specifically through the lens of food production, anthropologists argue that genetic engineering intersects with deeply perso-nal realms of consumption, cultural values, and human health. Within this space, they have explored perceptions and attitudes towards these food pro-ducts. Their ethnographic and qualitative research methods have enabled a nuanced exploration of cultural factors shaping these attitudes. One notable study (Stone & Glover, 2016) into the introduction of GMO-derived "Golden Rice" in the Philippines highlights how the social construction of risk is influenced by cultural norms, media narratives, and personal values. Their research points to the complexity of public opinion, which cannot be reduced to mere ignorance or irrational fear. Another paper (Flachs, 2019) argues that the anthropological approach of studying GMO crops is super-ior to the putatively "objective" focus on yields that is prevalent in studies from the field of economics, as it surfaces and contextualizes local nuances and identifies competing attitudes and definitions of the very concept of crop yield.

A notable theme that arguably cuts across most of the discourse is the concept of "biocapital" (Sunder Rajan, 2006) as a critique of the scientific and corporate structures that surround the development of biotechnologies. Sunder Rajan describes the densely interconnected realms of biotechnology conducted in universities (often state-sponsored) and corporate interests, including venture capital. He characterizes Western biocapitalism as being a field suffused with a spirit of techno-utopianism that operates on two different regimes of truth: That of scientific fact and the other, more mutable truth of PR hype aimed to gain investment.

> Scientific fact produced by biotech companies goes through the same peer-reviewed mechanisms that academic scientists go through, yet it is considered perfectly natural, at the same time, to issue press releases that are indeterminate, sometimes even misleading (if never, legally, fraudulent).
>
> (Sunder Rajan, 2006, 118)

GMOs and the Regulatory Landscape

The regulatory landscape for GMOs is a battleground of competing interests, power dynamics, and cultural values. David Theo Goldberg's analysis (2001) probes into the intersection of technology and food, scrutinizing how GMOs challenge traditional regulatory frameworks. He suggests that GMOs demand a rethinking of food regulations, which have historically been based on clear distinctions between natural and artificial. These lines are blurred in the case of GMOs, necessitating new anthropological approaches to regulation that consider cultural meanings of food purity and integrity.

Philip Conford (2001) takes a closer look at the complexities involved in regulating GMOs, arguing that the intricate relationship between technology and agriculture requires a nuanced understanding. Conford's perspective acknowledges the limitations of a one-size-fits-all regulatory approach and suggests that regulations should be informed by the sociocultural contexts of food production. He emphasizes the importance of incorporating local and indigenous knowledge systems into regulatory frameworks to ensure that they are equitable and culturally sensitive.

These studies highlight that, from an anthropological standpoint, GMO regulations cannot be dissociated from the cultural and social realms. Effective regulation of GMOs should not only mitigate potential risks but also respect and integrate the diverse agricultural practices and cultural beliefs about food.

GMOs: What the People Think

Public perceptions of GMOs are shaped by a myriad of factors, including media narratives, cultural beliefs, and personal values. Ronald J. Herring's work (2008) delves into the contentious debates on GMOs in India, revealing a disconnect between empirical evidence and public perception. Herring's anthropological lens shows how local knowledge and experiences can conflict with global scientific discourses, leading to skepticism and resistance towards GMOs.

Rachel Nugent (2018) addresses the intersection of GMOs with demographic changes, particularly the aging population. Nugent's research suggests that different age cohorts may perceive GMOs differently, influenced by their lived experiences and the changing societal narratives around food and health. She postulates that understanding these generational perspectives is crucial for navigating the public discourse on GMOs.

The anthropological inquiry into public perceptions uncovers the deep-seated cultural narratives and personal experiences that inform opinions on GMOs. It is clear that public acceptance cannot be divorced from these complex social and cultural dynamics. An anthropological approach to GMOs, therefore, must consider the plurality of voices and the nuanced beliefs that define the public stance on this controversial technology.

My familiarity with these ethical debates, coupled with my desire to use my skills to "do some good," made working with Egg 2.0 a compelling prospect. I was asking myself: Was this a case of techno-utopian PR, or was there substance to back up their claim? How receptive would they be to conducting a strategic research project using an anthropological approach? Would they be prepared to take on board research findings that might complicate or even negate their mission? I was in.

Egg 2.0: Doing Well by Doing Good

Egg 2.0 is a Scandinavian deep-tech genetic-engineering startup aiming to revolutionize the egg industry in pursuit of a more sustainable food system. While many tech firms hype flashy innovations devoid of substance, Egg 2.0 seemed to stand apart in their commitment to environmental and social responsibility. Its technology, precision fermentation, held the potential to disrupt industrial animal farming a major contributor to issues like climate change, pollution, and antibiotic resistance.

Precision fermentation is a half-century-old technology that allows microorganisms, such as *Trichoderma reesei*, to produce complex molecules identical to natural proteins. In the case of Egg 2.0, this process creates ovalbumin, the main protein found in egg white. Similar to brewing beer, the method involves feeding sugar to the microorganism, resulting in a powdered egg white protein made without animals.

The company was founded on the hypothesis that this method of food production could be a significant leap towards more sustainable and efficient food production. Traditional egg farming has particular sustainability issues that precision fermentation would not (Stephens et al., 2018), such as greenhouse gas emissions, land use, water scarcity, and exposure to antibiotics. Its origins were rooted within a national research institution, where the product was developed over years of research and development. In my mind, I had found the opportunity to use my skills to help a company with a product that had the potential to do good. After our initial kick-off meeting, I was personally sold on the potential of the technology to make a difference and, more importantly, I felt the team at Egg 2.0 were genuine and committed people, with shared values, equally interested in doing well by doing good.

The Market and Challenges

Egg 2.0's growth plan involved initially targeting the US market, a strategic move due to the regulatory landscape allowing for faster market entry. Put another way, the European regulatory landscape is more stringent than its counterpart in the United States (US), especially when it pertains to the regulation of GMO foods (Lynch & Vogel, 2001), and when launching a new product, there are more regulatory hoops to jump through. Theoretically, it would be easier to launch Egg 2.0 in the US, scale the company into profitability, and make the case afterwards to expand into Europe. However, introducing such a groundbreaking product is not without its hurdles, even in the US. As discussed above, the perception of genetic engineering and lab-grown food products can vary widely among consumers. For some, the idea may align with values of sustainability and ethical animal treatment, while others might harbor skepticism or distrust of genetically engineered products.

The Ask: Understanding the Market

Egg 2.0 recognized the need for a nuanced cultural understanding of the US market and its various consumer perceptions. They felt they needed this because, up until that point, they had only worked within the Scandinavian and European context. Early-stage startups often have to scale and grow through partnerships with other companies as well as investors and accelerators. The more they knew about how their product would perform in the US, the better equipped they would be to handle different types of conversations.

Before a typical consulting engagement, there is a period where senior consultants meet with prospective clients and discuss their challenges and how best to design the project structure and methodology to tackle them. With Egg 2.0, these discussions resulted in the eventual framing of the project in the following terms: How could Egg 2.0 identify their ideal customer, and what would this new product mean for different types of audiences? Should they adopt a B2B or B2C approach? How best to talk about their product in order to overcome the hurdles around GMO food? To answer these questions, they would need expertise in uncovering insights into the lives and mindsets of food professionals who would be their future partners and in building an authentic and relevant brand. They engaged Stripe Partners to provide this expertise.

Methodology

In the Egg 2.0 project, I utilized ethnographic interviews to delve into the perspectives of both professional and home users. I was responsible for conducting the majority of these interviews (around 80% of them), with support from my colleagues on the project team. To be clear, this was not in-person, long-term research. The interviews were "ethnographic" in terms of their structure and subject matter. While I created a discussion guide to help guide the conversations, I had the freedom to deviate from the guide according to the flow of the conversation and the particular background of the individual. Furthermore, I asked the participants to send pre-work, asking them questions about their use of eggs and egg whites, and asked them to show us photos of their "food environments." For example, I asked food scientists to show pictures of their labs and chefs to show their kitchens, restaurants, and menus. Building up this kind of biographical knowledge before the interviews took place helped build rapport quickly and made the conversations as specific to the individual's context as possible.

This approach allowed us to explore the nuanced relationships that people have with egg whites and the potential for egg alternatives. The detailed insights collected from the interviews across various geographies provided a unique window into the underlying motivations and reservations about using animal-free egg whites.

Four-Step Approach

Our methodology for Egg 2.0 was framed around a four-stage approach that allowed for a comprehensive understanding of the market landscape while also providing specific insights and actionable recommendations for brand and communication strategy. These stages were:

1 *Frame*: Initiation through workshops, market audits, and semiotic analysis.
2 *Explore*: Deep exploration through individual and group interviews.
3 *Sense-make*: Data analysis leading to insights, brand recommendations, and actionable strategies.
4 *Activate:* Finalization through activation workshops and agency briefing sessions.

This process provided a framework for a multifaceted exploration of Egg 2.0's needs.

I used two research methods that could be described as anthropological, aiming to learn insights that are both "wide" and "deep" through semiotic analysis and ethnographic research, respectively. The combination of ethnographic interviews, which helped me understand the lived experiences and attitudes of potential users, and semiotics, which helped me decode the cultural meanings and trends, enabled a robust, holistic insight into the market landscape. These techniques have a rich history in anthropology, especially in food studies, and provide a nuanced and contextual understanding of the subject.

The ability to move between these macro and micro perspectives is characteristic of anthropology, allowing us to understand the culture of food consumption and production, as well as individual needs and motivations. Egg 2.0 chose our approach precisely for this ability to offer both breadth and depth, providing them with a multifaceted understanding that could inform every aspect of their brand strategy.

Anthropological Method 1: Semiotics Analysis for "Width"

Semiotics is the study of signs and symbols and their use or interpretation (Saussure, 1959). This method has been employed by various anthropologists to understand cultural meanings embedded in everyday practices – the link between the realm of signs (including language) and the material world (Cavanaugh & Shankar, 2017), including food consumption. For example, Fischler's (1988) seminal work on food habits and social structure relied on semiotics to decipher food's social symbolism.

In the Egg 2.0 project, I conducted a semiotic analysis to understand the complex visual and verbal signifiers around their product, egg white protein, created through precision fermentation. This involved looking at the various other food brands related to this space, analyzing brand assets like color, typography, and symbols, and identifying cultural cues such as naturalness, cruelty-free, vegan, etc. By conducting this kind of semiotic analysis of food categories, there is the potential to create a deeper understanding of how food is framed, interpreted, and internalized within a society than relying on speaking to people alone. It helps contextualize data from interviews by linking them to latent cultural codes. By juxtaposing Egg 2.0's product with existing cultural codes, I was able to develop initial territories for the product and position it within the larger framework of food choices and ethics.

Semiotics was chosen so that I could map the cultural codes and territory landscapes that are essential in positioning Egg 2.0's product. As a method, it has been used to offer valuable insights into the shifting attitudes and behaviors within emerging food categories (Chandler, 2017). For this project it was also intended to help develop initial territories that were visually and verbally congruent with the desired space that Egg 2.0's product aimed to occupy.

Anthropological Method 2: Ethnographic Interviews for "Depth"

The ethnographic interviews provided a nuanced understanding of both professional and home users' needs, behaviors, and perceptions. The approach consisted of remote interviews with pre-work, conducted with an initial sample of 18 people, later extended to 24. Since Egg 2.0 was still an early-stage startup, they had the option to target their product at anyone. During the initial conversations with them, we collectively agreed on casting a broad net, trying to recruit a sample of participants that would provide diverse perspectives from the food industry. This included chefs (from large corporate kitchens to boutique award-winning hotels), nutritionists, sports scientists, R&D professionals who develop consumer products for large corporations, and vegan home cooks.

Ethnography offered rich insights into the potential use cases of the envisioned product and the behaviors around "egg-switching" – understanding what it would take for people to use alternative egg sources.

Findings and Analysis: Semiotics

An important note: The semiotic analysis was only the first step in the process. Its findings were only meant to help create some product concepts to test during the ethnographic interviews. After this phase of the project was complete, I put aside semiotics in favor of the ethnographic interviews.

The semiotic analysis process, following the example of previous work in cultural anthropology, began with identifying potential applications for Egg 2.0's egg white product across 11 diverse food categories. These categories, derived from the conversations with Egg 2.0 about the product's capabilities, were as follows:

1 Drinks, powders, bars
2 Meal replacement
3 Performance foods
4 Cultured meat
5 Alternative proteins
6 Ingredient alternatives
7 Protein powders
8 Fungus-made proteins
9 Vegan/veggie meals
10 Baking ingredient alternatives
11 Dairy free

Using a wide-reaching sweep of more than 60 brands in these categories, I built a comprehensive "corpus" of images and texts. To facilitate collaborative work, this corpus was created on a digital whiteboard, Miro.

Coding and Clustering

As outlined by Hunt and Barton (2014, 449), the "power of commercial semiotics comes when interpreting patterns that emerge through a larger corpus of cultural texts. We look for how similar ideas are communicated and expressed across texts, theming and clustering as we go."

Following this process, the next stage involved the extraction of multiple codes from the images and text. Each code represented a signifier in the semiotic sense, a building block of meaning that contributes to the overall message conveyed by the brand. Upon the collection of codes, I clustered them to identify emerging overarching themes.

Figure 8.1 One of the Miro Boards Used in the Project

Plotting onto a Map: Constructing a Framework for Understanding

In the analysis, I developed a framework that could anchor our understanding of potential brand territories and their associated meanings. My tool of choice was a 2×2 diagram, a graphical method that allows for the spatial plotting of elements. The main reason for choosing this diagram was its simplicity and familiarity within the professional world. After all, there have been entire books written on the subject (Lowy & Hood, 2004), and I felt that it would help communicate our ideas to our clients in a way that they would recognize.

The axes of the diagram were as follows:

• *Ingredient focus vs. Process focus*: Here, I examined codes centered on the product ingredients – their uniqueness, origin, and attributes – and juxtaposed them against those focused on the product's creation and delivery

IMPACT

INGREDIENT ———————————————— PROCESS

EXPERIENCE

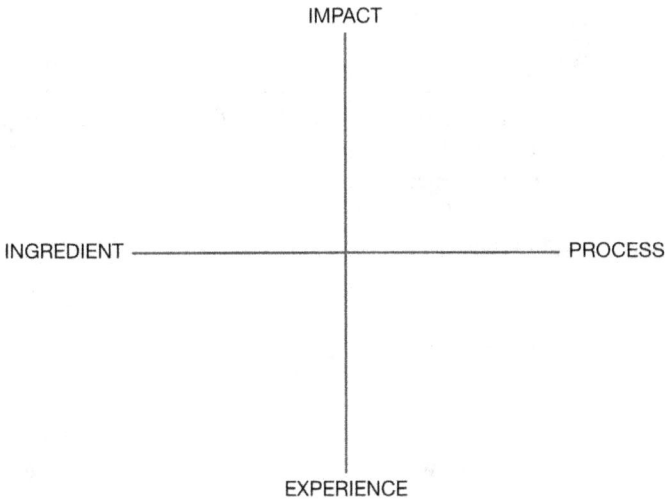

Figure 8.2 The 2×2 Diagram to Visualize our Framework

processes. This axis reveals the balance between what the product is and how it came to be.

- *Impact focus vs Experience focus*: The other axis contrasts codes expressing the product's wider impact (community, systemic, planetary) with those focusing on the individual's experience of the product (sensory qualities, personal impact). This lens explores the tension between the macro and micro perspectives of the product's significance.

Visualizing Brand Territories

Upon completion of the semiotic map, I collaborated with a designer to visualize the potential brand identities for Egg 2.0. These "territories" – collections of images articulating unique brand narratives akin to mood boards – would be subsequently evaluated with potential customers during the ethnographic phase of our research.

An initial eight territories were proposed, which we later streamlined to four following a workshop with the client team. Involving the clients throughout this process was paramount. Since it was the first time they had seen this kind of work in action, by conducting many workshops and meetings, I was able to answer their questions and show them how I did the work. As well as being in line with best practices suggested by scholars advocating for collaborative approaches in anthropology (Boyer & Marcus, 2021), this is also the consulting approach favored by Stripe Partners.

This iterative and thorough semiotic analysis allowed us to build a solid foundation for brand development. An important point to note is that while I relied on academic theory to shape the research and define the approach, I took care not to overload the client with too many academic concepts – many of them came from a science or marketing background and to speak in these terms would have led to unnecessary confusion. In my experience, this can be one of the most challenging aspects of making the transition from academic settings to the world of work, but it is an essential aspect of communication to master in order to run projects smoothly with minimal interference.

In the following section, I will delve deeper into my ethnographic research methods, further illuminating the robust, anthropologically rooted approach that attracted Egg 2.0 to our services.

Findings and Analysis: Ethnography

I created a comprehensive discussion guide aimed at understanding the business practices, relationships with food and ingredients, decision-making processes, and particularities about egg whites and alternatives usage of the participants, who seemed to be professionals in the food industry. This was shared in advance with the client, and a meeting was held to explain the justifications behind the approach, answer any questions, and provide clarifications where necessary.[2]

Overview of the Discussion Guide

1   *Business Goals and Challenges.* The guide starts with establishing an understanding of the participants' business goals, milestones, challenges, and typical work environments. This provides context about their professional environments and operations.
2   *Relationship with Food and Ingredients.* This section explored their relationship with food, focusing on their day-to-day tasks, preferred ingredients, their process of food preparation, and the evolution of their practices. The questions uncover their views on food categories, processes, and the importance of understanding the science behind food products. The guide also prompted discussion on topics like price efficiency, supply chain, sustainability, and alternative meat and dairy products, offering insights into the participants' values and priorities.
3   *Brands and Decision Making.* This section probed into the participants' brand preferences, changes they made in suppliers or ingredients, and the factors they considered while selecting a brand. Here, the focus was on understanding their decision-making processes, their experiences with the brands, and their perceptions of brand communication and advertising.
4   *Relationship with Egg Whites/Alternatives.* This section narrowed down to the usage and selection process of egg whites and alternatives, their importance, and preferred qualities.
5   *Exploring the Territories.* The last section involved understanding their views on alternative production methods (like precision fermentation) and creating an ideal supplier profile by choosing between different brand elements.

The guide employed elements from the anthropology of food, which is a sub-discipline focusing on the social, economic, and cultural factors that influence food choice. The questions about food preparation practices, ingredient preferences, and relationship with food were informed by the anthropological concept of "foodways" – the ways in which humans use food, including everything from how it's chosen, acquired, and distributed to who prepares, serves, and eats it (Mintz & Du Bois, 2002).

Overall Findings: On "Good Food"

Anthropological inquiries into contemporary food systems illuminate the intricate ways in which humans perceive, interact with, and transform their alimentary landscapes. From the globalization of gastronomy to the emergence of sustainable food cultures and health-conscious dietary regimes, individuals increasingly demand their nourishment to serve multifaceted functions (Mintz & Du Bois, 2002). As observed in this study, our understanding of food is gaining additional complexity as knowledge and technology evolve.

This turn triggers new definitions of "good food." Today's food attitudes indicate a convergence of the following three components: Gastronomy/pleasure ("Does this taste good?"), health ("Is this good for me?"), and sustainability ("Is this good for the planet?"). This consolidation signifies a shift from the traditional compartmentalized view of food's role. In this evolution, technology and the availability of information have played a critical role, illuminating the implications of food choices on personal health and the environment – part of the rise of so-called "alternative foods" seen as being part of "alternative worlds" (Goodman, Dupuis, & Goodman, 2014).

Simultaneously, new definitions of "good food" are emerging. What once was simply "healthy" or "sustainable" now entails nutritionally complete diets devoid of antibiotics and locally sourced, organic products independent of monocultures. This changing dynamic is evidence of Appadurai's (1981) concept of "gastro-politics," where the politics of consumption, production, and representation of food become intertwined with contemporary societal values.

Significance of Eggs and Their Limitations

Scientifically speaking, eggs are regarded as a "multifunctional food" able to cause widely-used effects such as foaming, emulsification, adhesion, and gelation (Dong & Zhang, 2020). They embody nutritional perfection, cultural ubiquity, and convenience. However, under the increasingly sophisticated lens through which people view food, some drawbacks of eggs have started to emerge. While their nutritional richness is undeniable, questions about sustainability, supply chain issues, and other concerns have surfaced in contemporary food discourse. The supply chain issues, in particular, seemed to cause problems for chefs and food scientists – in the words of a chef at a five-star restaurant:

> *There was a kill-off of chickens recently in the area because of avian flu or bird flu. I had to go some different routes, call some mainstream producers, and get some eggs out of Illinois. Am I proud of that? No, not necessarily. But here in [his small resort town], there isn't a supplier who can get me 30 dozen eggs every single week. It's just tough. It's hard to find.*
>
> John, Head Chef of a fine dining restaurant in the Midwest

Despite the availability of egg alternatives aiming to address some of these concerns, they often fall short in replicating the broad performance of eggs, especially in terms of taste and versatility. The prevalence of such issues provides a fertile ground for new food brands, like Egg 2.0, to innovate and meet these evolving consumer needs.

Emergence of Food Mindsets

A critical dimension of this study is the introduction of "food mindsets," a conceptual framework for understanding the mental models driving individuals' engagement with food brands. These mindsets encapsulate contextual information about consumers' circumstances and their actions, leading to desired results.

Various factors influence people's food mindsets, including participation in communities, overall life goals, cultural or religious affiliation, and their belief system regarding food. In recent years, the role of science in shaping food perceptions has wavered as individuals can find scientific validations for their viewpoints.

Rather than identifying one "foodie type," the concept of food mindsets encapsulates the variability in food situations and behaviors. The main determinants of food mindsets include prioritizing functionality or experience and possessing a narrow or broad sphere of influence.

The study identified five primary food mindsets:

1 *Trend-setters.* Explorers of new frontiers, curating the best food experiences to delight their audiences.
2 *Safeguarders.* Protectors of high food quality, meeting rigorous standards set both internally and externally.
3 *Producers.* Creators at scale, depending on reliable and large-scale production.
4 *Nourishers.* Providers of balanced meals to close relationships, reflecting an extension of those bonds.
5 *Instructors.* Advocates for performance, recommending specific nutrients for beneficial outcomes.

The application of these mindsets can guide food brands like Egg 2.0 to identify their target market segment and evaluate potential opportunities. In this case, the "trend-setter" mindset was identified as the most suitable for Egg 2.0's focus.

This study underscores the transformative impact of anthropological insights on modern food systems, revealing the dynamism of food perceptions, the complex relationships individuals maintain with food, and the emergence of new consumption patterns shaped by "food mindsets."

We argued that by comprehending these changes, Egg 2.0 can effectively navigate the contemporary food landscape, contributing to the creation of a gastronomically satisfying, health-conscious, and sustainable future.

Impact of the Project

The anthropological insights and strategic recommendations gleaned from this project have profoundly influenced Egg 2.0's product positioning and brand perception. By understanding the shifting landscape of consumer preferences and needs in relation to food, Egg 2.0 was equipped to position itself in a manner that resonated with these evolving attitudes. The application of ethnographic findings allowed the company to navigate the complex cultural narratives surrounding food, health, and sustainability, thereby strengthening its value proposition. Furthermore, the project led to the recognition that Egg 2.0's offerings are more than just egg substitutes – they are multifunctional foods that meet the multifaceted needs of the contemporary consumer. This insight propelled the brand into a realm of differentiation that transcends typical product categorizations.

In terms of market positioning, the project played an instrumental role in establishing Egg 2.0 as a leader in the rapidly emerging "next-generation foods" category within the US market. The anthropological lens applied during this investigation provided Egg 2.0 with an unparalleled depth of understanding regarding customer mindsets, offering valuable perspectives on how consumers approach food choices. Armed with these insights, the company was able to anticipate and align with the future trajectories of food trends, effectively placing itself at the vanguard of this burgeoning food movement.

The success of the project was further underscored by Egg 2.0's subsequent achievement in securing funding. Investors were evidently inspired by the robustness of the company's market entry strategy, a confidence that can be attributed in part to the rich, ethnographically-informed insights underpinning their approach. This endorsement not only provides a strong foundation for Egg 2.0's market entry but also signifies an appreciation of the anthropological methodologies employed in the project. It signals a growing recognition within the business community of the value that anthropological insights can bring to the formulation of business strategies.

Overall, the project stands as a testament to the power of anthropological inquiry in business contexts. It illuminates how a deep, nuanced understanding of cultural and consumer mindsets can lead to innovative, market-leading strategies. By centering its approach around ethnographic insights, Egg 2.0 has positioned itself to continue succeeding in a market that is as complex and dynamic as the consumers it serves.

Notes On Ethnography in Professional Practice

Readers familiar with anthropology will already be aware of the value of ethnography as a methodology. It is, however, employed differently within the realms of professional practice and academic anthropology, revealing distinct facets of its potential and limitations.

In academia, ethnography originates from a tradition of in-depth, long-itudinal study of societies and cultures. Time is a critical factor in academic ethnography; researchers often immerse themselves in the field for months or even years, offering them the possibility to witness and participate in the ebb and flow of social life (Ingold, 2017).

In contrast, the world of professional practice – such as in business consulting, design, and market research – embraces a more applied approach to ethno-graphy. This often involves addressing a specific business problem, improving a product or service, or understanding consumer behaviors (Cefkin, 2010). Here, ethnography serves to contextualize products and services within the wider social and cultural lives of consumers. The timelines of such projects are usually much shorter – from personal experience, most of the projects I have worked on have been less than three months long from start to finish.

This compression of timelines can invite criticism. There are some scholars who argue that such practices may not allow for the depth of understanding that a more traditional academic ethnography can offer (Baba, 1998; Cefkin, 2016). On the other hand, there are other perspectives, including the idea that a little ethnography is better than none at all (Isaacs, 2016).

My view is this: Despite its limitations, ethnography in professional practice can provide robust and rich insights that other methods may overlook. For graduate students entering the field of professional anthropology, trying to compare our approach to academic anthropologists is misguided. Rather, the more useful comparison to make is between professional anthropology and other types of professional research, especially traditional qualitative research (such as focus groups). First, as a qualitative method, it allows for an in-depth understanding of human behavior, often capturing the nuances and contexts that surveys or focus groups might miss – to quote Daniel Miller, anthropology is "a world apart from those who are satisfied with questionnaires and focus groups and seek to conduct experiments" (Miller, 2010, 24). Second, by immersing researchers within the lived experiences of people, ethnography provides insights into the tacit, taken-for-granted aspects of life that people themselves may not be consciously aware of (Miller, 2010). Last, it fosters empathy among its practi-tioners, facilitating a deeper understanding of, and connection with, the indivi-duals or communities being studied (Cefkin, 2010).

For consulting projects specifically, the compressed version of ethnography we do can contribute towards a more nuanced understanding of consumer behaviors, aspirations, and needs. It can reveal the motivations behind consumption practices, the meanings attributed to products or brands, and the social and cultural contexts within which these are embedded (Cefkin, 2010). Furthermore, ethnographic insights can stimulate innovation by highlighting gaps in the market or suggesting new directions for product development.

While ethnography in professional practice differs from its academic counterpart in its objectives, timelines, and depth of exploration, it still remains a powerful tool for gaining nuanced insights into human behavior and culture. Despite its limitations, it offers a valuable perspective that can complement other methodologies and contribute meaningfully to business strategy and decision making.

For those looking to break into this type of applied anthropology, I would suggest preparing for this style of work by doing the following:

- *Building a Portfolio of Shorter Projects*: Start with small projects, even if they're self-initiated, to showcase your ability to apply ethnographic methods in real-world settings. This portfolio should showcase the ability to gather and analyze data efficiently in a shorter amount of time than in academia.
- *Enhancing Communication Skills*: Learn to present your findings in a concise and impactful manner tailored to a business audience. Creating slides, diagrams, and frameworks is an important skill to learn in order to translate complex cultural insights into actionable business strategies.
- *Seeking Mentors and Building Networks*: Find seasoned anthropologists who have successfully transitioned into professional practice and seek their guidance and advice. Connect with professionals in the industry and attend relevant workshops, seminars, and conferences to get a sense of the current market dynamics and needs.
- *Diversifying Methodological Skills*: While ethnography is central, be open to learning complementary qualitative and quantitative research methods that are often used in professional settings.
- *Staying Updated with Industry Trends*: Understand the latest trends in the industries you're interested in. This knowledge will make your ethnographic insights more relevant and actionable.

By embracing these strategies, anthropologists can position themselves effectively in the professional world, leveraging their unique skills to offer valuable insights.

Conclusion

The history of genetic engineering in the US food market is a rich tapestry of scientific innovation, public controversies, and cultural complexities. Anthropologists, through their unique methodologies and perspectives, have contributed to a deeper understanding of this multifaceted field. Their research underscores the need for responsible innovation, transparent communication, and a recognition of the diverse values and beliefs that shape public perceptions of genetic engineering in food.

In this chapter, I sought to contribute to this conversation by showing how, as a consultant for Stripe Partners, I navigated the complex intersection of genetic engineering, food, and culture while trying to do well by doing good. Using a case study based on Egg 2.0's quest to introduce their genetically-engineered egg white product to the market. I discussed how deep ethnographic insights could illuminate people's multifaceted relationships with food, revealing the cultural, health, and environmental considerations that underpin food decisions. I explored how these insights informed Egg 2.0's product positioning and messaging, ultimately contributing to its success in the US market.

In the process, I emphasized the crucial role of anthropological methods in understanding and addressing cultural barriers in the adoption of genetically engineered food products. By offering a holistic, human-centric lens, anthropology can unravel the complex web of meanings, beliefs, and practices surrounding food. The power of anthropology lies in its ability to contextualize food decisions within broader cultural, social, and personal narratives, thus enabling more nuanced strategies for product introduction and adoption.

Reflecting on the future, it is clear that the role of anthropology in the food tech industry is just beginning to take shape. As technological advancements continue to revolutionize our food systems, anthropological insights will become increasingly critical in ensuring these innovations align with the values, needs, and lifestyles of their intended consumers.

This research carries broader implications for the food tech industry at large. It underscores the importance of deep cultural understanding in introducing novel food products, particularly those born out of complex scientific processes. This perspective reminds us that food is more than a physical substance – it is an embodiment of our identities, traditions, and relationships.

Furthermore, this work opens up exciting future directions for anthropological research. As the genetic engineering and food tech landscape continues to evolve, new cultural dynamics, ethical considerations, and consumer behaviors will undoubtedly emerge. Anthropologists are uniquely positioned to explore these changes, providing the necessary cultural context and human insights to ensure the acceptance and success of genetically engineered food products in diverse markets.

In conclusion, the journey of Egg 2.0 underscores the transformative potential of anthropological approaches in the biotech and food tech sectors. By bridging the gap between the technical world of genetic engineering, biotechnology, and the lived experiences of consumers, anthropology can foster a more nuanced understanding of the cultural landscapes within which these innovations are embedded.

More broadly, this chapter illuminates the value of anthropological perspectives in enhancing innovation and success within rapidly evolving sectors. By bringing humanity back into the heart of technological innovation, anthropology not only increases the chances of product adoption but also helps build a future where technology truly serves the needs, values, and aspirations of people.

In an increasingly interconnected and complex world, anthropology's human-centric approach will continue to be an essential tool for understanding, navigating, and shaping the future of emerging technologies, food included, and in the process, will help us to "do some good" in the words of Briody and Meerwarth Pester.

Notes

1 For those unfamiliar with the British university system, an applicant needs to choose their major right at the beginning of the application process – and changing subjects after starting at the university is often discouraged.
2 It is worth noting here that the interviews were all recorded and these recordings were viewed by the client afterwards, who was impressed to the point of asking us to conduct six additional interviews and paying for the privilege. To quote them directly: "watching these is more fun than Netflix!" While this statement can certainly be explained as a hyperbolic compliment, I am unaware of the specific regional differences between Scandinavian Netflix compared with the UK, and as such have no choice but to take the statement at face value.

Bibliography

Aistara, Guntra A. 2018. *Organic Sovereignties: Struggles over Farming in an Age of Free Trade*. University of Washington Press.

Appadurai, Arjun. 1981. "Gastro-politics in Hindu South Asia." *American Ethnologist* 8 (3): 494–511. https://doi.org/10.1525/ae.1981.8.3.02a00050.

Baba, Marietta L. 1998. "The Anthropology of Work in the Fortune 1000: A Critical Retrospective." *Anthropology of Work Review* 18 (4): 17–28. https://doi.org/10.1525/awr.1998.18.4.17.

Boyer, Dominic, and George E. Marcus. 2021. *Collaborative Anthropology Today*. Ithaca, NY: Cornell University Press.

Briody, Elizabeth, and Meerwarth Pester, Tracy. 2017. "Redesigning Anthropology's Ethical Principles to Align with Anthropological Practice." In: *Ethics in the Anthropology of Business: Explorations in Theory, Practice, and Pedagogy*, eds. Timothy de Waal Malefyt and Robert J. Morais. New York, NY: Routledge, Taylor & Francis Group.

Bruening, George, and James M. Lyons. 2000. "The Case of the FLAVR SAVR Tomato." *California Agriculture* 54 (4): 6–7. https://doi.org/10.3733/ca.v054n04p6.

Bucchini, Luca, and Lynn R. Goldman. 2002. "Starlink Corn: A Risk Analysis." *Environmental Health Perspectives* 110 (1): 5–13. https://doi.org/10.1289/ehp.021105.

Burke, D. C. 2012. "There's a Long, Long Trail A-winding: The Complexities of GM Foods Regulation, a Cautionary Tale from the UK." *GM Crops & Food* 3 (1): 30–39. Taylor & Francis Online.

Cavanaugh, J., and Shankar, S. (Eds.). 2017. *Language and Materiality: Ethnographic and Theoretical Explorations*. Cambridge: Cambridge University Press. doi:10.1017/9781316848418.

Cefkin, Melissa. 2010. *Ethnography and the Corporate Encounter.* Berghahn Books.

Cefkin, Melissa. 2016. "The Limits to Speed in Ethnography." *Advancing Ethnography in Corporate Environments.* pp. 108–121. Routledge.

Chandler, Daniel. 2017. *Semiotics: The Basics.* 3rd ed. New York: Routledge.

Charles, Daniel. 2001. "*Lords of the Harvest: Biotech, Big Money, and the Future of Food.*" Perseus Publishing.

Conford, Philip. 2001. "From Organic Principle to Complex Practice: An Anthropological Perspective on GMO Controversies." *Journal of Rural Studies* 17 (3): 321–328.

Dong, Xuan, and Yu-Qing Zhang. 2020. "An Insight on Egg White: From Most Common Functional Food to Biomaterial Application." *Journal of Biomedical Materials Research Part B: Applied Biomaterials* 109 (7): 1045–1058. https://doi.org/10.1002/jbm.b.34768.

Fernandez-Cornejo, Jorge, Seth Wechsler, Mike Livingston, and Lorraine Mitchell. 2014. "*Genetically Engineered Crops in the United States.*" USDA-ERS Economic Research Report 162.

Fischler, Claude. 1988. "Food, Self and Identity." *Social Science Information/sur les Sciences Sociales*27: 275–292. https://doi.org/10.1177/053901888027002005.

Flachs, Andrew. 2019. "The Factish in the Field." *Science & Technology Studies* 32 (3): 26–43. https://doi.org/10.23987/sts.63306.

Frewer, Lynn J., Ivo A. van der Lans, Arnout R. H. Fischer, Machiel J. Reinders, Davide Menozzi, Xiaoyong Zhang, Isabelle van den Berg, and Karin L. Zimmermann. 2013. "Public Perceptions of Agri-food Applications of Genetic Modification – A Systematic Review and Meta-analysis." *Trends in Food Science & Technology* 30 (2).

Gillam, Carey. 2017. "*Whitewash: The Story of a Weed Killer, Cancer, and the Corruption of Science.*" Washington, DC: Island Press.

Goldberg, David Theo. 2001. "Food as Technology and Technology as Food: Interrogating the GMO Controversy." *Identities: Global Studies in Culture and Power* 7 (4): 565–589.

Gómez-Barbero, Manuel, Julio Berbel, and Emilio Rodríguez-Cerezo. 2008. "Bt Corn in Spain—The Performance of the EU's First GM Crop." *Nature Biotechnology* 26 (4): 384–386.

Goodman, David, E. Melanie Dupuis, and Michael K. Goodman. 2014. *Alternative Food Networks: Knowledge, Practice and Politics.* London/New York: Routledge.

The Guardian. 2015. "Tens of Thousands March Worldwide against Monsanto and GM Crops." *The Guardian*, May 24, 2015. https://www.theguardian.com/environment/2015/may/24/tens-of-thousands-march-worldwide-against-monsanto-and-gm-crops.

Gunn, Wendy, Ton Otto, and Rachel Charlotte Smith. 2020. *Design Anthropology: Theory and Practice.* Abingdon, Oxon: Routledge, Taylor & Francis Group.

Herring, Ronald J. 2008. "Whose Numbers Count? Probing Discrepant Evidence on Transgenic Cotton in the Warangal District of India." *The International Journal of Multiple Research Approaches* 2 (2): 145–159.

Howard, Philip H. 2009. "Visualizing Consolidation in the Global Seed Industry: 1996–2008." *Sustainability* 1 (4): 1266–1287.

Hunt, Cato, and Sam Barton. 2014. "Decoding Culture: Cultural Insight & Semiotics in Britain." In: *Handbook of Anthropology in Business* ed. Rita Denny and Patricia Sunderland pp. 447–462. Abingdon: Routledge.

Ingold, Tim. 2017. "That's Enough About Ethnography!" *Moment Journal* 4 (1): 173–188. https://doi.org/10.17572/mj2017.1.173188.

Isaacs, Ellen. 2016. "The Value of Rapid Ethnography." *Advancing Ethnography in Corporate Environments.* pp. 92–107. Routledge.

Klümper, Wilhelm, and Matin Qaim. "A Meta-analysis of the Impacts of Genetically Modified Crops." *PloS One* 9 (11): e111629.

Lowy, Alex, and Phil Hood. 2004. *The Power of the 2×2 Matrix: Using 2×2 Thinking to Solve Business Problems and Make Better Decisions.* San Francisco: Jossey-Bass.

Lynch, Diahanna, and David Vogel. 2001. *The Regulation of GMOs in Europe and the United States: A Case-study of Contemporary European Regulatory Politics.* Council on Foreign Relations.

Miller, Daniel. 2010. *Stuff.* Cambridge: Polity Press.

Mintz, Sidney W., and Christine M. Du Bois. 2002. "The Anthropology of Food and Eating." *Annual Review of Anthropology* 31 (1): 99–119. https://doi.org/10.1146/a nnurev.anthro.32.032702.131011.

National Human Genome Research Institute. *"What is Genetic Engineering?"* Last modified 2020. https://www.genome.gov/genetics-glossary/Genetic-Engineering.

Nugent, Rachel. 2018. "Genetically Modified Organisms and the Ageing Population: Anthropological Insights into GMO Debates." *Journal of Population Ageing* 11 (2): 165–180.

Rabinow, Paul. 1996. *Making PCR: A story of Biotechnology.* Chicago: University of Chicago Press.

Roberts, Simon. 2022. *The Power of Not Thinking: How Our Bodies Learn and Why We Should Trust Them.* Lanham, MD: Rowman & Littlefield Publishing Group.

Roy, S. J., E. Negrão, and M. Tester. 2014. "Salt Resistant Crop Plants." *Current Opinion in Biotechnology* 26: 115–124.

Saussure, Ferdinandde. 1959. *Course in General Linguistics.* Edited by Charles Bally and Albert Sechehaye. Translated by Wade Baskin. New York: Philosophical Library.

Scott, Sydney E., Yoel Inbar, and Paul Rozin. 2016. "Evidence for Absolute Moral Opposition to Genetically Modified Food in the United States." *Perspectives on Psychological Science* 11 (3): 315–324. https://doi.org/10.1177/1745691615621275.

Stephens, Neil, Luca Di Silvio, Illtud Dunsford, Marianne Ellis, Abigail Glencross, and Alexandra Sexton. 2018. "Bringing Cultured Meat to Market: Technical, Socio-political, and Regulatory Challenges in Cellular Agriculture." *Trends in Food Science & Technology* 78: 155–166.

Stone, Glenn Davis. 2007. "Agricultural Deskilling and the Spread of Genetically Modified Cotton in Warangal." *Current Anthropology* 48 (1): 67–103.

Stone, Glenn Davis, and Dominic Glover. 2016. "Disembedding Grain: Golden Rice, the Green Revolution, and Heirloom Seeds in the Philippines." *Agriculture and Human Values* 34 (1): 87–102. https://doi.org/10.1007/s10460-016-9696-1.

Sunder Rajan, Kaushik. 2006. *Biocapital: The Constitution of Postgenomic Life.* Durham, NC: Duke University Press.

Tett, Gillian. 2021. *Anthro-Vision: A New Way to See in Business and Life.* New York: Avid Reader Press.

9 Biotechnology and Anthropology

Bringing Human Experience into Focus

Thomas Scott Hughes

Introduction: Biotechnology and the Anthropological Lens

In the realm of groundbreaking advancements, few sectors hold as much transformative promise as biotechnology. Biotech companies, drawing inspiration from the very essence of life and its intricate science, are positioned at the forefront of reshaping the landscape of healthcare (Collins & Varmus, 2015), agriculture (Tilman et al., 2011), environmental management (Rockström et al., 2009), industrial processing (Stephanopoulos, 1998), consumer goods (Trivedi et al., 2017), and possibly defense (Armstrong, 2010). These organizations have the potential to redefine our understanding of life, health, and well-being, using tools and techniques that once seemed the stuff of science fiction. The work they are engaged in isn't just innovative; it has the potential to fundamentally alter our perspectives on illness, wellness, and the human experience.

Having dedicated a significant portion of my academic and professional work to the multifaceted experience of illness, I was intrigued by those organizations that have the profound capability to enhance and even redefine patient experiences: Biotech companies. Their pioneering endeavors resonated with my own passion for understanding the often-complex human narratives and experiences surrounding illness. Throughout my career trajectory, my interactions with biotech and life science entities have been twofold – as an academic researcher and as an anthropology-based management consultant. This dual engagement has allowed me to immerse myself in both the technical and human aspects of the business of biotech innovations.

Anthropology, with its emphasis on human experiences, behaviors, and cultures, brings a unique lens to the world of biotech. In an industry teeming with technological brilliance and innovation, it is easy to overlook the human element. Yet, this human element is critical. The technologies birthed in biotech labs are not just abstract scientific achievements; they grapple with profound anthropological questions – questions about the lived experiences of illness, the nature and nuances of care, and the overarching impact on human lives. My work, informed by theories from phenomenology and organizational anthropology, has strived to bridge this gap, to infuse the world of biotech with rich human insights.

DOI: 10.4324/9781003458555-9

For anthropologists, the biotech sector offers a fertile ground. We have the privilege, and indeed the responsibility, to bring the vast tapestry of human experiences into sharp focus for these organizations. As I will highlight, anthropology is not just equipped to deepen our understanding of how bio-technologies interface with the world but also to better understand and shape the organizational cultures that produce these groundbreaking innovations. Our expertise doesn't just help biotech companies better understand the patient groups they serve; it also sheds light on their own organizational cultures, dynamics, and ethos. My foundation in applied medical anthropology, I believe, has found its most impactful application in this exciting intersection of science, technology, and humanity.

This chapter explores the landscape and origins of biotechnology as a field and discusses the importance of an anthropological lens in this field. It also explores a case study of my most recent research project that shows how anthropology can not only provide value in understanding the impact of bio-tech products but also the innovative organizations that create them. There are many phenomena and aspects shaping biotechnological innovation itself, but in this chapter, one critical and anthropologically salient one I will focus on is organizational culture and specifically diversity, equity, and inclusion's (DEI) role in shaping it. A deep understanding of how to shape organiza-tional culture and the tools at hand for doing this, particularly from the field of DEI, is an essential element for supporting ethical innovations in these organizations, both in terms of products and the processes that create them.

Finally, I explore how anthropology can shape a more ethical future for the biotech industry. Throughout my career in research and the life science industry, ethics have been the cornerstone of my engagements. My guiding principles – confidentiality, volunteerism, and a heartfelt concern for the well-being of my informants – have been essential. I have always endeavored to ensure that my research not only respects but actively safeguards the interests and well-being of those I work with. It's a commitment that extends beyond the immediate research process to encompass the broader implications of the organizations and innovations I support, meaning that it is my responsibility to ensure not only that my work is ethical but also that it supports ethical organizations that are having a positive impact on the world.

As we delve deeper into this chapter, I invite you to journey with me into the heart of biotechnology – not just as a realm of scientific marvels but as a space where human stories, experiences, and aspirations intersect with cut-ting-edge innovation. This story begins with my own first experiences of wonder and inspiration in this exciting field.

My Own Journey Through Anthropology and Life Sciences

In the vast and ever-evolving landscape of applied research and business strategy, my journey over the past decade has been an exploration of the intricate interplay between qualitative research methods and the dynamic field of life sciences. What first ignited my passion for this field was the opportunity to examine experiences at the intersection of life and death, health and illness, providing me with a visceral understanding of the human condition in its most vulnerable state. This topic is close to my heart, likely due to my experience watching my father struggle with a physically and socially debilitating chronic illness throughout his life. Here, I could see that his illness was only one factor in the burden he experienced – the most salient was actually social exclusion. I have always pursued this interest in my work, be it volunteering in nonprofit clinics and community centers or working in nursing homes as a caregiver. However, I was first able to pursue this topic academically at the University of Copenhagen's Department of Anthropology. There, I did my master's project exploring the experience of mental illness and ethnic otherness in the Danish healthcare system.

My initial foray into working with life science organizations was during my engagement with The Ida Institute in Copenhagen, an independent, nonprofit think tank that works with clinicians, academics, and people with hearing loss around the world to support the development of knowledge, skills, and confidence in order to better manage hearing loss. This period was more than just a professional stint; it was a deep dive into the profound connections between medical science and the vast tapestry of human experiences. Here, my intrigue with the complexities of life and illness continued to flourish. The Institute's focus on the vital importance of the social in understanding the utility of audiological technologies provided the perfect platform to nurture my budding interest in the narratives surrounding illness and care.

However, it was my tenure at ReD Associates, a human science-based management consulting house straddling the cities of Copenhagen and New York, that truly sharpened my applied research skills and broadened my horizons as an anthropologist in the life science industry. As a strategy consultant, I was immersed in using social science methods and theory to derive unique human insights, address complex challenges, and craft people-centered strategies for some of the life science industry's leading names. One particularly powerful use of anthropology here was using ethnographic methods to bring to these life science companies a profoundly deep understanding of the lived experiences of the patients that includes a wide lens of the environments they are in and the challenges they face (see Hughes et al., 2020a–2020d). This work served to inform the creation of better technologies and support services. With the opportunity to lead projects and use social science to spearhead foundational insights, research, and advising on pivotal organizational change strategies for biotech companies, I began to solidify my niche at the intersection of anthropology and biotech. There were always new life science clients with new interesting problems that required adaptability but also allowed for rapid learning about the industry.

In the winter of 2021, I embarked on an amazing new career opportunity at the heart of the intersection of biotech and academic anthropology when I accepted a postdoctoral research position at the Department of Anthropology at the University of Copenhagen to lead a collaboration with a prominent Danish biotech firm that I will refer to as The Danish Biotech. The company was interested in understanding how its organizational culture and DEI related to its continued ability to produce exceptionally innovative biotech discoveries and products. This opportunity was the culmination of my experiences in academia and industry and turned out to be one of my most cherished collaborations. This wasn't merely an academic endeavor. I was actively involved in shaping and refining culture-strengthening initiatives and DEI strategies, drawing from the insights that our project unearthed. The insights from this project, which will be explored as a case study below, support the growing body of research connecting strong organizational culture and DEI programs with an organization's continued innovation potential (Cox & Blake, 1991; Hunt et al., 2015) and in the field of drug development in particular (Bresman & Edmondson, 2022). In addition to the many other ways anthropology can play a vital role in the biotech industry, supporting a continued culture of innovation within the organizations is a critical one that is relatively unexplored.

This engagement as a postdoc provided more than just professional growth. I had the privilege of dialogue on culture and DEI matters with the The Danish Biotech's leadership, including enriching interactions with the CEO and the global leadership team. These moments underscored for me the immense value of anthropology in deciphering, nurturing, and guiding organizational cultures, especially in the fast-paced realm of the biotech industry. For example, providing insight into how to build bridges and leverage the inevitable cultural differences seen in a high-growth organization. The project also showed the powerfully creative potential of anthropology when combined with expertise from other disciplines, for example, scientific research. One such partnership was explored in a recent article describing my collaboration with a scientist and a filmmaker, where we endeavored to render the experience of people who work in biotech labs in a short film (Hughes et al., 2022).

Reflecting on my path overall, I see it as a testament to the immense potential that lies at the crossroads of disciplines. My academic pursuits, complemented by my roles across varied organizations, equipped me with a multifaceted skill set: Anthropology's keen eye for deep drivers of behavior and critical stance on the norm can be extremely impactful when combined with an understanding of the norms, communication style, and organizational dynamics of the commercial organizations that shape our world. This skill set, continually enriched by learning and meaningful connections, has empowered me to make impactful contributions to the biotech sector, championing the lens of anthropology.

As I look toward the future, what continues to excite me is the transformative impact that is possible when anthropological perspectives and insights are applied within the industry. The confluence of anthropology and biotechnology doesn't just result in theoretical discussions; it leads to tangible, life-altering outcomes. Ethnographic methods and phenomenologically informed theory from the world of anthropology (e.g., Kleinman & Kleinman, 1991) have afforded me the unique opportunity to dig deeper into the lived experiences of patients, caregivers, and healthcare professionals. This adds a crucial layer of understanding to the empirical data that life science companies often rely upon. And I see our role as critical in shaping ethical innovation for biotech organizations and the biotech industry as a whole.

This is not merely a professional pursuit for me; it's a personal one. Every strategy I craft, and every project I lead, brings me one step closer to affecting change at that significant intersection of life and death, the very aspect that drew me into this field in the first place. The ability to not just study human experiences but to actually improve them is what fuels my curiosity and drive each day. As I continue my work, my focus remains steadfast on creating a symbiotic relationship between life sciences and anthropology, aiming to humanize the former and give actionable purpose to the latter. I am excited by the endless possibilities this integration offers to enable the development of innovative medical technologies that consider the holistic needs of patients. My journey is far from over; in many ways, as I have now joined the ranks of The Danish Biotech I researched as a postdoc, it feels like it's just beginning.

As we delve deeper into the fascinating confluence of biotechnology and anthropology, I hope my experiences serve as both an inspiration and a guide, shedding light on the myriad ways in which science and humanity can harmoniously converge.

Biotechnology and the Anthropological: An Overview of its Historical Interplay and Current State of the Art

"Biotechnology" refers to the use of biology to create products, often for human benefit. This field amalgamates biology with technology to develop products and solutions for a myriad of sectors, most notably healthcare, agriculture, and the environment (Bhatia, 2018). Its emergence and subsequent evolution offer a riveting tale of scientific advancement and innovation. While fundamentally rooted in molecular biology, genetics, and other scientific disciplines, biotechnology is not isolated from the sociocultural fabric it operates within. There has always been a significant interplay between biotechnological advancements and the practical realm of social science. Whether it's the development of genetically modified organisms (GMOs) and the ensuing public debates around food safety and ethics or the challenges and considerations of gene editing via CRISPR in human embryos, the technologies of biotech are deeply intertwined with societal values, beliefs, and structures.

As the field continues to shape our medical treatments, food systems, and even our environmental interventions, the social implications of these technologies become increasingly prominent. Understanding biotechnology's trajectory requires not just a grasp of the science but also an appreciation for its impact on human identity, cultural values, ethical debates, and societal systems. This review delves into the historical progression of biotechnology, its current state, and its societal implications from a social science perspective in order to show an opening for anthropological investigation and intervention. I argue that a cultural understanding of the biotech organizations that are shaping our world from the inside out is essential for supporting ethical outcomes and their business success.

While biotechnology is often perceived as a modern innovation, taking an anthropological viewpoint reveals that the utilization of biology as a technology dates back to ancient civilizations. Moreover, it's essential to acknowledge that these early applications transcended mere technological advancements; they were profoundly intertwined with societal and cultural dynamics. For instance, the Sumerians and Babylonians employed biotechnological processes in fermentation to produce beer (Arnold, 2005). This wasn't merely a chemical process; it was a social one, intrinsically tied to community gatherings, religious ceremonies, and even economic exchanges (Mintz & Du Bois, 2002). Similarly, ancient Chinese civilizations utilized microbial fermentation for food and beverage applications, which were deeply embedded in cultural traditions and rituals (Ibid.). One concrete example is the production of "Jiu," a term that encompasses various types of alcoholic beverages like rice wine. These drinks have been made for thousands of years and are not only consumed for pleasure but also have ceremonial and ritualistic significance, for example, in traditional Chinese weddings, ancestral rites, and festivals (Newman, 2004). It's considered a symbol of joy and a way to connect with the divine or ancestral spirits (Ibid.). These practices are not just culinary but are deeply ingrained in the fabric of Chinese cultural and spiritual life. From an anthropological perspective, these early forms of biotechnology served as more than just practical applications; they were conduits for social interaction, cultural expression, and even the dissemination of traditional knowledge. They were community endeavors that bridged generational gaps, facilitated social cohesion, and contributed to the formation of collective identities.

It wasn't until the late 19th and early 20th centuries that biotechnology began its journey as a formal scientific endeavor. The term "biotechnology" itself was coined in 1919 by Karl Ereky, a Hungarian engineer, envisioning a process of converting raw materials into a more useful product through biological systems (Ereky, 1919). Even here, the anthropological dimension persists. Ereky's vision wasn't merely a technical one; it was reflective of broader shifts in industrial society, labor relations, and human interaction with the natural world, e.g., the era's broader movement toward applying scientific knowledge to solve complex industrial problems, as outlined by Rasmussen (2014). The subsequent decades witnessed seminal discoveries that laid the foundation for modern biotech, such as the structure of DNA in 1953 by Watson and Crick, with the pivotal contributions of Rosalind Franklin (Watson & Crick, 1953; Cobb & Comfort, 2023). While modern biotechnology is not exclusively DNA-centered, this scientific leap ushered in a new era of ethical and social questions that are deeply anthropological in nature, from concerns about genetic privacy to the cultural implications of gene editing.

Another monumental leap in the field came with the development of recombinant DNA technology in the 1970s. This allowed scientists to manipulate DNA and led to the creation of the first genetically engineered organism (Cohen et al., 1973). The implications were vast: The possibility of producing human insulin using bacteria, pioneering work that was realized by Genentech in 1978 (Goeddel et al., 1979). This breakthrough heralded the inception of the modern conception of the biotech industry, with companies focusing on developing drugs using recombinant DNA technology. The rise of recombinant DNA technology in the 1970s was not just a scientific milestone but also a societal conundrum. The potential to alter DNA opened debates around ethics, identity, and the very essence of life. While the technology promised solutions to diseases, it also raised profound questions about the manipulation of life, societal acceptance, and the boundaries of human intervention.

The late 20th century saw another transformative endeavor – the Human Genome Project (HGP). Launched in 1990 and completed in 2003, the HGP aimed to map all the genes in the human genome (Collins et al., 2003). This endeavor revolutionized biotech, giving rise to the genomics era. The information from HGP has been instrumental in identifying genes associated with diseases, enabling targeted drug development and personalized medicine. This mapping of the entirety of the human genome prompted more societal introspection around privacy, data ownership, and potential misuse. Moreover, it evoked discussions on identity, ancestry, and the very notion of what it means to be human in a world where one's genetic code could be read like a book (Nelkin & Lindee, 1995; Nelson, 2016). Anthropology, with its expertise in studying human societies, cultural norms, and ethical considerations, can offer valuable insights and guidance on navigating the ethical complexities arising from these advancements in genomics, helping to shape responsible practices and policies.

The current state of biotech is marked by rapid advancements and innovations. One of the most notable breakthroughs in recent years has been the development of CRISPR-Cas9 genome editing technology. This technique allows precise modification of genes in living organisms and holds potential for therapeutic applications, including treating genetic disorders (Doudna & Charpentier, 2014). The CRISPR-Cas9 genome editing breakthrough stands at the intersection of promise and ethical dilemma. While it offers revolutionary therapeutic potentials, it also ventures into morally ambiguous territories, like designer babies and the alteration of the human germline. For example, the recent case of He Jiankui, the Chinese scientist who drew global attention with his announcement in 2018 of his involvement in the creation of genetically modified babies, serves as a cautionary tale, emphasizing that the pursuit of biotech breakthroughs must always be guided by a strong ethical framework to prevent reckless and potentially harmful applications of technology (Normile, 2019). Societal debates around CRISPR encapsulate the broader struggle of balancing scientific potential with ethical considerations (Jasanoff & Hurlbut, 2018).

Biotechnology, from its humble beginnings in ancient civilizations to the cutting-edge innovations of today, has profoundly impacted humanity. Its trajectory is a testament to human ingenuity and the relentless pursuit of knowledge. As we stand on the cusp of new discoveries, e.g., in precision medicine, the future of biotech promises even greater advancements, holding the potential to reshape our world in ways previously deemed the realm of science fiction. What is clear from a social science viewpoint is that biotechnology is not an isolated scientific endeavor; it's a societal dialogue (Mayer & Sandøe, 2002). Its advancements continually shape and are shaped by societal norms, ethics, and values. As biotech propels us into an era of unparalleled possibilities, society's role in grounding these advancements in ethical, moral, and value-driven frameworks becomes paramount. For example, the confluence of the biotech industry with emerging digital and artificial intelligence technologies will present many more ethical questions about privacy, agency, access, and even what it means to be human (Bennet, 2017; Floridi, 2023). That is why a deep cultural understanding of the organizations that create these innovations, and even a position within them, is critical, not only for their success but to help foster a dialogue on how these organizations are shaping our society and to help steer the organizational culture toward ethical outcomes.

The narrative of biotechnology told through its scientific milestones and ethical quandaries can help us understand the context of where the field is today. Yet, a crucial dimension remains relatively unexplored: The organizational cultures and internal dynamics that shape these innovations and their societal impacts. Understanding biotechnology from this vantage point is not just advantageous; it's a business imperative. Biotech organizations are not monolithic entities but complex socio-technical systems. They are inhabited by a diverse array of individuals – from bench scientists to business strategists, from ethicists to engineers – each bringing their own perspectives, values, and cultural backgrounds into the mix. This diversity shapes not only how work is done but also what kinds of questions are asked and what solutions are deemed acceptable or viable.

Biotech organizations are intricate ecosystems in themselves, comprising a variety of roles – scientists, ethicists, business strategists, and more – that contribute to both its innovative capacity and ethical considerations. As Pettigrew (1979) laid the groundwork for understanding organizational culture, anthropology had already long been committed to understanding the complex nuances of human cultures, dating back to foundational works such as Malinowski's (1944). As opposed to managerial studies, which have often reduced organizational culture to a set of normative beliefs serving organizational interests (Martin, 1992; Czarniawska & Joerges, 1996), anthropology views it as deeply embedded within its broader social, historical, and political context

(Smircich, 1983; Alvesson, 2002). In the context of ethical decision making within biotech, this anthropological perspective is invaluable (Schein, 2010).

From the inside, the decision to pursue a specific line of research or to commercialize a particular technology is often the outcome of intricate social negotiations. These negotiations take place in the context of internal hierarchies, professional norms, market pressures, and sometimes even the personal ambitions and ethical orientations of those involved. Therefore, the technologies that eventually emerge – be it CRISPR, recombinant DNA, or bioengineered agriculture – are as much a product of these social dynamics as they are of scientific ingenuity. Moreover, the internal culture of biotech organizations can significantly influence how ethical considerations are integrated into research and development. For example, an organization with a strong culture of social responsibility may be more inclined to prioritize projects with clear public health benefits and to engage more deeply with ethical, legal, and social implications. On the other hand, an organization driven primarily by profit motives and shareholder value may navigate ethical landscapes differently.

DEI is a critical component of an ethical framework that guides innovation. Anthropology's unique contribution to DEI becomes evident when we consider how it delves into the covert power structures, assumptions, and social dynamics governing organizational behavior (Martin, 1992; Alvesson & Sveningsson, 2015). Such a multifaceted understanding of culture provides a roadmap for leveraging DEI not just as a set of initiatives but as a core element of an ethical culture of innovation. Anthropological methods, especially ethnographic approaches, with its focus on deeply embedded local complexities of culture, power dynamics, and social relations, offers invaluable perspectives in this domain (Cefkin, 2009; Lamont & Molnár, 2002; Martin, 1992; Schwartzman, 1993; Van Maanen, 1991; Vallas, 2006). They can provide comprehensive insights into the experiences of a diverse workforce and contribute to more equitable hiring and management processes (Ladson-Billings, 1998; García Bedolla & Michelson, 2012). In essence, anthropology offers a magnifying glass that brings the complexities of organizational culture into sharp focus – complexities that are often obscured in traditional management studies but are crucial for ethical decision making in biotech.

As we will see in the coming case study, anthropological research within these organizations can offer invaluable insights into these processes. By employing methods such as participant observation, interviews, and organizational ethnography, anthropologists can unearth the implicit assumptions, values, and norms that guide decision making. This understanding is critical not just for the organizations themselves, as they strive for more responsible innovation, but also for society at large, as we seek to understand the kinds of institutions that are shaping our collective future. As biotechnology continues to advance, bringing with it both transformative possibilities and complex dilemmas around scientific progress and ethical concerns, e.g., genetic privacy, genetics-based inequality, and access to medicine, the need for this inside perspective becomes ever more urgent. Only by understanding biotech organizations from within can we fully grasp the multidimensional impacts of their work, from the laboratory bench to the broader realms of society and ethics. This inside look is essential for anyone committed to steering biotechnology toward more equitable, ethical, and socially responsible outcomes.

An "inside-out" perspective enriched by anthropological insights allows biotech organizations to navigate the intricate cultural and ethical landscapes they inhabit. By understanding their own internal cultures, norms, and ethical frameworks, biotech organizations can innovate more effectively and ethically, avoiding crises and fostering a culture that is inclusive, equitable, and attuned to the broader social implications of their work. Anthropology, with its deep-rooted understanding of culture, stands as a powerful ally in this endeavor, ensuring that the biotechnological innovations of tomorrow are born from ethical, inclusive, and equitable cultures today. In biotechnology, it's crucial to look not just at the end results but also at how organizations arrive at these outcomes. The "grounded ethics" approach highlighted by Dull et al. (2020) suggests we should study real-world behavior and choices to understand ethical issues. Anthropology helps us do this by examining the culture within biotech organizations. This is especially useful for making DEI more than just buzzwords; it helps to integrate these concepts into the fabric of the organization's ethical decision making. By using a grounded approach, we get a a more complete picture of the ethics in biotechnology, making it easier to innovate in a way that is not only effective but also ethical and socially responsible.

In the section that follows, this understanding is brought to life through an anthropological research case study that delves into the organizational culture driving innovation in a leading biotech firm. This case study serves as a concrete example of the intricate interplay between internal dynamics, ethical considerations, and scientific advancements within biotech organizations. It illustrates how an anthropological lens can offer insights into the often unseen, but profoundly influential, cultural factors that shape not only what biotech firms do but also how they think. As you read, consider this case study as both an illustration and a call to action, demonstrating the need for anthropological engagement in shaping the future of biotechnology.

Applied Anthropology Case Study: Biotech Innovation through Deep Cultural Understanding

Understanding biotech organizations from the inside is more than just an academic pursuit; it's a business imperative. The following case focuses on how the culture-strengthening insights can support a continued culture of innovation in a biotech. As you delve into this case study, view it from two interconnected perspectives: A detailed examination of a specific scenario within biotechnology and a broader commentary on the pivotal role of anthropology in guiding biotechnology toward outcomes that are more equitable, ethical, socially responsible, and ultimately more innovative.

Conducted over two years, at a rapidly growing international biotech firm, The Danish Biotech, this research project aimed to provide an in-depth view of the organization from the inside. In the project, I was embedded as an anthropologist in the newly formed DEI team, thereby gaining insights into how culture and DEI are not only a set of policies but also a crucial part of the company's innovative ethos. Taking cues from anthropological methods and theories, this study delves into the complexities of what I refer to as The Danish Biotech's unique "critical collectivist" culture. It is an ecosystem where inclusivity, critical thinking, and personal trust form the bedrock of innovation. The research argues that leveraging anthropological understanding of the intricate social, cultural, and political factors can greatly enrich biotech organizations' innovative potential. It shows that investing in effective culture works and DEI practices can lead not just to greater diversity but also to stronger collaborations and more robust innovation within biotech organizations. This case study is not merely an isolated instance but a compelling exemplification of the broader argument for the anthropological imperative to understand and shape the field of biotechnology from within.

Setting the Stage: The Danish Biotech in a Period of Rapid Growth

For modern high-growth biotech organizations, fostering a cohesive culture is an inevitable challenge. Biotechnology firms that are at the forefront of scientific innovation are often operating in a fast-paced, high-stakes, and international environment. This pace and intensity can offer little room for error, especially when navigating the nuanced landscapes of culture, ethics, and diversity. For success, these organizations need a broad range of internationally diverse subject area specialists to work in concert, for example, in the life science space to move a discovery from the lab bench to the patient. A strong culture of collaboration across these differences is essential for the continued success of these organizations.

Amid this rapid expansion across diverse cultural terrains, the call for a culture strategy that resonates universally yet caters individually becomes particularly loud. The challenges, such as retaining trust, psychological safety, and mutual respect in the face of inevitable cultural misunderstandings and constrained resources, are daunting but not insurmountable. This is where anthropology comes in, offering a unique approach that can help organizations to better understand the deep locally embedded complexities of culture, power dynamics, and social relations that underpin these potential conflicts.

The Danish Biotech, recognized for its culture of innovation, also finds itself at a critical juncture. As the company expands, it faces the complex task of scaling its innovative capacity while also preserving the core elements of its organizational culture that made its growth possible in the first place. It's a delicate balance, calling for strategies that are not just scientifically robust but also culturally sensitive and ethically grounded. A misstep in the company's culture could not only compromise its internal cohesion but also impact its innovative output, thereby influencing its standing in the highly competitive biotech industry. If they are unable to continue moving discoveries to market at their exceptional rate, they risk being outpaced by competitors. But with the right anthropological insights, The Danish Biotech has the opportunity to intentionally shape and safeguard its organizational culture in a way that is both effective and resonant, contributing to stronger collaborations and sustaining its innovation amid rapid organizational growth.

This case study delves into how The Danish Biotech addresses these challenges, guided by anthropological methods and theories. As you read on, you'll gain a comprehensive understanding of how anthropology can offer practical solutions to real-world organizational challenges, particularly in sectors as dynamic and complex as biotechnology.

Enter Anthropology: A Postdoctoral Research Project from the University of Copenhagen

As The Danish Biotech found itself at the crossroads of rapid expansion and eager to maintain its culture of innovation, an applied anthropological research intervention emerged as a timely solution. Spearheaded by the Department of Anthropology at the University of Copenhagen, this intervention took the form of a two-year postdoctoral research project aimed at dissecting the complexities of organizational culture in the face of rapid growth, with a specific focus on the power of DEI.

Study Design and Setting

Drawing from ethnographic traditions (Chatman & O'Reilly, 2016) and the "grounded ethics" framework (Dull et al., 2020), this qualitative research project was embedded within the international biotech company for a span of two years. The primary objective was to explore the intricate dynamics of organizational culture, focusing in particular on DEI's role in a setting characterized by rapid growth and diversification. The application of grounded ethics provided an empirical, field-based perspective that guided the study's ethical and methodological rigor, considering the complex and consequential nature of biotech industries. While many companies in the field of emerging technologies have begun trying to address ethical considerations, their techniques are often hindered by the classical approach of moral philosophy and ethics – namely normative philosophy – which prescribes an approach to resolving ethical dilemmas from the outset based on assumed moral truths (Dull et al., 2020). In contrast, "grounded ethics" proposes to do the opposite: To discover them by going out into the world to study how relevant people resolve similar ethical dilemmas in their daily lives (Ibid.).

Data Collection

By integrating both ethnographic methodology, action research, and grounded ethics, this study aimed to offer a multidimensional, empirically grounded insight into the complex organizational culture and ethical considerations of organizational culture and DEI within biotech settings. By incorporating ethnographic methods such as participant observation and semi-structured interviews, the study reveals the nuances and hidden levers that influence both decision making and ethical frameworks within biotech companies (Martin, 1992; Lamont & Molnár, 2002). Qualitative research techniques such as coding and thematic analysis were used to interpret the gathered data.

The most essential element of the data-gathering process was my long-term embedded role in the organization. For 24 months, intensive ethnographic fieldwork was carried out. As an embedded researcher on the biotech's DEI team, I was involved in various capacities within the organization, from an initial observer to participating in daily activities and eventually contributing to strategy setting based on early research insights. This approach allowed for a nuanced "inside-out" understanding of the organization, capturing its ethical, social, and cultural dimensions (Schein, 2010; Cameron & Quinn, 2011).

Aligned with the "grounded ethics" approach, I also conducted a series of semi-structured interviews throughout this fieldwork. In total, I conducted interviews with 53 employees across different levels and sites of the organization to uncover employee assumptions and beliefs (Kvale, 1996). Each interview lasted approximately 60 minutes and aimed to delve into individual perspectives, experiences, and ethical considerations concerning DEI. Interviews were audio-recorded with explicit consent from the participants. In addition to these interviews, a rigorous document analysis was conducted to provide a more comprehensive understanding of the formal organizational stance on DEI. This included scrutinizing DEI policy guidelines, training manuals, and internal communications. This aspect of the research design helped in contrasting the formal rhetoric with actual practices, an element that grounded ethics argues is crucial for understanding real-world ethical dilemmas (Dull et al., 2020).

The data gathered was then analyzed through a process of coding and thematic analysis (Berg & Lune, 2012). This bottom-up approach facilitated a deeper understanding of the ethical frameworks and DEI practices within the organization (McCarthy et al., 2006). An action research element of the project, described below, allowed further learning from this embedded position, where early insights were put into practice, and the observed results informed the overall findings of the project (Reason & Bradbury, 2001).

Ethical integrity was a major concern in this work, especially given the sensitive nature of DEI topics. All participants provided informed consent, and confidentiality was maintained through the use of pseudonyms and stringent anonymization protocols. The study received ethical clearance from the University of Copenhagen and adhered to international ethical standards outlined by ICC/ESOMAR (2016).

What the Project Found: The Fabric of "Critical Collectivism"

The concept of "critical collectivism" emerged as a powerful descriptor for the organizational culture at The Danish Biotech. This culture is a complex tapestry woven from threads of inclusivity, critical thinking, and trust. Together, these attributes not only define the company's core ethos but also seem to fuel its innovation engine.

The Pillars of Critical Collectivism

1. TRUST: THE CORNERSTONE OF COLLABORATION

In an environment where rapid growth is the norm, trust serves as a stabilizing force. It not only sustains the organization's innovative capabilities but also acts as the social glue binding teams together.

Executive, US: "High trust levels are essential to maintaining our innovative edge as we expand."

2. COLLABORATING ACROSS DIFFERENCES: THE SPARK OF INNOVATION

Diversity within the organization is not just a tick-box exercise; it's strategically essential. Diverse teams bring in multiple novel perspectives, enriching the company's problem-solving capabilities (Bresman & Edmondson, 2022; Cox & Blake, 1991; Hunt et al., 2015).

Director, Enabling, DK: "Diversity is like having multiple lenses to look at a problem, enriching our problem-solving and ideation processes."

3. INCLUSIVITY AND CRITICAL THINKING: A POWERFUL COMBINATION

The data revealed an intriguing relationship between inclusivity and critical thinking. An inclusive culture fosters a safe space for constructive critical discussions, driving robust decision making.

Project Manager, RD, NL: "Inclusivity leads to a culture where every idea is dissected critically."

Challenges Facing Critical Collectivism: Navigating Growth and Culture

While The Danish Biotech thrives on its "critical collectivist" ethos, the challenge lies in maintaining this culture amidst rapid growth and global expansion. The organization's global expansion brings both opportunities and challenges. On the one hand, it enriches the workforce's diversity, creating a fertile ground for "creative friction." On the other, it also raises concerns about cultural dilution and introduces the risk of internal conflicts.

Director, Commercial, US: "There's a worry that the one culture may dominate over another as we grow."

Director, RD, NL: "Preserving our 'One Team' spirit becomes a critical task as we continue to grow."

Locally Contextualized DEI Presents a Way Forward

Why is locally contextualized DEI indispensable in supporting a culture of innovation in high-growth biotech organizations? It serves as the protective shield against the cultural erosion that rapid growth and globalization can bring. When DEI is embedded within local geographic and business area contexts – taking into account local norms, sensitivities, and specific challenges – it ensures that the foundational elements of trust, diversity, and inclusivity are not only maintained but also enriched. It allows for a "glocalized" approach – global reach with a local touch – that preserves the core attributes of critical collectivism. Moreover, locally tailored DEI initiatives serve as cultural anchors that reinforce the organization's collectivist values. They provide a structured framework for integrating new team members into the prevailing culture, ensuring that growth does not dilute the organizational ethos but enriches it.

In essence, these DEI efforts are not mere add-ons but essential gears in the innovation engine of The Danish Biotech. They serve as the cultural scaffolding that supports not only the integrity of the unique organizational culture but also its future viability. As the company stands on the precipice of unprecedented expansion, a localized and deeply integrated DEI strategy can help provide a cultural compass and propeller to ensure that the organization both excels and remains true to its foundational values. This research makes it clear: For The Danish Biotech, preserving its "critical collectivist" culture in the face of growth isn't just an aspiration; it's a strategic necessity. Furthermore, localized, contextually informed DEI work is the essential ingredient in ensuring that this unique culture not only survives the challenges of expansion but thrives and evolves through them.

Concluding Thoughts

The findings reveal a complex landscape of organizational dynamics that drive The Danish Biotech's innovative prowess, where an increasingly diverse set of actors, both in terms of personal background and professionalism, need to effectively collaborate, and their cultural differences need to be not only managed but leveraged for the continued success of the organization. The interplay between trust, critical thinking, diversity, and inclusivity – elements of what we term "critical collectivism" – creates a fertile ground for innovation. However, as the company scales, the stakes are high. Will it manage to preserve this unique culture that has been its competitive edge? In the action research element of the project, I observed how DEI initiatives, informed by anthropological insights, could well be key in guiding this journey.

Putting Anthropological Insights into Action: A Three-Pronged Approach to Supporting Biotech Innovation

The project findings illuminate how the unique "critical collectivist" culture at The Danish Biotech provides fertile ground for innovation. However, growth presents a double-edged sword, offering both opportunities and challenges for preserving this organizational culture. Leveraging these anthropological insights and the results of action research, I will outline a three-pronged approach for how to harness the tools of DEI for fostering innovation during periods of organizational growth in biotech organizations.

1. Invest in Connections Across Boundaries

Understanding the complex cultural landscapes within the biotech organization is key to fostering a culture of trust and inclusion. The research revealed opportunities for leveraging existing bridges across cultural differences, thereby fostering a greater sense of inclusion.

Action Taken: As an embedded researcher on The Danish Biotech's DEI team, we introduced various initiatives – events, games, films, and workshop series – to promote mutual understanding and trust. One example is an internal workshop series that focuses on enhancing collaborations through cultural self-awareness and mutual understanding. The series, informed by empirical data, has received overwhelmingly positive feedback from participants, acknowledging the utility of the tools they were provided for more effective collaboration across cultural boundaries.

2. Co-create Culture Work to Drive Adoption

Culture should not merely be a top-down initiative but a shared organizational value. For example, anthropological insights revealed a complex picture of DEI concepts across different layers of the organization that could ultimately be coupled together to great benefit in processes of initiative and, ultimately, meaning, co-creation. This approach is particularly ineffective in our environment, where a prevalent "rebel spirit" often leads to the rejection of top-down directives, especially in such aspects as personal as culture. Employees are more receptive to top-down messages when they align with their values or benefit them directly. In recognizing that culture can't be "done to" someone, our team's strategy has been to use a co-creation approach.

Action Taken: As part of the DEI team, we utilized co-creation as a strategy to drive DEI work adoption and ownership in the organization. The team actively engaged employees in defining DEI concepts, facilitated open discussions, and included employee voices in DEI awareness events. This co-creation strategy led to increased engagement and a groundswell of interest in DEI work within the organization, visible in the number of views on DEI intranet content and event attendance.

3. Adopt a Social Movement Paradigm for Culture Strategy

The Danish Biotech has a rich history of leaders inspiring employees by embracing unorthodox approaches to achieve their goals and employees taking the initiative to pursue an opportunity for the organization. Capitalizing on this phenomenon of a social movement cultivated by inspiration, culture work can be most effective when treated as a grassroots movement rather than a top-down initiative.

Action Taken: We laid the foundations for a DEI social movement by enabling employee resource groups (ERGs) as platforms for internal organization. These ERGs are designed to be democratic, bottom-up initiatives supported but not directed by executive leadership. Since their launch in Q4 2022, the ERGs have continued to rapidly grow in membership, indicating a strong internal commitment to culture and DEI.

Conclusion: An Anthropology Powered Culture of Biotech Innovation

The anthropological insights gained from this study have not just enriched my understanding of The Danish Biotech's unique organizational culture that resulted in its exceptional innovative capacity but have also informed the three actionable strategies outlined above for sustaining this innovative capacity in the face of growth and change. By investing in cross-boundary connections, co-creating DEI, and adopting a social movement paradigm, we are not merely preserving but enriching the "critical collectivist" culture that drives the organization's innovative prowess.

Anthropology's Role in Guiding the Ethical Future of Biotechnology

The case study of The Danish Biotech serves as an instructive microcosm, illustrating how anthropological methods and the theory and concepts it generates can be applied to the complex and fast-paced world of biotechnology. Yet, the implications of this study reach far beyond one organization or even one sector. It raises a broader question that is both timely and timeless: What role does anthropology play in guiding the ethical and innovative future of biotechnology?

In a sector as dynamic and consequential as biotechnology, understanding the organizational culture is an ethical imperative. As biotechnology increasingly shapes our world, from medical advancements to environmental solutions, the sociocultural and ethical dimensions of its development become ever more critical. Anthropology offers a unique lens through which we can examine these dimensions. This section delves into anthropology's unique vantage point, emphasizing how it can guide organizations in developing effective strategies that maintain an ethical orientation within these organizations and, thereby, the technologies they produce. In doing so, anthropology helps shape not just the trajectory of individual organizations but also the ethical contours of biotechnology as a field. This is crucial for anyone committed to steering biotechnology toward more equitable, ethical, and socially responsible outcomes, for example, on the topics of genetic privacy, inclusion in clinical trials, access to new technologies, or the broader socio-economic implications of introducing bioengineered food.

The case study of The Danish Biotech serves as a compelling illustration of the power of anthropological insights in shaping an organizational culture of innovation, particularly with the tools of DEI. The case study not only illuminated the intricate interplay of social, cultural, and ethical factors within a high-growth biotech organization but also revealed actionable strategies for leveraging DEI as a conduit for innovation. Yet, The Danish Biotech example is not an isolated phenomenon. Rather, it stands as a testament to the broader, indispensable role that anthropology can play in the biotechnology sector. As biotechnology continues to advance at an unprecedented pace, bringing along a host of ethical dilemmas and societal challenges, the need for a nuanced understanding of the organizational cultures driving this innovation becomes increasingly urgent.

The Biotech Need for a Grounded "Inside-Out" Perspective

The public discourse on biotechnology often centers around its external impacts – be it the medical advancements it fosters, the environmental solutions it promises, or the ethical quandaries it raises. While these aspects are undeniably crucial, focusing solely on them risks overlooking the internal organizational cultures and social dynamics that actually give rise to these innovations and ethical considerations. Here, anthropologists have a role in not just delivering "innovation-as-a-service" (Wolf et al., 2020) but in supporting an ecosystem where ethical innovation can flourish. Understanding biotechnology through an "inside-out" perspective is, in this way, an ethical imperative.

This is where anthropology can offer fresh perspectives. Inspired by the concept of "grounded ethics," anthropologists argue for an empirical, field-based approach to understanding ethical dilemmas (Dull et al., 2020). Unlike classical ethics, which often starts with predefined moral principles, grounded ethics advocates for studying human behavior and choices as they unfold in real-world contexts. This could involve studying communities where new biotechnological solutions are introduced, analyzing how they align or clash with existing ethical norms, and how people navigate these moral mazes. Such an approach allows for ethical frameworks that are not only theoretically sound but also socially and culturally sensitive.

Anthropologists have the opportunity to become pivotal players in shaping biotechnology's ethical landscape, leading to the creation of more ethical products. By providing empirically grounded, culturally nuanced insights, they can contribute to the creation of ethical guidelines that are both practical and equitable. The multifaceted lens of anthropology allows for an enriched understanding of ethical questions, incorporating not just moral but also social, cultural, and economic dimensions. This offers a more comprehensive ethical framework that can guide scientists, policymakers, and practitioners in making decisions that are both scientifically innovative and ethically responsible.

As biotechnology continues to push the boundaries of what is scientifically possible, it is essential that ethical considerations evolve in tandem. Anthropology, with its emphasis on human-centric and context-specific understanding, provides a much-needed framework for navigating the ethical complexities of this burgeoning field. By adopting a grounded ethics approach, we can work toward a future where biotechnological innovations are not only groundbreaking but also ethically and socially sustainable.

Advice for Other Anthropologists Breaking Into this Field

Anthropologists have an opportunity to be at the forefront of policymaking in the biotechnology sector. By providing empirically grounded insights, they can help shape ethical guidelines that are both practical and socially just. We can contribute to more ethical innovation in biotech by engaging with affected communities and stakeholders to ensure such guidelines are feasibly sound and socially just in the worlds of those impacted by these technologies. As explored above, we can play a critical role within biotech organizations to support an organizational culture where not just innovation flourishes but ethical innovation. Moreover, anthropology's multidisciplinary approach allows for a more holistic view of ethical questions, incorporating social, cultural, and even economic dimensions. This offers a richer and more comprehensive framework that can guide biotechnology practitioners in developing products and technologies that are ethical, equitable, and socially responsible.

1. Focus on Applied Research

One of the most rewarding aspects of my career has been the emphasis on applied research. I encourage those looking to move into applied roles to look beyond the theoretical to how anthropological work can have a real-world impact. In the ever-evolving field of biotechnology, this is especially crucial.

My time at the University of Copenhagen and collaboration with The Danish Biotech offered a unique perspective that you can only get from straddling the line between research and industry. I highly recommend seeking out such partnerships as they can offer you the best of both worlds.

2. Embrace Multidisciplinary Collaboration with Industry

My career has been a blend of academic research and business strategy, focusing not just on anthropology but also on DEI and life sciences. One of the most rewarding projects I have worked on was the interdisciplinary endeavor to create an ethnographic film about science with other experts because we continually inspired each other (Hughes et al., 2022). The lesson here is to not pigeonhole yourself; the more fields you can traverse, the richer your work will be.

3. Step into Leadership

Being a postdoc and project lead has taught me that anthropology and bio-technology both require strong leadership skills. You'll need to be adept at coordinating research and overseeing complex projects, so start honing these skills early.

4. Specialize but Stay Adaptable

I've found a niche at the intersection of anthropology and life sciences. It's been rewarding, and I urge you to find your own specialized area within bio-technology. However, also remain flexible enough to shift your focus as the field evolves; it's a fast-moving space. New opportunities for anthropologists to provide value are always emerging.

5. Never Stop Learning

With over a decade in the field, I can say that continuous learning is not optional; it's a necessity. The landscape of biotechnology is ever-changing, and to stay relevant, you'll need to keep up. This also applies to the field of tech in general, where every new technological disruption presents a new opportunity for anthropologists to show their value in understanding the organizations that produced this innovation and the many questions of how it interfaces with society.

The journey through anthropology and biotechnology is as challenging as it is rewarding. It requires a multidisciplinary approach, a focus on real-world applications, and an unending curiosity. But for those willing to navigate its complexities, the rewards are immense.

Conclusion

In this chapter, we've navigated the complex intersection of anthropology and biotechnology – a confluence of disciplines that holds enormous potential for shaping the ethical, social, and cultural dimensions of scientific innovation. We began with an overview that set the stage for understanding the historical and current interplay between biotechnology and anthropological inquiry. Through the detailed case study of The Danish Biotech, we illustrated how anthropology can delve into the organizational culture of biotech firms, thereby influencing DEI initiatives and ethical frameworks.

We then considered the broader role of anthropology in guiding the ethical future of the entire biotechnology sector. The chapter highlighted the importance of adopting an "inside-out" perspective enriched by anthropological insights, advocating for grounded ethics as a comprehensive framework for tackling the ethical complexities of biotech innovations. Finally, we offered practical advice for anthropologists entering this field, emphasizing the need for applied research, multidisciplinary collaboration, leadership, specialization with flexibility, and continuous learning.

The overarching message is clear: Anthropology has a critical role to play in the biotechnology sector. Not only can it help decode the complex social and cultural dynamics within biotech organizations, but it can also guide the ethical trajectory of biotechnological advancements. In a world where biotechnology increasingly shapes our lives, healthcare, and environment, the anthropological lens offers insights for steering this field toward more equitable, ethical, and socially responsible outcomes.

For those willing to engage with the challenges and opportunities at this interdisciplinary juncture, the rewards – both intellectual and societal – are immense. This chapter serves as both a guide and an invitation to explore this compelling landscape where science meets society and where anthropology can serve as a moral and cultural compass in the ever-evolving realm of biotechnology.

Disclaimer

The research case mentioned was conducted by the University of Copenhagen in collaboration with The Danish Biotech. The author maintains a financially dependent relationship with the company. The views expressed in this presentation are solely those of the presenter and do not represent the views of The Danish Biotech, its subsidiaries, and/or affiliates.

Bibliography

Alvesson, Mats. 2002. *Understanding Organizational Culture.* London: Sage.
Alvesson, Mats, and Stefan Sveningsson. 2015. *Changing Organizational Culture: Cultural Change Work in Progress.* London: Routledge.
Armstrong, Robert E., ed. 2010. *Bio-inspired Innovation and National Security.* Washington, DC: National Defense University Press.
Arnold J. P. 2005. *Origin and History of Beer and Brewing: From Prehistoric Times to the Beginning of Brewing Science and Technology.* Cleveland, OH: BeerBooks.
Bennett, Gaymon. 2017. *The Ethics of Biotechnology.* London, UK: Routledge.

Berg, Bruce Lawrence, and Howard Lune. 2012. *Qualitative Research Methods for the Social Sciences*. Harlow, England: Pearson.

Bhatia, Saurabh. 2018. "History, Scope and Development of Biotechnology." In: *Introduction to Pharmaceutical Biotechnology, Volume 1: Basic Techniques and Concepts*. IOP Publishing Ltd.

Bresman, Henrik, and Amy C. Edmondson. 2022. "Research: To Excel, Diverse Teams Need Psychological Safety." *Harvard Business Review*.

Bull, A. T., G. Holt, and M. D. Lilly. 2000. *Biotechnology: International Trends and Perspectives*. OECD Publishing.

Cameron, Kim S., and Robert E. Quinn. 2011. *Diagnosing and Changing Organizational Culture: Based on the Competing Values Framework*. 3rd ed. San Francisco: Jossey-Bass.

Cefkin, Melissa. 2009. *Ethnography and the Corporate Encounter: Reflections on Research in and of Corporations*. New York: Berghahn.

Chatman, Jennifer A., and Charles A. O'Reilly. 2016. "Paradigm Lost: Reinvigorating the Study of Organizational Culture." *Research in Organizational Behavior* 36:199–224.

Cobb, Mathew, and Nathaniel Comfort. 2023. "What Rosalind Franklin Truly Contributed to the Discovery of DNA's Structure – Franklin was no Victim in How the DNA Double Helix was Solved. An Overlooked Letter and an Unpublished News Rrticle, Both Written in 1953, Reveal that She Was an Equal Player." *Nature* 616 (7958): 657–660.

Cohen, S. N., A. C. Chang, H. W. Boyer, and R. B. Helling. 1973. "Construction of Biologically Functional Bacterial Plasmids In Vitro." *Proceedings of the National Academy of Sciences of the United States of America* 70 (11): 3240–3244. https://doi.org/10.1073/pnas.70.11.3240.

Collins, Francis S., and Harold Varmus. 2015. "A New Initiative on Precision Medicine." *New England Journal of Medicine* 372 (9): 793–795.

Collins, F., E. Green, A. Guttmacher, et al. 2003. "A Vision for the Future of Genomics Research." *Nature* 422: 835–847. https://doi.org/10.1038/nature01626.

Cox, Taylor H., and Stacy Blake. 1991. "Managing Cultural Diversity: Implications for Organizational Competitiveness." *The Executive* 5 (3): 45–56. http://www.jstor.org/stable/4165021.

Czarniawska, Barbara, and Bernward Joerges. 1996. "Travels of Ideas." In: *Translating Organizational Change*, edited by Barbara Czarniawska and Guje Sevón, pp. 13–48. Berlin/New York: De Gruyter. https://doi.org/10.1515/9783110879735.13.

Doudna, J. A., and E. Charpentier. 2014. "The New Frontier of Genome Engineering with CRISPR-Cas9." *Science* 346 (6213): 1258096.

Dull, Ian, Fani Ntavelou Baum, and Thomas Hughes. 2020. "Where Can We Find an Ethics for Scale?: How to Define an Ethical Infrastructure for the Development of Future Technologies at Global Scale." *EPIC Proceedings*, 98–114. ISSN 1559–8918. https://epicpeople.org/where-can-we-find-ethics-for-scale/.

Ereky, K. 1919. "*Biotechnologie*." Verlag von Gustav Fischer.

Floridi, Luciano. 2023. *The Ethics of Artificial Intelligence – Principles, Challenges, and Opportunities*. Oxford: Oxford University Press.

García Bedolla, L., and M. R. Michelson. 2012. *Mobilizing Inclusion: Transforming the Electorate Through Get-Out-The-Vote Campaigns*. New Haven, CT: Yale University Press.

Goeddel, D. V., D. G. Kleid, F. Bolivar, et al. 1979. "Expression in Escherichia Coli of Chemically Synthesized Genes for Human Insulin." *Proceedings of the National*

Academy of Sciences of the United States of America 76 (1): 106–110. https://doi.org/10.1073/pnas.76.1.106.

Hughes, Thomas, Mikkel Brok-Kristensen, Yosha Gargeya, Anne Mette Worsøe Lottrup, Ask Bo Larsen, Ana Torres-Ortuño, Nicki Mackett, and John Stevens. 2020a. "What More Can we Ask For?: An Ethnographic Study of Challenges and Possibilities for People Living with Haemophilia." *The Journal of Haemophilia Practice* 7 (1): 25–36. https://doi.org/10.17225/jhp00151.

Hughes, Thomas, Mikkel Brok-Kristensen, Yosha Gargeya, Anne Lottrup, Ask Bo Larsen, Ana Torres-Ortuño, Nicki Mackett, and John Stevens. 2020b. "He's a Normal Kid Now: An Ethnographic Study of Challenges and Possibilities in a New Era of Haemophilia Care." *The Journal of Haemophilia Practice* 7 (1): 150–157. https://doi.org/10.17225/jhp00167.

Hughes, Thomas, Mikkel Brok-Kristensen, Yosha Gargeya, Anne Lottrup, Ask Bo Larsen, Ana Torres-Ortuño, Nicki Mackett, and John Stevens. 2020c. "Treating for Stability: An Ethnographic Study of Aspirations and Limitations in Haemophilia Treatment in Europe." *The Journal of Haemophilia Practice* 7 (1): 165–172. https://doi.org/10.17225/jhp00169.

Hughes, Thomas, Mikkel Brok-Kristensen, Yosha Gargeya, Anne Lottrup, Ask Bo Larsen, AnaTorres-Ortuño, NickiMackett, and John Stevens. 2020d. "Navigating Uncertainty: An Examination of How People with Haemophilia Understand and Cope with Uncertainty in Protection in an Ethnographic Study." *The Journal of Haemophilia Practice* 7 (1): 158–164. https://doi.org/10.17225/jhp00168.

Hughes, Thomas, BradyWelch, JanineSchuurman. 2022. "The Making of Pieces of the Puzzle: Reflections on a Collaborative Ethnographic Filmmaking Process." *Journal of Ethnographic Studies* 11 (02).

Hunt, Vivian, et al. 2015. "Why Diversity Matters." McKinsey & Company.

ICC, ESOMAR. 2016. "ICC/ESOMAR International Code on Market, Opinion and Social Research and Data Analytics." https://www.esomar.org/uploads/pdf/profes sional-standards/ICCESOMAR_Code_English_.pdf.

James, C. 1997. "Global Review of Commercialized Transgenic Crops: 1997." *ISAAA Briefs No. 5*. Ithaca, NY: ISAAA.

Jasanoff, S., and J. B. Hurlbut. 2018. "A Global Observatory for Gene Editing." *Nature* 555 (7697): 435–437.

Kleinman, Arthur, and Joan Kleinman. 1991. "Suffering and its Professional Transformation. Toward an Ethnography of Interpersonal Experience." *Culture, Medicine and Psychiatry* 15 (3): 275–301.

Kvale, Steinar. 1996. "*InterViews: An Introduction to Qualitative Research Interviewing.*" Thousand Oaks, CA: Sage.

Ladson-Billings, Gloria. 1998. "Just What Is Critical Race Theory and What's It Doing in a Nice Field like Education?" *International Journal of Qualitative Studies in Education* 11 (1): 7–24.

Lamont, Michèle, and Virág Molnár. 2002. "The Study of Boundaries in the Social Sciences." *Annual Review of Sociology* 28 (1): 167–195.

Malinowski, Bronisław. 1944. *A Scientific Theory of Culture, and Other Essays*. Chapel Hill, NC: University of North Carolina Press.

Martin, Joanne. 1992. *Cultures in Organizations: Three Perspectives*. Oxford: Oxford University Press.

Mayer, Gitte, and Peter Sandøe. 2002. "Scientists' Understanding of the Public." In: *Focus on Biotechnology. Issues Related to R&D in Biotechnology – Denmark in a*

Comparative Perspective. Aarhus: The Danish Institute for Studies in Research and Research Policy.

McCarthy, J., P. Sullivan, and P. Wright. 2006. "Culture, Personal Experience and Agency." *British Journal of Social Psychology* 45: 421–439.

Mintz, Sidney W., and Christine M. Du Bois. 2002. "The Anthropology of Food and Eating." *Annual Review of Anthropology* 31 (1): 99–119.

Nelkin, Dorothy, and M. Susan Lindee. 1995. *The DNA Mystique: The Gene as a Cultural Icon.* Freeman.

Nelson, Alondra. 2016. *The Social Life of DNA: Race, Reparations, and Reconciliation After the Genome.* Boston: Beacon Press.

Newman, Jacqueline M. 2004. *Food Culture in China.* Westport, CT: Greenwood Press.

Normile, Dennis. 2019. "Chinese Scientist who Produced Genetically Altered Babies Sentenced to 3 Years in Jail." *Science*, December 30, 2019. doi:10.1126/science. aba7347.

Pettigrew, Andrew M. 1979. "On Studying Organizational Cultures." *Administrative Science Quarterly* 24 (4): 570–581. https://doi.org/10.2307/2392363.

Rasmussen, S. 2014. *The Biotechnology Primer.* BioTech Primer Inc.

Reason, Peter, and Hilary Bradbury. 2001. *Handbook of Action Research: Participative Inquiry and Practice.* SAGE Publications.

Rockström, Johan, Will Steffen, Kevin Noone, Åsa Persson, F. Stuart Chapin III, Eric Lambin, et al. 2009. "Planetary Boundaries: Exploring the Safe Operating Space for Humanity." *Ecology and Society* 14 (2): 32.

Schein, Edgar H. 2010. *Organizational Culture and Leadership.* San Francisco: Jossey-Bass.

Schwartzman, Helen B. 1993. *Ethnography in Organizations.* Newbury Park, CA: Sage.

Smircich, Linda. 1983. "Concepts of Culture and Organizational Analysis." *Administrative Science Quarterly* 28 (3): 339–358.

Stephanopoulos, Gregory. 1998. "Metabolic Fluxes and Metabolic Engineering." *Metabolic Engineering* 1 (1): 1–11.

Tilman, David, Christian Balzer, Jason Hill, and Belinda L. Befort. 2011. "Global Food Demand and the Sustainable Intensification of Agriculture." *Proceedings of the National Academy of Sciences* 108 (50): 20260–20264.

Trivedi, D. K., Hollywood, K. A., and Goodacre, R. 2017. "Metabolomics for the Masses: The Future of Metabolomics in a Personalized World." *New Horizons in Translational Medicine*, 3 (6), 294–305. https://doi.org/10.1016/j.nhtm.2017.06.001.

Vallas, Steven Peter. 2006. "Empowerment Redux: Structure, Agency, and the Remaking of Managerial Authority." *American Journal of Sociology* 111 (6): 1677–1717. https://doi.org/10.1086/499909.

Van Maanen, John. 1991. "The Smile Factory: Work at Disneyland." In: *Reframing Organizational Culture*, edited by P. J. Frost, L. F. Moore, M. R. Louis, C. C. Lundberg, and Joanne Martin, pp. 58–76. Sage Publications, Inc.

Watson, James D., and Francis Crick. 1953. "Molecular Structure of Nucleic Acids: A Structure for Deoxyribose Nucleic Acid." *Nature* 171: 737–738. https://doi.org/10. 1038/171737a0.

Wolf, Christine T., and Jeanette Blomberg. 2020. "Innovation-as-a-Service: Emergent Lessons from an AI Innovation Management Project." In: *Advances in the Human Side of Service Engineering* pp. 50–56. Cham: Springer.

10 The Space Between

Charting the Past and Future Relationships between Anthropology and Emerging Technologies

Kate Sieck

And. It's a tiny word, but one of the most common in the Oxford English Corpus. Rarely capitalized, rarely attended to, we often just gloss past it. Yet it is a connector, linking the words on either side, positing a relationship – and thus a history and possible future between two disparate things. Therein lies its power – because relationships always include dynamics of power. Yet *And* remains frustratingly elusive, recognizing connection without articulating how or why. All we know is that it's not *Or* – not an exclusionary choice, but a space for engagement and entanglement. In signaling a relationship without details or context, *And* invites readers and practitioners to consider a multitude of ways in which disparate elements could coexist.

In this volume, the authors have provided their perspectives on anthropology *And* emerging technologies. Through detailed narratives of their careers situated within the wider discipline, each has shared insights into how these concepts connect. In this conclusion, I aim to coalesce these perspectives through a framework that disaggregates *And* with words that further suggest how (and thus why) anthropology is related to emerging technologies. I will focus on five potential pairings: *Of, For, With, By,* and *Within.* In choosing these, I don't presume to offer a definitive list, but rather, I would invite readers to consider other dynamics as well. The more we explore and play with the dynamic, shifting the existing relationship between anthropology *And* emerging technologies, the more we unlock new potentials for how they might continue to be in relationship going forward.

Anthropology OF Emerging Technologies

The historical foundations of anthropology as an academic discipline lie in understanding the dynamics of social and cultural systems. Emerging technologies emerge from, and are situated within, these sociocultural systems, hence, it is of little surprise that much of our disciplinary work has long centered on the anthropology *OF* emerging technologies: Where they come from and how they change us.

In fact, we could argue that the American strains of anthropology, in particular, were largely an anthropology *OF* emerging technologies. The turn of

DOI: 10.4324/9781003458555-10

the twentieth century saw the growing power of the eugenics movement and, with it, a host of technologies to measure, rank, and judge people, but often in ways that supported existing biases and hierarchies (Gould, 1980). Boas and his students championed anthropology as a means to challenge spurious science-ism with rigorous, rich contextual studies (King, 2019; Stocking, 1991).

This attention to the impact of technologies did not stop with cultural anthropology. The history of archaeology can similarly be read as an anthropology *OF* emerging technologies. For example, the emergence of tool-making has long been held as the defining feature of the human ancestral line, marking the distinction between *Homo habilis* and *Australopithecus*. It is built into the very name of our ancestral line: "handy-man" or "tool-maker." The development of agriculture – and the technologies required to farm *in situ* – heralded the "Neolithic Revolution," resulting in the purported birth of the city-state, radical shifts in political economy, and attendant shifts in family and communal relationships. Thus, much of our reading of deep human history is through the lens of emerging technologies and their subsequent impact on human life.

These threads continue. From the anthropological studies *OF* industrialization (Taussig, 1980; Haraway, 1991) to new medical technologies (Rapp, 1999), communications (Horst & Miller, 2005), social media (Broadbent, 2020), and algorithms (Eubanks, 2018; Seaver, 2022), ethnographers continue the important task of tracing and articulating the ways in which emerging technologies impact – and make – communities across the globe. This makes sense – as frontiers continue to shift, there will always be a need for studying the anthropology *OF* emerging technologies.

Anthropology FOR Emerging Technologies

Where the anthropology *OF* emerging technologies excels in identifying disjunctures and gaps, the anthropology *FOR* emerging technologies specializes in using ethnographic praxis to address problems and needs by informing the design of products and processes. Rather than just watch as emerging technologies upended communities, these researchers typically begin by asking if there is something we can and should do about it to ensure not just a voice but clear influence from those who will be impacted.

There are typically two core questions that fuel this work. First, what could be done to products and systems to address the gaps and disjunctures facing communities? Madsbjerg & Rasmussen's (2014) work on using ethnographic praxis to inform the redesign of products for colostomy patients is a classic example of this approach. By elucidating where current products were failing to support a well-lived life for these individuals, the research team was able to help the corporate client rethink – and redesign – their offerings.

A second approach within the anthropology *FOR* emerging technologies centers on how we make this new product or process acceptable or tolerable within a community when its launch or redesign is inevitable. This might entail identifying people who could be local "champions" for the new. Alternatively, it might center on identifying how to communicate change in ways that are more sensical within a community. Heitman et al.'s (2018) efforts on identifying the opportunity space for digital financial markets is a clear example of how ethnographic praxis can be employed to smooth the introduction of new technologies.

In the anthropology *FOR* emerging technologies, the praxis extends the traditional role of "informant" into one of collaborator, co-designer, and/or co-researcher. This critical shift has important implications as more products and services rely on algorithms and AI models. How might anthropology better inform the design of algorithms and AI models? Where can we use our collaborative approach to guide on data selection, the establishment of parameters, and the validation of outcomes? How can our specialized knowledge influence algorithms to consider and understand human data and human lives? How can we clarify what is missing in large data sets, and when that missing information is critical to the outcomes? This work remains a too-open terrain and should be one that anthropologists consider moving forward. The chapters herein by Artz and Musgrave are an important contribution toward this growing this field.

Anthropology WITH Emerging Technologies

While Malinowski (1922, 20) may have sufficed with a "camera, notebook, and pencil" as his tools for data gathering, anthropologists have long been at the forefront of conducting fieldwork *WITH* emerging technologies. Within cultural anthropology, ethnographers were some of the first to use film to extend and expand our documentary efforts. From Flaherty's (1922) early efforts to Bateson and Mead's use of film in the early 1940s to capture life-as-lived (versus staged recreations) (see Henley, 2013) to Maya Deren's (1953) experimental documentary style, film has been a way to convey the experiences of other lives when travel was far more difficult for the wider population. Today, the rapid spread of handheld, high-quality photographic devices (via mobile phones) supports documentary images and videos in ways that bring richness, depth, and diversity to our praxis.

Beyond film, cultural anthropologists have embraced other technologies in their praxis. For example, the Electronic Cultural Atlas Initiative uses GIS and other mapping technologies to "enhance understanding and preservation of human culture." Neff and Nafus (2016) leveraged the data collected through health-tracking apps as a tool for reflection and conversation in their ethnographic work. Work using Extended Reality platforms, such as Milk and Arora's (2015) virtual reality film about Syrian refugees, shifts the experiential distance between "field" and "home" in unique and powerful ways.

As the emergence of web- and app-based platforms has enabled ethnographers to connect with people across the globe, ethnographic research can look quite different. Rather than immersion in a field-as-physical-place, these platforms enable immersion in a field-as-lived-experience. For example, platforms such as Patients Like Me can be a way to connect with people who share a rare medical diagnosis, regardless of their physical geography, thus enabling a better understanding of rare(r) experiences (see Tempini & Teira, 2019). The rise of platforms like dscout and Qualtrics similarly enable researchers to get a curated glimpse into participants' lives, often in advance of more traditional fieldwork.

The use of emerging technologies is a key part of the developments in biological anthropology and archaeology as well. The incorporation of neuroimaging technologies – from fMRIs to PET scans – has enabled new understandings of the human experience, including comparative neuroanatomy (Rilling, 2014; Pang et al., 2022) and studies of the brain during trance states (Seligman & Brown, 2009; Seligman et al., 2015). Bioassays provide additional data for understanding things like stress responses (DeCaro 2016, 2022), differences in aging (Finlay et al., 2019), and growth trajectories (Kuzawa & Sweet, 2009; Kuzawa & Thayer, 2011) across populations. Archaeologists now use lidar and a host of electron microscopy techniques to limit the damage to landscape and found objects (c.f., Chase et al., 2011; Masini et al., 2013).

I will speak separately to the integration of algorithms, and particularly the rise of generative AI platforms (such as large language models), as these rightly shift the relationship of engagement from "with" to "by." That said, we have every reason to expect the continued integration of emerging technologies into the toolkits of anthropologists.

Anthropology BY Emerging Technologies

The anthropology *BY* emerging technologies embraces the possibilities of engaging technology as our collaborators in the creation of ethnographic work. Perhaps one of the earlier examples might be Arnold et al.'s study of life at home among families across Los Angeles (2012). The participants' homes were outfitted with cameras to monitor movement, conversations, and behaviors, much as you would track in proximity studies, but enabling 24-hour access to what happened in the home and where in the home it occurred. In this regard, the cameras became surrogate "researchers," serving as the eyes and ears of the team during moments when the anthropologists could not rightly be present. Koycheva's (2023) concept for scaling co-presence through the deployment of teleoperated robots, capable not only of "seeing" but of gathering other sensory data, provides an intriguing and updated twist on ethnographic collaborations *BY* emerging technologies.

Today, we face the transformative possibilities of anthropological research conducted *BY* large language models (LLMs) and large vision models (LVMs). These technologies, which underlie platforms like ChatGPT, Bard, DALL-E, and CLiP, enable radical new kinds of partnerships with human ethnographers, as detailed by Artz (2023). For example, you can query any of the major LLMs for insights about how or why people in X place might navigate Y issue. Drawing from data across the Internet – including published ethnographies, government reports, gray literature, news media, social media, historical documents, etc. – the responses from LLMs can certainly contain elements of truth. Similarly, the LVMs excel at pattern recognition in image-based datasets and can "see" things that an ethnographer might otherwise miss or can confirm at scale what the human might struggle to articulate or document.

The second way in which LLMs and LVMs are upending traditional field-work is in the analysis phase of our work. Historically, the process of decoding fieldnotes – the sensemaking that is a foundational part of finding the patterns and threads that place our findings in dialogue with existing theoretical work – has been where many people see the "magic" within rigorous research. The ability of researchers to find these themes and connect them in unique ways to the body of ethnographic work has long been a way that we distinguish the quality of the research (and researcher). However, LLMs and LVMs play an increasingly influential role in this step. Researchers can input their fieldnotes and videos/images into an LLM or LVM, and these models are trained to find patterns within the material. That is what they do.

Granted, there are a range of challenges with this approach. The most important consideration is the match between the training dataset and what is needed to analyze fieldnotes and images. The emergence of tailored LLMs and LVMs that provide more relevant geographic/historical/cultural context – such as Latimer and Spark Plug, emphasizing the experiences of BIPOC communities – offers a path forward for how anthropologists might better engage with large modes as collaborators. Additionally, they do not yet include data that is not captured on the Internet. It is critical that anthropologists consider the relative impact of this on their particular topic and community. Finally, LLMs and LVMs excel in pattern recognition, often to the exclusion of outlier data. Hence, they should not be relied on for a complete understanding of what is happening within our data. However, as a first pass at framing the work, LLMs and LVMs can be very powerful tools for ethnographers. These kinds of platforms will continue to advance, and as such, they hold radical new options for true collaboration between ethnographers and emerging technologies

Anthropology WITHIN Emerging Technologies

In this final terrain, I want to come full-circle to deeply engage in the contributions anthropology might make to the governance discussions regarding emerging technologies. Ostensibly, governance might imply a power dynamic of anthropology dominating emerging technology. What I'd rather suggest is that we explore the ways in which deeply embedding our expertise into the boundaries and structuring of emerging technologies might advance conversations about whether and how to manifest them. Building on our ability to trace systems dynamics, map causal analyses, and bring desired futures to the table, how might anthropology offer a much-needed perspective on the impact of emerging technologies in contexts currently dominated by law, politics, and economics? How might our "collective-centric" way of thinking – beyond the individual, to include communities and ecosystems – provide a different framework for opportunity assessments, risk analyses, and governance structures?

To do this well, we need to understand the previous four areas: What are these technologies, and what are the socio-technical systems they exist within; why did they emerge, who was impacted, and who benefitted; what can we learn from similar tech evolutions elsewhere in place or time; and where are they augmenting and/or replacing humanity? Could we build an anthropological history of what triggers new technologies and what contextual factors shape their impact on communities and ecosystems? With a framework like that, anthropologists would be well-positioned to advise and guide discussions on how to design and govern such technology. For example, if anthropologists had been serious players during the building of social media platforms, how might we have provided different counsel regarding access and monetization? What could we have leveraged from ethnographic work on gossip, social dynamics, power, anonymity, value – topics well-covered by previous researchers – to consider the likely impact of social media on human relationships?

In a way, interventional anthropology WITHIN emerging technologies brings a crucial balancing force to the conversations. Beyond the technical discussions of what can be done, or the "voice of the consumer" work on how to make emerging technologies acceptable, this approach asks deeper questions: Why something should be pursued, who might be impacted, and how it will change the worlds in which we live (inclusive of the ecosystems that sustain us). By integrating more into strategic planning and business intelligence, we can deploy the same skills to ask questions about systemic risks and problems arising from emergent technologies. Moreover, we can build upon the robust findings of our field to attend to the language and cultural models underlying the scenario, to consider how mitigation efforts might be received by different stakeholders, and to offer novel strategies from different contexts (e.g., How have communities addressed stigma? How have communities navigated shifting power relationships?).

Finally, to be successful in this endeavor, we need to become ethnographers WITHIN the organizations that build and launch new tech. As with all fieldwork, it requires a seat at the table, fluency in the languages that matter (business metrics, materials selection, production design, supply chains, engineering, etc.), and, above all else, basic trust and rapport with our colleagues. These are all the same things we cultivate within any field project, and are well within the toolset of every ethnographer. In interventional anthropology, these skills are especially relevant if we expect to bring along stakeholders to embrace new framings of risks and opportunities. It requires seeing this as a valuable space for anthropology (c.f., Nader, 1972). If we do this well, we have the ability to shift interventional anthropology from its historic roots as the "handmaiden of colonialism" to a rigorous, collective-centric balancing force on the systems and organizations whose products and services are building our futures.

Conclusion

This chapter is intended as a call to action to consider the many possible ways that anthropology AND emerging technologies might co-exist. I suggested five fairly standard ways that we tend to connect these fields, but many others remain. For example:

- Anthropology BEHIND emerging technologies: Conducting historical ethnographies on how technologies came to be.
- Anthropology OVER emerging technologies: Extending our work in governance to lead the frameworks that channel or contain technological advancements.
- Anthropology ACROSS emerging technologies: Assessing the collective impact of multiple emerging technologies on our global communities.

Whatever path we pursue to connect anthropology AND emerging technologies, all paths will require deep engagement with technology and partnership with those who fund and build them. And this will require shifts in how anthropologists train. For example, our historical emphasis on language studies might shift to include programming languages, design languages, or the technical languages of engineering. Our Area Studies component might be better conceived as tied to particular broad industries. These newer competencies will enable ethnographers to earn a seat at the table, just as we earn a place in our fieldsites through demonstrating competencies, respecting systems, and building rapport.

As a discipline that ostensibly cares about human communities – as one grounded in active empathy (Hollan, 2008) – there is a unique opportunity presented through interventional anthropology AND emerging technologies. We see and experience the scope and scale of emerging technologies' impacts on our communities and our globe – including social and environmental degradation. We also have the skills to change these, as demonstrated by every author in this volume. Critiquing the impact while standing on the sidelines *after the fact* ignores the power inherent in anthropology to shape the situation from the outset. My hope – our hope – in writing this volume is to demonstrate that there are ways to do stellar ethnographic research that influence the development and deployment of technologies in order to create more equitable, liveable, collective futures. As the next generation of scholars grows in their voice and power, I am excited for what they will produce and how they will choose to connect these terrains.

Bibliography

Arnold, J. E., A. P. Graesch, E. Ochs, and E. Ragazzini. 2012. *Life at Home in the Twenty-First Century: 32 Families Open Their Doors*. Los Angeles, CA: Cotsen Institute of Archaeology Press.

Artz, Matt. 2023. "Ten Predictions for AI and the Future of Anthropology." in *Anthropology News* website, May 8, 2023.

Broadbent, Stefana. 2020. "Approaches to Personal Communication." In: *Digital Anthropology*, pp. 127–145. Routledge.

Chase, A. F., D. Z. Chase, F. J. Weishampel, J. B. Drake, R. L. Shrestha, K. C. Slatton, J. J. Awe, and W. E. Carter. 2011. "Airborne LiDAR, Archaeology, and the Ancient Maya Landscape at Caracol, Belize." *Journal of Archaeological Science-*February 2011, 38 (2): 387–398.

DeCaro, J. A. 2016. "Beyond Catecholamines: Measuring Autonomic Responses to Psychosocial Context." *American Journal of Human Biology* 28: 309–317.

DeCaro, J. A., and C. Helfrecht. 2002. "Applying Minimally Invasive Biomarkers of Chronic Stress across Complex Ecological Contexts." *American Journal of Human Biology* 34: e23814.

Deren, Maya. 1953. "*Divine Horsemen: The Living Gods of Haiti.*" Full video available here: https://www.youtube.com/watch?v=HhkQHQDel2o.

Eubanks, Virginia. 2018. *Automating Inequality: How High-Tech Tools Profile, Police and Punish the Poor*. New York: Macmillan.

Finlay, B. B., S. Pettersson, M. K. Melby, and T. C. Bosch. 2019. "The Microbiome Mediates Environmental Effects on Ageing." *BioEssays* October 2019, 41 (10).

Flaherty, Robert J. 1922. "*Nanook of the North.*" Film accessible through: https://naturedocumentaries.org/2637/nanook-north-1922/.

Gould, Stephen J. 1980. *The Mismeasure of Man*. New York: W.W. Norton.

Haraway, Donna. 1991. *Simians, Cyborgs and Women: The Reinvention of Nature*. New York: Routledge.

Heitmann, Soren, Sinja Buri, Gisela Davico, and Fabian Reitzug. 2018. "*Operationalizing Ethnographic Resarch to Grow Trust in Digital Financial Services.*" In: Ethnographic Praxis in Industry Conference.

Henley, Paul. 2013. "From Documentation to Representation: Recovering the Films of Margaret Mead and Gregory Bateson." *Visual Anthropology* 26 (2): 75–108.

Hollan, Dorothy. 2008. "Being There: On the Imaginative Aspects of Understanding Others and Being Understood." *Ethos* December 2008: 36 (4): 475–489.

Horst, Heather, and Daniel Miller (eds). 2005. *Digital Anthropology*. New York: Routledge.

King, Charles. 2019. *Gods of the Upper Air: How a Circle of Renegade Anthropologists Reinvented Race, Sex and Gender in the Twentieth Century*. New York: Penguin Random House.

Koycheva, Lora. 2023. "*Ethnography for an Accessible Future – Scaling Embodiment as a Paradigm for Anthropology in the Digital World through Telepresence Robots.*" Report for UNESCO and LiiV Center for Innovating Digital Anthropology, Document Code SHS/MOST/DA/2023/PI/6.

Kuzawa, Christopher, and E. Sweet. 2009. "Epigenetics and the Embodiment of Race: Developmental Origins of US Racial Disparities in Cardiovascular Health." *American Journal of Human Biology* 21 (1): 2–15.

Kuzawa, Christopher, and Z. Thayer. "The Timescales of Human Adaptation: The Role of Epigenetic Processes." *Epigenomics* 3 (2): 221–234.

Madsbjerg, Christian, and Mikkel B. Rasmussen. 2014. *The Moment of Clarity: Using the Human Sciences to Solve Your Toughest Business Problems.* Cambridge, MA: Harvard Business Review Press.

Malinowski, Bronislaw. 1922. *Argonauts of the Western Pacific: An Account of Enterprise and Adventure in the Archipelagoes of Melanesian New Guinea.* London: Routledge.

Masini, Nicola, and Rosa Lasaponara. 2013. "Airbonre Lidar in Archaeology: An Overview and Case Study." In: Murgante, B., et al. *Computational Science and Its Applications – ICCSA 2013.* Lecture Notes in Computer Science, vol. 7972. Berlin/Heidelberg: Springer.

Milk, Chris, and Gabo Arora. 2015. *"Clouds over Sidra."* Immersive VR film, accessible through UNICEF: https://www.unicefusa.org/stories/clouds-over-sidra-award-winning-virtual-reality-experience.

Nader, Laura. 1972. "Up the Anthropologist: Perspectives Gained from Studying Up." In: Dell Hymes (ed.) *Reinventing Anthropology.* New York: Random House.

Neff, Gina, and Dawn Nafus. 2016. *Self-Tracking.* Boston: MIT Press.

Pang, James C., James K. Rilling, James A. Roberts, Martijn P. van den Heuvel, and Luca Cocchi. 2022. "Evolutionary Shaping of Human Brain Dynamics." *eLife*October 2022, 26:11.

Rapp, Rayna. 1999. *Testing Women, Testing the Fetus: The Social Impact of Amniocentesis in America.* New York: Routledge.

Rilling, James. 2014. "Comparative Primate Neuroimaging: Insights into Human Brain Evolution." *Trends in Cognitive Science*2014 January; 18 (1): 46–55.

Seaver, Nick. 2022. *Computing Taste: Algorithms and the Makers of Music Recommendations.* Chicago: University of Chicago Press.

Seligman, R., and R. Brown. 2009. "Theory and Method at the Intersection of Anthropology and Cultural Neuroscience." *Social, Cognitive, and Affective Neuroscience* 5 (2–3): 130–137.

Seligman, Rebecca, S. Choudhury, and L. J. Kirmayer. 2015. "Locating Culture in the Brain and in the World: From Social Categories to an Ecology of Mind," In: *Oxford Handbook of Cultural Neuroscience.* Oxford: Oxford University Press.

Stocking, George. 1991. *Victorian Anthropology.* New York: Free Press.

Taussig, Michael T. 1980. *The Devil and Commodity Fetishism in South America.* Chapel Hill: University of North Carolina Press.

Tempini, Niccolò, and David Teira. "Is the Genie Out of the Bottle? Digital Platforms and the Future of Clinical Trials." *Economy and Society* 48 (1): 77–106.

Index

For Product Safety Concerns and Information please contact our EU
representative GPSR@taylorandfrancis.com
Taylor & Francis Verlag GmbH, Kaufingerstraße 24, 80331 München, Germany

www.ingramcontent.com/pod-product-compliance
Lightning Source LLC
Chambersburg PA
CBHW070324270326
41926CB00017B/3746

9 781032 602998